Selected Essays

Selected Essays

NUALA NÍ DHOMHNAILL

NEW
ISLAND

Selected Essays
First published 2005
by New Island
2 Brookside
Dundrum Road
Dublin 14
www.newisland.ie

ISBN 1 904301 32 0

Typeset by New Island
Cover design by New Island
Printed in the UK by CPD, Ebbw Vale, Wales

New Island received financial assistance from The Arts Council
(An Chomhairle Ealaíon), Dublin, Ireland

10 9 8 7 6 5 4 3 2 1

Contents

For the past several decades, Nuala Ní Dhomhnaill's poetry has enthralled readers in Ireland and, increasingly, around the world. The critical praise that trailed after her first two collections, *An Dealg Droighin* (1981) and *Féar Suaithinseach* (1984), led to what was then the progressive and innovatory idea of publishing a *Selected Poems* in dual-language format (*Rogha Dánta*, revised edition 1990). The success of that volume's marriage of Irish originals and Michael Hartnett's English translations did much to confirm Ní Dhomhnaill's singular talent among non-Irish speakers and readers, as well as among those whose Irish wanted, perhaps, the inspiration of facing-page translations that sent one diving after particular words. *Feis* (1991), the Irish-language collection that followed, confirmed Ní Dhomhnaill's reputation as an inspired, lyrical poet with a gift for probing and invigorating folklore and mythology. And if more confirmation of her talent was needed, it came in the guise of Paul Muldoon's accompanying translations in *The Astrakhan Cloak* (1992), and the elegant *Pharaoh's Daughter* (1993), in which Ní Dhomhnaill's poems were translated and so re-envisioned by thirteen of Ireland's foremost poets. By the early 1990s, in other words, Ní Dhomhnaill's reputation, like that of the best writers, had gone beyond the marvellous specificities of her particular language and had been transported, via translation, into the minds of non-Irish speakers and readers; her individual reputation had also done much to raise the general awareness of Irish-language poetry, and played no small role in sending flurries of scholars back to their Irish grammars and in encouraging other, younger writers to continue their Irish-language work. Not content to rest upon her established reputation, Ní Dhomhnaill has gone on to produce the much admired *Cead Aighnis* (1998), selected poems from which appeared as *The Water Horse* in 1999, a volume that reiterates the interest generated by Ní Dhomhnaill's poetry for her fellow poets in both Irish and English.

Since publication of *The Water Horse*, critical praise of Ní Dhomhnaill's work has continued unabated; her poetry garners more and more attention from scholars and critics of both Irish- and English-language poetry, so that it would be intensely difficult to consider the Irish poetic landscape without her. This fact seemed to be recognised when Ní Dhomhnaill was named the second Ireland Professor of Poetry in 2001, an appointment supported by Trinity College Dublin, University College Dublin and Queen's University Belfast in recognition of the international achievements of Irish poets. This appointment, which allows for a year in residence at each of the three supporting institutions, affirmed Ní Dhomhnaill's importance as a writer and lecturer within the bounds of academic communities while also distinguishing her as among the most significant of Irish poets. Beyond the borders of Ireland, Ní Dhomhnaill had previously served as Visiting Professor at Villanova University, Boston College, New York University and Smith College, and she has lectured and read her poetry in countries as diverse as Newfoundland and Japan. Ní Dhomhnaill's poetic success is evident too in the translation of her work into English by poets as respected as Seamus Heaney, Medbh McGuckian and Paul Muldoon, and in the translation of her work into other languages that include Breton, French, German, Italian, Japanese, Russian, Swedish and Turkish.[1] While Ní Dhomhnaill is herself increasingly well known, and while her poetry is thus increasingly available, her essays and lectures have been frustratingly difficult to come by; many students of her work, as well as many scholars, remain unaware of this body of material in its entirety, and have rarely encountered more than a handful of her prose pieces. This volume attempts to rectify this situation by making available twelve essays, articles and lectures of one of Ireland's major poets.

Ní Dhomhnaill's essays are interesting for many reasons, but their language is an obvious point at which to begin a discussion of them. That Ní Dhomhnaill's poetry has been written exclusively in Irish since her schooldays is well known; half-way through a poem in English, she began writing the same poem in Irish and 'immediately saw that it was much better'. Ní Dhomhnaill is not alone amongst Irish writers in changing tongues and discovering a new voice; Samuel Beckett is largely supposed to have turned to French as a way of counteracting the influence and weight of the English-language literary tradition on his work which was, at the time, particularly indebted to Joyce. Both Beckett and Ní Dhomhnaill, then, find freedom and expression in turning away from English. But while Beckett turned away from English to fly by certain nets of literary language and committed himself to writing in a language to which he had no national or familial tie, Ní Dhomhnaill's decision – which these essays attest was a conscious one – to turn to Irish involves an *immersion* in literary language. And that language, as Ní Dhomhnaill's poetry has consistently demonstrated, offers the opportunity not to escape nets, but to recover and mend them, and to recognise them not as limiters of freedom, but as webs and links between one person and another, a bind of community that stretches beyond the individual's time and into an epochal linguistic heritage that Ní Dhomhnaill has described as a veritable goldmine for a poet. Far from functioning as a way out of influence, Ní Dhomhnaill's decision to compose her poetry in Irish was in fact a commitment to a different set of influences that engender the Irish-language literary tradition stretching back to the seventh century, as well as to the language's oral traditions.

Ní Dhomhnaill's commitment to the Irish language is, these essays reveal time and again, an emotive, creative one, first and foremost. Irish, for Ní Dhomhnaill, is her language in a way that no other language can be; it is the language of happiest, thrilling, exploratory childhood, the language of relationship and belonging, the language of self, the language in which it becomes most possible to communicate essentials of the mind and body's experience. The political statement that writing in Irish is taken to be is a secondary, although still important, issue for the poet, who has had to answer not only the queries of those with little or no experience of Irish culture, but also the harder questions of those who also define themselves as Irish but who have doubted the purpose of writing in Irish, or remain suspicious of Irish as a 'dead' language that speaks only of the past and never the present. Being an Irish poet who writes in Irish has meant that Ní Dhomhnaill has often been treated to what her well-known essay 'Why I Choose to Write in Irish, the Corpse that Sits Up and Talks Back', with which this volume begins, outlines as an ideological pummelling. Ní Dhomhnaill has thus been forced, as many other poets never are, to justify her language, her choice of words; that choice has been subjected to a scrutiny that would be unthinkable about, say, Seamus Heaney's poetry in English. Ní Dhomhnaill has eloquently written about the results of this scrutiny, and the sometimes exhausting repercussions of existing as an Irish-language poet in an Ireland in which English dominates the majority of everyday discourse, particularly in urban centres and the east of the country.

And yet, extraordinarily, Ní Dhomhnaill has remained unflaggingly open to this dialogue about language and her decision to write in Irish, producing insightful and revealing essays and lectures that cut close to the heart of these matters, to the emotion and necessity that drives her poetry – and, even more extraordinarily, she has done so largely in English. With the exception of one, all of the essays this volume comprises were originally composed in English. Ní Dhomhnaill's ideological stance, which holds her to the Irish language as a means of poetic expression, does not disallow the communication of that stance through another medium, another tongue: whether in Irish or in English, Ní Dhomhnaill's work seems to commit itself to a thoroughly generous type of conversation and exchange. These essays, I am suggesting, while written in English, disclose a contiguity with her poetry in theme and in tone and thus can, for the student and scholar alike, reveal a good deal about Ní Dhomhnaill's poetic process.

I noted above that Ní Dhomhnaill's essays communicate largely in English. What is remarkable about Ní Dhomhnaill's

English prose is that it does not, in fact, draw merely upon the English language for its expression. Just as Ní Dhomhnaill's poetry is sometimes scattered with English words that function to remind us of an Irish historical situation in which two languages vied and reflected political tensions, here her prose is scattered with Irish – and, indeed, with French, with Latin and with Turkish. These essays, in other words, testify not merely to the bilingual experience of which her poetry has long spoken, but also to a truly macaronic, multi-linguistic way of writing and thinking. In a world that Ní Dhomhnaill believes is often in danger of reifying particular languages like English over others deemed to be 'minority' or 'marginal' tongues, Ní Dhomhnaill's own experience and linguistic abilities offer insight not only into what might be lost should those 'minority' languages be elided from our consciousness, but also into the immense creative advantages that come with fluency of thought across cultures.

This macaronic capacity is something that is mirrored not solely in the actual, graspable language of these essays, but also in their themes and concerns. When Ní Dhomhnaill first began publishing poetry while studying Irish and English at University College Cork, the use of the Irish language was an 'issue'. Irish was considered by many to be one of those minority languages perceived as a mode of communication that was marginal and outdated and, some would have it, actually dead, having suffered an undated defeat. That the supposedly dead language was still in use – employed by neighbours discussing sundries such as weather and news as well as by writers creating poems, novels and plays of aesthetic and cultural value – was a broken cog in the ideological wheel that first denied and then defied the Irish language to prove it was otherwise. Ní Dhomhnaill's writings in essays such as 'Cé Leis Tú?' offer explorations of that situation, ponder the reasons why Irish had become a language to be lashed out against. Her essays also trace the ways in which that situation of the 1970s might be perceived as having changed now, three decades on. Ní Dhomhnaill's charges in her 1995 essay 'Why I Choose to Write in Irish' offer a proof positive that the Irish language has indeed recovered ground since then: when Ní

Dhomhnaill wondered in 1995 about the idea of an Irish television station becoming reality, we have the happy circumstance, in 2005, of being able to confirm its creation and ongoing success.

The battles for linguistic freedom and recognition outlined by Ní Dhomhnaill are also ongoing, of course, and these essays are important in positing many, many reasons why the Irish language remains a significant, and still undervalued, cultural resource. While Irish is a private sanctuary for the poet, it is also much more than that, a repository for both the oral and literary traditions of Ireland over many centuries. Ní Dhomhnaill offers the Irish language to readers of these essays as an entrance into an otherworld, and that otherworld is the imaginatively specific and fantastically constructed imaginative space that recurs in Irish literary lore, the liminal site at which myth and reality meet – but it is also an unconscious of the nation, a continually enlivened form of cultural memory. To deny the place and import of the Irish language, Ní Dhomhnaill suggests, is to ignore the existential semantic of Ireland's cultural heritage – which was shaped, after all, Ní Dhomhnaill points out, by that very language. Ní Dhomhnaill thus sees the frequent silence on the Irish language by critics, cultural historians and popular culture as a form of repression that has dramatic consequences for the psychological make-up of the Irish population. When after the Famine, she writes in 'A Ghostly Alhambra', the Irish language found itself bereft of many of its speakers, a psychological shift took place that equated the English language with modernity and with the open-palmed possibilities that immigration seemed to offer, and the Irish language with the vagaries of weather, disease, poverty, starvation, mistreatment and colonial conditions. This shift, Ní Dhomhnaill contends, amounts to a defiant act of psychic reconstruction whose results Ireland is only beginning to face in this new century. Ní Dhomhnaill explores the dramatic effects of the loss of the Irish language as the primary tongue, forcing us to address what has often gone unexamined: the fact that the Irish language was 'lost' to speech in such a short space of time must, she argues, be counted among the tragedies to have befallen Ireland, and must be faced as a trauma if the nation is to move forward.

In their concern with the psychological state of the nation as well as with bringing the mythologies and folktales of Ireland back to consciousness, Ní Dhomhnaill's essays demonstrate a conceptual savvy. As rooted in international folktales and myths as she is in the place-specific, local Irish lore that provides her work with its uncurving spine, Ní Dhomhnaill is also comfortable, these essays attest, drawing upon influential theoretical works by French feminists and psychoanalytic thinkers, by ethnologists and literary critics. If the classic Munster poets of Irish literature provided early inspiration, that inspiration was augmented by exposure to an impressive range of poetry, from Shakespeare and John Berryman to Yeats, as well as to the range of Turkish poetry to which Ní Dhomhnaill introduces the reader in 'Sojourn to the Eastern World'. In its discussion of sources and the ways in which various influences made their way into the poet's work, this volume provides scholars of Ní Dhomhnaill's work with new insights that might not have been apparent in reading the essays in their scattered form: as a collection they allow, for the first time, a solid glimpse into the formation of this poet's aesthetic.

As readers familiar with Ní Dhomhnaill's poetry will know, the Irish literary and oral tradition of *dinnsheanchas*, or placelore, is of utmost importance to her work. Like Yeats one hundred years before, Ní Dhomhnaill is convinced of the need to root poetry in place, as witnessed by her consistent fascination with stories of local lore. Unlike Yeats, however, Ní Dhomhnaill has the advantage of an intense and long-term association with one particular place, Cahiratrant, which provides her work not merely with inspiration, but also with impetus, movement and an often profoundly moving personal basis. There is a sense, in these essays, of entering another world quite literally: images begin to form of particular people, of paths, of fields and strands and stretches of recovered time to which the writer introduces us, outsiders. It is a position of privilege that we as readers have, here, invited into the world of Ní Dhomhnaill's West Kerry childhood and allowed to hear the stories that she hears, allowed to participate in her discoveries of how stories of place function. We are privy to the ways in which these stories explain and order the world, giving it a meaning that is not merely personal but also communal; we accompany the poet on pilgrimages to Glendalough and Kerry, and are submersed in lore. Ní Dhomhnaill's talent, in essays such as 'Cé Leis Tú?', 'Holy Wells and Psychic Depths', 'The Naming of High and Holy Places', 'Patterns' and 'Unalive Beings and Things That Don't Exist', is to stretch the community to include the reader: and that is, after all, what the *dinnsheanchas* tradition has done for hundreds, if not thousands, of years – explained our own place in the world through a remembrance of past experiences in that same place, providing a continuity over time and marking us as inheritors of a particular form of knowledge and tradition.

Through her involvement in *dinnsheanchas* and folklore, Ní Dhomhnaill manages not only to preserve myth, however, but also to instil in the reader a sense of the importance mythologies have for us as humans. While she is concerned to demonstrate the contemporary value and relevance of myth and folklore, however, Ní Dhomhnaill is by no means a conservative preservationist. Essays such as 'The Woman Poet in the Irish Tradition' as well as reflections on her personal experiences in 'Cé Leis Tú?' provide a resounding critique of Irish cultural traditions that kept women's writing out of the canon and which continued, well into the twentieth century, to define Irish women's roles with reference to a variety of stereotypes and images. Ní Dhomhnaill's introduction to the selection of contemporary women's poetry in *The Field Day Anthology of Irish Women's Writing*, which appeared in 2002, attests to the changes taking place in this area as well, outlining the ways in which Irish women's poetry has flowered in recent decades, as well as how the country's attitude towards women has been changed by women themselves. And this is not simply a matter of women making changes, Ní Dhomhnaill insists; the entire culture needs to participate in the phenomenon of such a change, as she outlines in 'Mis and Dubh Ruis'. In such essays, we bear witness to the poet's use of centuries-old Irish material that transforms itself in her hands into lessons for our own time, lessons that reveal to us the damage done by the continuing repression of women and what Ní Dhomhnaill deems a feminine energy.

Written over a period of approximately fifteen years, these essays are offered as starting points for further analysis of Ní Dhomhnaill's work in the context of the sources and influences revealed here. If this volume sends readers back to Ní Dhomhnaill's poetry, it is hoped that it will also provide a way of thinking about a changing Irish world, a way of tapping into what the poet calls the 'psychic realities' of Irish culture. Lest we forget, these essays suggest, Ireland was not always a place of English-speaking, text-based culture, and remains, to this day, steeped in other traditions that have not been lost, but which are too often uncelebrated. Ní Dhomhnaill's essays mend the nets that allow us to catch hold of the elusive traditions of Irish culture that rely on oral lore and the awareness of myth, providing revelations about what it means to be part of not only a linguistic community, but also an imaginative one.

Oona Frawley

[1] I am grateful to Maureen Murphy for sharing her ongoing bibliographic work on Ní Dhomhnaill, which provided me with this information.

Why I Choose to Write in Irish, the Corpse That Sits Up and Talks Back

Not so long ago I telephoned my mother about some family matter. 'So what are you writing these days?' she asked, more for the sake of general conversation than anything else. 'Oh, an essay for *The New York Times*,' I said as casually as possible. 'What is it about?' she asked. 'About what it is like to write in Irish.' There was a good few seconds' pause on the other end of the line; then, 'Well, I hope you'll tell them that it is mad.' End of conversation. I had got my comeuppance. And from my mother, who was the native speaker of Irish in our family, never having encountered a single word of English until she went to school at the age of six, and well up in her teens and in boarding school before she realised that the name they had at home for a most useful household item was actually two words – 'safety pin' – and that they were English. Typical.

But really not so strange. Some time later I was at a meal hosted by the American Embassy in Dublin for two of their writers, Richard Wilbur and Toni Morrison. We stood in line and took our buffet suppers along to the nearest available table. An Irishwoman across from me asked me what I did. Before I had time to open my mouth her partner butted in, 'Oh Nuala writes poetry in Irish.' And what did I write about? she asked. Again before I had time to reply he did so for me: 'She writes poems of love and loss, and I could quote you most of them by heart.' This was beginning to get up my nose, and so I attempted simultaneously to deflate him and to go him one better. 'Actually,' I announced, 'I think the only things worth writing about are the biggies: birth, death and the most important thing in between, which is sex.' 'Oh,' his friend says to me archly, 'and is there a word for sex in Irish?'

I looked over at the next table, where Toni Morrison was sitting, and I wondered if a black writer in America had to put up with the likes of that, or its equivalent. Here I was in my own country having to defend the first official language of the state from a compatriot who obviously thought it was an accomplishment to be ignorant of it. Typical, and yet maybe not so strange.

Let me explain. Irish (as it is called in the Irish Constitution; to call it Gaelic is not politically correct at the moment, but seen as marginalising) is the Celtic language spoken by a small minority of native speakers principally found in rural pockets on the western seaboard. These Irish-speaking communities are known as the 'Gaeltacht', and are the last remnants of an earlier historical time when the whole island was Irish-speaking, or one huge 'Gaeltacht'. The number of Irish-speakers left in these areas who use Irish in most of their daily affairs is a hotly debated point, and varies from 100,000 at the most optimistic estimate to 20,000 at the most conservative. For the sake of a round number let us take it to be 60,000, or about two per cent of the population of the Republic of Ireland.

Because of the effort of the Irish Revival movement, and of the teaching of Irish in the school system, however, the language is also spoken with varying degrees of frequency and fluency by a considerably larger number of people who have learned it as a second language. So much so that census figures over the last few decades have consistently indicated that up to one million people, or thirty per cent of the population of the Republic, claim to be speakers of Irish, to which can be added the 146,000 people in the six counties of Northern Ireland who also are competent in Irish. This figure of one million speakers is, of course, grossly misleading and in no way reflects a widespread use of the language in everyday life. Rather it can be seen as a reflection of general goodwill towards the language, as a kind of wishful thinking. Nevertheless that goodwill is important.

The fact that the Irish language (and by extension its literature) has a precarious status in Ireland at the moment is a development in marked contrast to its long and august history. I believe writing in Irish is the oldest continuous literary activity in western Europe, starting in the fifth century and flourishing in a rich and varied manuscript tradition right through the middle ages. During this time the speakers of any invading language such as Norse, Anglo-Norman and English were assimilated, becoming 'more Irish than the Irish themselves'. But the Battle of Kinsale in 1601, in which the British routed the last independent Irish princes, and the ensuing catastrophes of the turbulent seventeenth century, including forced population transfers, destroyed the social underpinning of the language. Its decline was greatly accelerated by the Great Famine of the mid-nineteenth century; most of the one million who died of starvation and the millions who left on coffin ships for America were Irish speakers. The fact that the fate of emigration stared most of the survivors in the eye further speeded up the language-change to English – after all, 'What use was Irish to you over in Boston?'

The indigenous high-culture became the stuff of the speech of fishermen and small farmers, and this is the language that I learned in West Kerry in the 1950s at the age of five, in a situation of total immersion, when I was literally and figuratively farmed out to my aunt in the parish of Ventry. Irish is a language of enormous elasticity and emotional sensitivity; of quick and hilarious banter and full of a welter of references both historical and mythological; it is an instrument of great imaginative depth and scope, which has been tempered by the community for generations until it can pick up and sing out every hint of a tint of emotional modulation that can occur between people. Many international scholars rhapsodise that this speech of ragged peasants seems always on the point of bursting into poetry. The accident that had me learn this language at an early age can only be called a creative one.

The Irish of the Revival, or 'book Irish', was something entirely different, and that I learned at school. Although my first literary love affair was with the Munster poets Aodhagán Ó

Rathaille and Eoghan Rua Ó Suilleabháin, and I had learned off reams and reams of poetry that wasn't taught at school, when I myself came to write it didn't dawn on me that I could possibly write in Irish. The overriding ethos had gotten even to me. Writing poetry in Irish somehow didn't seem to be intellectually credible. So my first attempts, elegies on the deaths of Bobby Kennedy and Martin Luther King published in the school magazine, were all in English. They were all right, but even I could see that there was something wrong with them.

Writing Irish poetry in English suddenly seemed a very stupid thing to be doing. So I switched language mid-poem and wrote the very same poem in Irish, and I could see immediately that it was much better. I sent it in to a competition in *The Irish Times*, where it won a prize, and that was that. I never looked back.

I had chosen my language, or more rightly, perhaps, at some very deep level, the language had chosen me. If there is a level to our being that for want of any other word I might call 'soul' (and I believe there is), then for some reason that I can never understand, the language that my soul speaks, and the place it comes from, is Irish. At sixteen I had made my choice. And that was that. It still is. I have no other.

But if the actual choice to write poetry in Irish was easy, then nothing else about it is, especially given the hypocritical attitude of the state in its approach towards the language. On the one hand, Irish is enshrined as a nationalistic token (the ceremonial *cúpla focal* – few words – at the beginning and end of speeches by politicians, broadcasters and even airline crews is an example). On the other hand, however, it would not be an exaggeration to speak of the state's indifference, even downright hostility, to Irish-speakers in its failure to provide even the most basic services in Irish for those who wish to go about their everyday business in that language.

'The computer cannot understand Irish' leads the excuses given by the state to refuse to conduct its business in Irish, even in the Gaeltacht areas. Every single service gained by Irish-speakers has been fought for bitterly. Thus the *Gaelscoileanna*, or Irish schools, have been mostly started by groups of parents, often in the very teeth of fierce opposition from the Department of Education. The only reason we have a single Irish-medium radio station is that a civil-rights group started a pirate radio twenty years ago in the West and thus shamed the Government into establishing this vital service. A single television channel is being tooted at present, but I'll believe it when I see it.

You might expect at least the cultural nationalists and our peers writing in English to be on our side. Not so. A recent television documentary about Thomas Kinsella begins with the writer intoning the fact that history has been recorded in Irish from the fifth century to the nineteenth. Then there is a pregnant pause. We wait for a mention of the fact that life, experience, sentient consciousness, even history is being recorded in literature in Irish in the present day. We wait in vain. By an antiquarian sleight of hand it is implied that Irish writers in English are now the natural heirs to a millennium and a half of writing in Irish. The subtext of this documentary is that Irish is dead.

So what does that make me, and the many other writers of the large body of modern literature in Irish? A walking ghost? A linguistic spectre?

Mind you, it is invidious of me to single out Thomas Kinsella; this kind of insidious 'bad faith' about modern literature in Irish is alive and rampant amongst many of our fellow writers in English. As a fellow poet in Irish, Biddy Jenkinson, has said, 'we have been pushed into an ironic awareness that by our passage we would convenience those who will be uneasy in their Irishness as long as there is a living Gaelic tradition to which they do not belong'. Now let them make their peace with the tradition if they wish to; I don't begrudge them a line of it. But I'll be damned if their cultural identity is procured at the expense of my existence, or of that of my language. I can well see how it suits some people to see Irish-language literature as the last rictus of a dying beast. As far as they are concerned, the sooner the language lies down and dies the better, so they can cannibalise it with greater equanimity, peddling their 'ethnic chic' with nice little translations 'From the Irish'. Far be it from them to make the real effort it takes to learn the living language. I dare say they must be taken somewhat aback when the corpse that they have long since consigned to choirs of angels, like a certain Tim Finnegan, sits up and talks back at them.

The fault is not always one-sided. The Gaels (Irish-language writers) often fell prey to what Terence Browne, a literary historian, has called an 'atmosphere of national self-righteousness and cultural exclusiveness', and their talent did not always equal the role imposed on them. Nevertheless, long after the emergence of a high standard of modern literature in Irish with Seán Ó Riordáin, Máirtin Ó Direáin and Máire Mhac an tSaoi in poetry and Máirtín Ó Cadhain in prose, writing in Irish was conspicuously absent from anthologies in the 1950s and '60s. Even as late as the '70s one of our 'greats', Seán Ó Riordáin, could hear on the radio two of his co-writers in English saying how 'poetry in Ireland had been quiescent in the '50s', thus consigning to mere nothingness the great work that he and his fellow poets in Irish had produced during that very decade. After a lifetime devoted to poetry, is it any wonder that he died in considerable grief and bitterness?

As for the cultural nationalists, Irish was never the language of nationalist mobilisation. Unlike other small countries where nationalism rose throughout the nineteenth century, in Ireland it was religion rather than language that mostly coloured nationalism. Daniel O'Connell, the Liberator, a native Irish-speaking Kerryman, used to address his monster mass meetings from the 1820s to the 1840s in English, even though this language was not understood by seventy per cent of the people he was addressing. Why? Because it was at the reporters over from *The Times* in London and their readers that his words were primarily directed. It is particularly painful to recall that while nationalism was a major motivator in developing modern literary languages out of such varied tongues as Norwegian, Hungarian, Finnish and Estonian, during that very same period the high literary culture of Irish was being reduced to the language of peasants. By the time the Revival began, the damage had already been done, and the language was already in decline (spoken by only 14.5 percent in 1880). The blatant myopia of the cultural nationalists is still alive and glaringly obvious in the disgraceful underrepresentation of Irish in the recently published three-volume *Field Day Anthology of Irish Writing*.

It should not be surprising, then, that we poets and fiction writers in Irish who are included in the anthology feel as if we are being reduced to being exotic background, like Irish Muzak. Thus the cultural nationalists, without granting Irish the intellectual credibility of rational discourse or the popular base of the oral tradition, enshrine it instead as the repository of their own utopian fantasies: pristine, changeless, 'creative', but otherwise practically useless.

How does all this affect me, as a poet writing in Irish? Well, inasmuch as I am human and frail and prone to vanity and clamoring for attention, of course it disturbs me to be misunderstood, misrepresented and finally all but invisible in my own country. I get depressed, I grumble and complain, I stand around in rooms muttering darkly. Still and all, at some fundamental level it matters not one whit. All I ever wanted was to be left alone so that I could go on writing poetry in Irish. I still remember a time when I had an audience I could count on the fingers of one hand. I was perfectly prepared for that. I still am.

But it has been gratifying to reach a broader audience through the medium of translations, especially among the one million who profess some knowledge of Irish. Many of them probably had good Irish when they left school but have had no chance of using it since, for want of any functional context where it would make sense to use the language. I particularly like it when my poetry in English translation sends them back to the originals in Irish, and when they then go on to pick up the long-lost threads of the language which is so rightly theirs. I also find it pleasant and vivifying to make an occasional trip abroad and to reach a wider audience by means of dual-language readings and publications.

But my primary audience is those who read my work in Irish only. A print run for a book of poems in Irish is between one thousand and fifteen hundred copies. That doesn't sound like much until you realise that that number is considered a decent run by many poets in English in Ireland, or for that matter even in England or America, where there's a much larger population.

The very ancientness of the Irish literary tradition is also a great source of strength to me as a writer. This works at two levels, one that is mainly linguistic and prosodic and another that is mainly thematic and inspirational. At the linguistic level, Old Irish, though undoubtably very difficult, is much closer to modern Irish than, say, Anglo-Saxon is to modern English. Anyone like me with a basic primary degree in the language and a bit of practice can make a fair hand of reading most of the medieval texts in the original. Thus a few lines into a text on, for example, Mór of Munster taken from the twelfth century Book of Leinster but dealing with seventh century material and written in, at the latest, tenth century Irish, I am hauled up short at a rather difficult word, '*admilliud*'. I understand the grammar of the sentence, and how the word functions in it, but what can it possibly mean? Then as I ponder the word, repeating it aloud and making allowances for more than one thousand years of linguistic development, suddenly I've got it: it is the word '*aimliú*'. This is not only still occasionally heard in West Kerry speech, but I can even remember the last time I heard it uttered, on the tongue of Mike Long, a farmer of Cahiratrant, as we sat chatting on his ditch while he took a break from bagging potatoes. Talking about a well-known local rascal who had quite coolly helped himself to a large quantity of his neighbour's hay, he declared, 'Fágfadsa aimliú air!' – he would leave a 'deformity' upon him if he caught him. This depth of resonance is of untold linguistic and psychological strength.

Thematically, too, the older literature is a godsend, though I am only now slowly but surely beginning to assess its unique possibilities to a modern writer. There are known to be well over four thousand manuscripts in Ireland and elsewhere of material from Old to modern Irish. Apart from the great medieval codices, only about fifty other manuscripts date from before 1650. Nevertheless, the vast majority of the material pain-stakingly copied down after this time is exemplary of much earlier manuscripts that have since been lost. A lot of this is still catalogued in ways which are unsatisfactory for our time.

Many items of enormous psychological and sexual interest,

for example, are described with the bias of the nineteenth century as 'indecent and obscene tales, unsuitable for publication'. On many such manuscripts human eye has not set sight since they were so described. Most scholarly attention has been paid to pre-Norman Conquest material as the repository of the unsullied well-springs of the native soul (those cultural nationalists again!), with the result that the vast area of post-Conquest material has been unfairly neglected. The main advantage of all this material to me is that it is proof of the survival until even a very late historical date of a distinct *Weltanschauung* radically different from the Anglo mentality that has since eclipsed it.

Because of a particular set of circumstances, Irish fell out of history just when the modern mentality was about to take off. So major intellectual changes like the Reformation, the Renaissance, the Enlightenment, Romanticism and Victorian prudery have never occurred in it as they did in the major European languages. One consequence is that the attitude to the body enshrined in Irish remains extremely open and uncoy. It is almost impossible to be 'rude' or 'vulgar' in Irish. The body, with its orifices and excretions, is not treated in a prudish manner but is accepted as '*an nádúir*', or 'nature', and becomes a source of repartee and laughter rather than anything to be ashamed of. Thus little old ladies of quite impeccable and unimpeachable moral character can tell risqué stories with gusto and panache and enter into an animated banter where every word is not only a double but often a triple or even quadruple entendre. The language is particularly rich in what the French call *polysémie*, words with many different meanings, which get stretched like elastic. And because it is a highly inflected language, word order is much less rigid than it is in English, say; the copula, for example, can be used instead of a substantive at the beginning of a sentence to allow for expectations to be set up and then demolished. Thus the skillful use of syntax alone can be the cause of wholesale hilarity, and has resulted in some of the best laughs of my life. It is with great personal difficulty that I buckle down to the relatively staid and straight-faced literalness that passes for civilised conversation anywhere in Ireland east of the Shannon. In Irish you can get away with murder. 'Is there a word for sex in Irish' indeed! Is there an Eskimo word for snow?

By now I must have spent whole years of my life burrowing in the Department of Folklore at University College Dublin, and yet there are still days when my hands shake with emotion holding manuscripts. Again, this material works on me at two levels. First is when I revel in the well-turned phrase or nuance or retrieve a word that may have fallen into disuse. To turn the pages of these manuscripts is to hear the voices of my neighbours and my relatives – all the fathers and uncles and grandfathers come to life again. The second interest is more thematic. This material is genuinely ineffable, like nothing else on earth.

Indeed, there is a drawer in the index entitled 'Neacha neamhbeo agus nithe nách bhfuil ann' ('Unalive beings and things that don't exist'). Now I am not the greatest empiricist on earth but this one has even me stumped. Either they exist or they don't exist. But if they don't exist why does the card index about them stretch the length of my arm? Yet that is the whole point of this material and its most enduring charm. Do these beings exist? Well, they do and they don't. You see, they are beings from '*an saol eile*', the 'otherworld', which in Irish is a concept of such impeccable intellectual rigour and credibility that it is virtually impossible to translate into English, where it all too quickly becomes fey and twee and 'fairies-at-the-bottom-of-the-garden'.

The way so-called depth-psychologists go on about the subconscious nowadays you'd swear they had invented it, or at the very least stumbled on a ghostly and ghastly continent where mankind had never previously set foot. Even the dogs in the street in West Kerry know that the 'otherworld' exists, and that to be in and out of it constantly is the most natural thing in the world. This constant tension between reality and fantasy, according to Jeffrey Gantz, translator of *Early Irish Myths and Sagas*, is characteristic of all Celtic art, but manifests itself particularly in the literature of Ireland. Mr Gantz believes that it is not accidental to the circumstances of literary transmission but is rather an innate characteristic, a gift of the Celts. It means that the 'otherworld' is not simply an anticipated, joyful afterlife; it is also

— even primarily — an alternative to reality. This easy interaction with the imaginary means that you don't have to have a raving psychotic breakdown to enter the 'otherworld'. The deep sense in the language that something exists beyond the ego-envelope is pleasant and reassuring, but it is also a great source of linguistic and imaginative playfulness, even on the most ordinary and banal of occasions.

Let's say I decide some evening to walk up to my aunt's house in West Kerry. She hears me coming. She knows it's me because she recognises my step on the cement pavement. Still, as I knock lightly on the door she calls out, 'An de bheoaibh nó de mhairbh thú?' ('Are you of the living or of the dead?') Because the possibility exists that you could be either, and depending on which category you belong to, an entirely different protocol would be brought into play. This is all a joke, of course, but a joke that is made possible by the imaginative strengths of the language itself.

I am not constructing an essentialist argument here, though I do think that because of different circumstances, mostly historical, the strengths and weaknesses of Irish are different from those of English, and the imaginative possibilities of Irish are, from a poet's perspective, one of its greatest strengths. But this is surely as true of, say, Bengali as it is of Irish. It is what struck me most in the Nobel Prize acceptance speech made by the Yiddish writer Isaac Bashevis Singer. When often asked why he wrote in a dead language, Singer said he was wont to reply that he wrote mostly about ghosts, and that is what ghosts speak, a dead language. Singer's reply touched a deep chord with his Irish audience. It reminded us that the existential precariousness of our language is not an Irish problem alone. According to the linguist Michael Krauss in a recent article in *Language* magazine, minority languages in the English-language sphere face a ninety per cent extinction rate between now and some time in the next century. Therefore, in these days when a major problem is the growth of an originally Anglo-American, but now genuinely global, pop monoculture that reduces everything to the level of the most stupendous boredom, I would think that the preservation of minority languages such as Irish, with their unique and unrepeatable way of looking at the world, would be as important for human beings as the preservation of the remaining tropical rainforests are for biological diversity.

Recently, on a short trip to Kerry with my three daughters, I stayed with my brother and his wife in the old house he is renovating at Camp, on the eastern end of the Dingle peninsula, under the beetling brow of Cathair Chonroí promontory fort. My brother said he had something special to show us, so one day we trooped up the mountain to Derrymore Glen. Although the area is now totally denuded of any form of growth other than lichens and sphagnum moss, the name itself is a dead giveaway: Derrymore from "Doire Mór" in Irish, meaning 'large oak grove'. A more desolate spot you cannot imagine, yet half-way up the glen, in the crook of a hanging valley, intricate and gnarled, for all the world like a giant bonsai, was a single survivor, one solitary oak tree. Only the top branches were producing leaves; it was definitely on its last legs, and must have been between two and three hundred years old. How it had survived the massive human and animal depredation of the countryside that occurred during that time I do not know, but somehow it had. It was very much a '*bile*', a sacred tree, dear to the Celts. A fairy tree. A magic tree. We were all very moved by it. Not a single word escaped us as we stood in the mizzling drizzle. At last Ayse, my ten-year-old, broke the silence. 'It would just give you an idea', she said, 'of what this place was like when it really was a 'Doire Mór' and covered with oak trees.' I found myself humming the air of 'Cill Cais', that poignant lament for both the great woods of Ireland and the largesse of the Gaelic order which they had come to symbolize.

> Cad a dhéanfaimid feasta gan adhmad?
> Tá deireadh na gcoillte ar lár.
> Níl trácht ar Chill Cais ná a theaghlach
> is ní chlingfear a chling go brách.

> What will we do now without wood
> Now that the woods are laid low?

Cill Cais or its household are not mentioned
and the sound of its bell is no more.

A week later, back in Dublin, that question is still ringing in the
air. I am waiting for the children to get out of school and writing
my journal in Irish in a modern shopping mall in the south
Dublin suburbs. Not a single word of Irish in sight on hoarding,
sign or advertisement, nor a single sound of it in earshot. All
around me are well-dressed and articulate women. I am intrigued
by snatches of animated conversation, yet I am conscious of a
sense of overwhelming loss. I think back to the lonely hillside,
and to Ayse. This is the answer to the question in the song. This
is what we will do without wood.

At some level, it doesn't seem too bad. People are warm and
not hungry. They are expressing themselves without difficulty in
English. They seem happy. I close my notebook with a snap and
set off in the grip of that sudden pang of despair that is always
lurking in the ever-widening rents of the linguistic fabric of
minority languages. Perhaps my mother is right. Writing in Irish
is mad. English is a wonderful language, and it also has the added
advantage of being very useful and of putting bread on the table.
Change is inevitable, and maybe it is part of the natural order of
things that some languages should die while others prevail.

And yet, and yet ... I know this will sound ridiculously
romantic and sentimental. Cringe-makingly awful. Yet not by
bread alone ... We raise our eyes to the hills ... We throw our
bread upon the waters. There are mythical precedents. Take for
instance Moses' mother; consider her predicament. She had the
choice of giving up her son to the Egyptian soldiery, to have him
cleft in two before her very eyes, or to send him down the Nile in
a basket, a tasty dinner for crocodiles. She took what under the
circumstances must have seemed very much like '*rogha an dá dhiogha*'
('the lesser of two evils'), and Exodus and the annals of Jewish
history tell the rest of the story, and are the direct results of an
action which even as I write is still working out its inexorable
destiny. I know it is wrong to compare small things with great, yet
my final answer to why I write in Irish is this:

Ceist na Teangan (in *Feis; Pharaoh's Daughter*)

Cuirim mo dhóchas ar snámh
i mbáidín teangan
faoi mar a leagfá naionán
i gcliabhán
a bhéadh fite fuaite
de dhuilleoga feileastraim
is bitiúman agus pic
bheith cuimilte lena thóin

ansan é a leagadh síos
i measc na ngiolcach
is coigeal na mban sí
le taobh na habhann,
féachaint n'fheadaraí
cá dtabharfaidh an sruth é,
féachaint, dála Mhaoise,
an bhfóirfidh iníon Fharoinn?

The Language Issue (in *Pharaoh's Daughter*)

I place my hope on the water
in this little boat
of the language, the way a body might put
an infant

in a basket of intertwined
iris leaves,
its underside proofed
with bitumen and pitch,

then set the whole thing down amidst
the sedge
and bulrushes by the edge
of a river

only to have it borne hither and thither,
not knowing were it might end up;
in the lap, perhaps,
of some Pharaoh's daughter.

Trans. Paul Muldoon

Dinnsheanchas: The Naming of High or Holy Places

Any discussion of *dinnsheanchas* is bound to be complicated. From time immemorial it has been of great significance in Irish oral and literary traditions, and from time immemorial, too, our ideas of our homeland, our place in the world, have been bound up in it. It is perhaps best, then, to begin at the root: *'dinnsheanchas'* is a compound word, from the two elements *'dinn'* and *'seanchas'*. *'Dinn'*, cognate with Old Norse *'tindr'*, may originally have signified 'a spike or a point', but in Old Irish had already acquired the primary meaning of 'a mountain, hill or hillock', and the extended one of a 'landmark, eminent or notable place'. *'Dinn'* thus early involved itself with the numinosity of place and the values of blood and soil which are fundamental tenets of cultural nationalism, indicating to us how or why a place comes to be 'notable'. The second element of the word, *'seanchas'*, is usually — and inadequately — translated as 'lore'. The meaning of *'seanchas'* is in fact wide enough to encompass all the work of the professional learned classes of early Gaelic society, which included the genealogies of powerful families, tribal lore, stories of conquest or migration, traditional laws and customs of the tribe. And in a similar way to *'dinn'*, the meaning of the word *'seanchas'* is complicated by the fact that idealisation of the 'lore' of the 'people' or 'folk' — 'folklore' — has been another stable tenet in cultural nationalisms, the rampant, violent nature of which, since the break up of the former Soviet Union and more especially Yugoslavia, give one at the very least call for pause when considering a phenomenon such as *dinnsheanchas* in Irish culture.

The bloodcurdling and bloody-handed spectre of Greater Croatia and Greater Serbia, and the possibilities of what we may yet witness in the emergence of a Greater Albania or Greater Macedonia, as well as the closer-to-home last decades in Northern Ireland, all must prove to us that terms such as 'folk' are not to be bandied about lightly. Maurice Goldring's conclusion in *Pleasant the Scholar's Life: Irish Intellectuals and the Construction of the Nation State* may be true: the nation may not be an essence but a social and historical construction, and most national history may be a fairy-tale invented for grown-up children in the nineteenth century. The fact remains, however, that the violence and bloodthirstiness which children know to belong to the region of fantasy in fairy-tales are right now, at this very moment – as Leopold Bloom puts it – being acted out in actual terms, a nightmare from which we have yet to awake.

Affected by the appalling vistas of the now empty landscapes of Bosnia, I have experienced a personal change of mode. This amounts to a movement inwards and downwards, to a form of introversion necessary for the writing of poetry, and especially for dealing with new material and inspirations which are as yet nebulous, free-floating. This is coal-face work which must go on in darkness and silence, down within the deeply black-veined recesses of the psyche. A part of the job-description, this necessary *abaissement du niveau mentale*, also, in a rather unfortunate corollary, unfits me for most social transactions as well as any other intellectual one besides the writing of poetry. I cringed recently when I heard broadcast on radio a lecture I had written in the last few weeks: it seemed self-indulgent, and it was obvious to me that I had been unable to haul myself up out of the depths to achieve what might be termed an objective perspective. So rather than attempt to fight the tendency here, I have decided to write of *dinnsheanchas* from a point of personal witness and as an act of *pietas*.

Dinnsheanchas has long been one of the great branches of knowledge of the Gaelic world. For countless millennia in the oral tradition and for the fifteen hundred years of the written Irish-language tradition, it has been central to the culture. Indeed *dinnsheanchas* is so endemic in early and medieval Irish literature as to be annoying for the modern reader, so woven into the fabric of myths and sagas as to almost entirely obscure the primary narrative, seeming to hold up the pace of the story. Thus just when one of the earliest and greatest sagas of the Ruaraíocht (Red-Branch Knight cycle), the *Táin Bó Cuailnge*, or Cattle-raid of Cooley, is about to hit its stride, the story is abruptly interrupted by toponomical asides that can seem quite gratuitous; a much later tale from the mythological cycle such as the *Aoidhe Chlainne Lir* has numerous similar interruptions. While *dinnsheanchas* thus weaves its way through Irish literature, the text that most exemplifies the tradition is the very beautiful and ecologically informed thirteenth-century Fenian text *Acallamh na Senórach*, or the Colloquy of the Ancients. In it two of the last remnants of Fionn Mac Cumhail's warrior band, Caoilte mac Rónán and Fionn's own son, Oisín, tell a series of stories about the landscape of Ireland that they travel through with the newly arrived St Patrick. While providing Patrick (and the reader, or audience: what the exact relation was between the written text of a medieval tale and the form in which it was transmitted we do not know) with information useful to him in his missionary activity, the text still manages to mount a fairly hefty critique of the religion that he preaches. This is done, one could argue, through *dinnsheanchas*: placelore offers an opportunity to praise the great deeds of the mighty Fianna, now no more, and composes a funerary ode to their talents, wisdom and especially their generosity. By comparison, the codes of conduct of the new faith and its obsession with ascetic practices like fasting and bodily denial are but paltry and niggardly excuses for existence. *Dinnsheanchas* thus allows for both a preserving of the past and a critique of the present, and this tradition lives through centuries of Irish literature, and continues to this day.

On the subject of *dinnsheanchas* in modern Irish, I have chosen to restrict myself to the oral tradition, and in it to a particular informant, Thomas Murphy, of the townland of Cahiratrant in the parish of Ventry, just west of Dingle, County Kerry. This is where I must ask you to bear with me for a moment, while I declare my personal stake in this material. When a return from England to Ireland was in the offing, it was the horror of having a child who could not speak Irish properly which caused my parents to send me out to my aunt May, my mother's only sister, in the village of Cahiratrant in the Kerry Gaeltacht, at the tender age of five. Now, this does seem a rather drastic step, and I'm sure it mustn't have been easy for me, but this particular accident of personal history left me with my deepest allegiance, which is to the Irish language. This chance also led to that language being fused for me with the landscape of Corcha Dhuibhne, the Gaeltacht area of the Dingle Peninsula, and, most especially, with the parish of Ventry. This is deeply limiting in ways, because it means that wherever else I live, I am always hankering after it. I am spoiled for everywhere else because of being so deeply bonded with this one particular place. What I experienced in Corcha Dhuibhne can only be described as an atavistic reaction: I felt a great sense of relief, of belonging, of being a link in a family chain which had been missing in my existence on a Lancashire coalmine.

Recently I came across a piece of writing which contains a lovely expression of my sense of a particular 'genius loci', without the connotations of blood and bloodlust that I find so terrifying in many formulations of cultural nationalism. In *My Golden Trades*, the Czech novelist Ivan Klíma describes making what many considered the mad decision to return to his country less than two years after the Soviet occupation. The thing that drew him back was not a sense of cultural nationalist loyalty, but a simple bond to place:

> The voice through which the spirit of place speaks to those who listen is common to us all: to me and to those people who moved from the backwaters of my homeland more than two millennia ago. By calling it a voice I don't mean anything mystical, a voice of blood and soil. I'm surprised that most people don't hear it, don't feel the natural reasons for affinity with each other. I'm surprised that they invent other reasons, more artificial ones, for sticking together: race, faith or ideas. They are more eager to believe their lives were influenced by the positions of the planets than by the shape of the mountains that surround their birthplace, or the height of the heavens above them, or the direction of the winds that bring the

clouds. Is it possible not to feel some affinity for people who have followed every day the meandering of the same river, climbed the same hills, seen the same flock of birds with each spring, and to whom darkness and light, the cold season and the fruitful season arrived at the same time? ('The Archeologist's Story')

It is something like this that I felt in West Kerry and that wedded me to Irish in a way that has proven, well, if not fatal, then at least decisive. But a further accident that involved me in the fascination with placelore was that my aunt's household was also that of Thomas Murphy, her husband, whom I was to know intimately during the following thirty-five years, until his death at the age of eighty-four.

Thomas Murphy's way of being in the world was primarily the way of *dinnsheanchas*. In describing him thus I do not wish to idealise him in the way of turn-of-the-century cultural national- ists like Padraig Pearse and Douglas Hyde, or in the way of anthropologists and literary historians like George Thomson and Robin Flower. Thomas was no oil painting, and least of all an idealistic, John Lavery one; he was also most unlike Yeats's vision of the Connemara fisherman as 'a wise and simple man'. In many ways he was, in fact, typical of the patriarchal head of household described in Conrad Arensberg and Solon Kimball's classic story of the Irish smallholding: his surviving sisters are scathing in their stories of his youthful high-handedness, and my aunt did not necessarily have an easy life with him. Seventeen years his junior, she was for a long time at the wrong end of the stick. A certain power-balance was eventually established between them, however, and the relationship was always one of a certain mutual respect, albeit within the rigid role-differentiated pattern of the rural family model.

If in his youth he was high-handed, in his old age he could be an irascible and cranky old so-and-so, especially in the years before his hip-replacement operation, when he was in considerable pain from arthritis. Still and all, we got on very well, on the whole, and I was always sure of a welcome in his house. One of the main things that brought us together was my all-consuming interest in placename lore. A level of banter and mutual leg-pulling was also part of our interaction, with he setting me up and mocking my 'book-learning', and I playing the dunderhead in order to get him to tell a well-loved story or anecdote for the umpteenth time. Much of this interaction was informal and, like all oral performance, characterised by its ephemerality and impermanence. Still, I do have any amount of entries on his stories in the forty-odd folklore and general working notebooks that I possess and it is on them that I rely to draw this quick sketch of an until very recently living exponent of *dinnsheanchas*.

Thomas Murphy was born in Cahiratrant on December 28, 1906. There was a fall of snow that night and hence he was often known as 'Thomáisín an tSneachta', 'Little Thomas of the Snows'. Early next morning his father Peaits took the short-cut – up through Mám na Gaoithe and over through the three villages of the Leataithe – to Cathair Deargan in the parish of Cill Mhaolchéadair, to inform his wife's people of the birth. We know this story because my grandmother was a young girl of twelve years of age, throwing snowballs from on top of the frozen-over *'buailé'* or dungheap when Peaits went by. Her father hailed him. 'Bhuel, a Phaits, an bhfuil aon scéal nua agat?' ('Have you any news?') 'Tá,' arsa Peaits, 'mac ó aréir. Abhar fathaigh, cnámha chapaill óig faoi is ní bhfaighidh sé aon fhuacht go brách' ('Yes,' said Peaits, 'a son since last night. The makings of a giant, the bones of a young horse under him, and he'll never get a cold'). The last part of the prediction proved remarkably true, because Thomas was one of the hardiest men who ever lived; he didn't even catch the great flu of 1918, though the whole village went down with it, including four of his uncles who were still living in the house with them. The rest of the statement, unfortunately, was not true, but he retained a great respect for height all his life. 'Níl aon teora leis an scrothaíocht,' he used to say: fine physique is a mighty thing.

Little did my grandmother think that the child who was born that snowy night would grow up, and that she herself would also grow up, marry and have a daughter who would in turn grow up to marry that child. If she had, she would have been horrified at the thought, and actually she was, and my Aunt May's wedding was the result of as subtle a bit of subterfuge as you could get away with in a rural area. She simply got the banns read out in Ventry, rather than in Dingle, so her mother had no inkling of the event until it was landed on her the night before as a *fait accomplit.* One of the reasons my Granny was horrified was that she considered Thomas Murphy to be of her own rather than her daughter's generation. This is not quite true – and in fact from the point of view of mindset, he belonged to an even older generation than herself.

My Granny was also upwardly mobile, and valued education primarily for its material advantages, to the extent that on her husband's death she mortgaged the farm to give most of her children a university education, something totally unheard of in the area. She herself always regretted bitterly that she had had only one year of formal schooling. So she was not at all impressed that Thomas Murphy had had no more than one year in National School in all. Though officially enrolled for four years, he was the eldest son, fated to inherit the farm, and was dragged out of school on any old excuse at all: to help with cows calving, to dig potatoes, to bring in the hay, to do the ploughing. He once admitted to me that any year that he was on the school rollbooks never meant more than four months' schooling in reality. This did not affect his Irish, as only English was taught in the schools in those days, and he could be disdainful of '*Gaeilge na leabhar*' or book-Irish as taught in the school system since Irish independence.

Despite this lack of formal education, Thomas had enormous knowledge of the local environment, a knowledge he continually sought out: there is no such thing as a natural tradition-bearer. You get to know an awful lot of stories, songs and lore only by having a thirst for them, a need to learn them at all costs. Thus the renowned storyteller Peig Sayers was reviled in her youth by her sister-in-law, Cáit Ní Bheoláin, as being a big lazy slob; she did nothing around the house all day but sit listening to stories. Thus also did Seán Ó Griffin of Cathair Boilg walk fourteen miles to Abhann an Scáil and back in one night – twenty-eight miles in all – because he dearly wanted to hear a certain story, and he had heard that a certain tailor was telling it in a house there that night.

Thomas Murphy's interest in placename lore was likewise of an encyclopaedic capacity. Though the son of a renowned Fenian storyteller and notable wit, Peaits Ó Murchu, he was not a *seanchaí* or storyteller as such, mainly because he had a bad stammer. While among the manuscripts of the Department of Irish Folklore at University College Dublin are countless stories from his father collected by Joe Daly, I have found only three stories by Thomas himself. In the notes to these stories he is described as a '*mac feirmeora*', a farmer's son, which is correct in that he had not yet been given the title to the land. I got photocopies of these stories once and presented them to him, but he was uninterested. I was therefore intrigued to be told later by Joe Daly himself that he had set out to collect stories from Thomas, and in particular had hoped to record the beginning of a story about the King of Ireland's Son and the Eagle where a battle of the birds and beasts is described that nobody on the whole peninsula remembered correctly except Thomas. (This story had been collected in English in the turn of the century and is the basis of Patricia Lynch's wonderful book for children, *The Turfcutter's Donkey*.)

At this point I would like to draw on the methods and categories developed by Séamas Ó Catháin and Patrick Flanagan in *The Living Landscape*, a study of the Irish-speaking townland of Kilgalligan in County Mayo, as much of their material is applicable to the world-view of Thomas Murphy. Ó Catháin and Flanagan seek to differentiate between two categories, Namelore and Placelore. Namelore, they suggest, embraces any explanation or comment on a name or name element, whether factual or fictitious. Thus I would categorise quite a lot of material given to me by Thomas – such as his comments on places such as 'Drom a' chapaill', a narrow ridge of cliff shaped a bit like a horse's back, or other such names such as 'Leacacha na bhFaoileán' or 'Ceann an Chloichir'.

Placelore, Ó Catháin and Flanagan continue,

includes a broad range of comment ranging from cultural appraisals of land, seashore and sea to the identification and location of hazards at sea in the form of reefs and hazards on land such as the haunts of otters. In addition, this kind of lore contains reference to events, real or imaginary, which are reputed to have taken place at specific locations. There is also frequent comment on the functional attributes of certain places, many of which still maintain their prominence in the context of life in Killgalligan today.

This is equally true of the placelore repertoire of Thomas Murphy and its relation to the townland of Cahiratrant. Rarely, for example, would he mention Lic Caoil, a large rock lying south off his own land, without telling me how it was the petrified body of a giant. He also always connected it with Tráig Chaoil, or Caol's Strand, a short beach about one mile away, saying that this was where Caol's body had first been found when it floated in on the tide after the Battle of Ventry. He seemed totally unfazed at any contradictions between the floating of the body onto the strand and its petrification back on the cliffs. These things were not to be scoffed at or questioned: at some level they were a form of gospel.

For all their attempts at categorisation, however, Ó Catháin and Flanagan, in studying the *dinnsheanchas* of Mayo, finally succumb to an umbrella term – 'placename lore' – equally applicable to what I learned from Thomas Murphy:

> The placename lore has its own peculiar style and structure, ranging as it does from truism to gossip and from the mundane to the fantastic, each item having its own validity though it is often difficult to differentiate between the real and the unreal. This kind of material has a specific function in Killgalligan and in Irish-speaking Ireland since it is recognised and acknowledged as a vehicle for the explanation of the structure of the local world.

For me the wonderful heterogeneity of material is one of its main attractions, amounting to a spontaneous eruption of unconscious material, with very little input from the organising, linear left brain: it is, in other words, a mode of thought that lends itself very easily to the associative register of poetry. Thus poems of mine grew naturally from the stories that I had heard from Thomas since my childhood.

Thomas Murphy was possessed of what Seamus Heaney has called a 'genealogical imagination'. Not only could he go back in his own bloodlines, but in those of every other member of the

townland, and also most of the parish, and their connections
with many people from other parishes as well, often at least to
the seventh generation. Thus he himself was 'Tomás Mhic
Phádraig Mhic Thomáis Mhic Sheáin Mhic Mhuiris Mhic
Mhuiris Uí Mhurchú': Thomas, son of Pádraig, son of Thomas,
son of Seán, son of Muiris, son of Muiris Murphy, and his sons
Pádraig and Seán were the seventh generation of those that he
knew about. He claimed that his line were originally from Fán,
but then had moved to Cill Fearnóg, where they lived until the
three villages of An Cuan Íoctarach, An Cuan Uachtarach and
An Cúilín Bán were evicted by a Corkman called Leahy in the
1860s. His grandfather was six and a half years old when they
moved to their present land in Cahiratrant, which was lying idle
after the Great Famine.

Thomas could also outline other people's relationships to
each other to a remarkable degree, and I have endless pages of
notes that I have taken down from him about my own family tree,
with all the ins and outs of it over many generations. These were
the basis of an almost endless source of comment, where the
simplest action of physical characteristic could be put back to a
certain long-dead relation or bloodline. When my second
daughter Ayse was born with curling toes, Thomas took one look
at her and declared, 'Hm! Tá méireanna marcaigh aici. Furaist a
aithint gur de shliocht Chill Uraidh í' ('She's got rider's toes.
Easily known that she's the progeny of Cill Uraidh'). Now, my
child's father is Turkish, and his mother was Bosnian, and my own
people haven't lived in Cill Uraidh since my great-grandmother
Cáit Ní Shé, yet Thomas was unmoved. The toes were the
giveaway. Later I found out that, yes, this physical feature is well-
attested for Cill Uraidh people, though I dare say it was more
from holding on to the flanks of donkeys and mules on the
precipitous *boithríns* of their townland, half-way up Mount Eagle,
that they developed such 'rider's toes' rather than from any great
acquaintance with pedigree bloodstock!

Placenames were a source of fascination to Thomas Murphy
at all times. A major source of distress to him, though, was the
fact that there were some free-floating placenames for which he

was not sure of the places. One of them was a place called 'Slí Uislí', which was, seemingly, a gap in the cliffs over near where Cuan Íóchtarach used to be that he had heard of from his Grandfather but had never been able to identify for himself. Another was a place called 'Seamair Bhuaile', which for reasons of his own, never really disclosed, he made out was on the northeast flank of Mount Brandon. Any time he went over the Connor Pass to that side of the peninsula he would ask anyone he met had they ever heard of this place 'Seamair Bhuaile' and did they know where it was. Years later in the Department of Irish Folklore I came across a fleeting reference to it, in a description of two Fairy Women — *Mná Sí* — who were glimpsed striding along the countryside on the north side of the Connor Pass in the dead of night. They were carrying *buarachs* — that is, lengths of rope for tethering cattle — and were obviously up to no good. One of them was overheard saying to the other one, 'Ní bheidh bó ar bith ná beidh bleáite againn as seo go Seamair Bhuaile' ('There will not be a single cow that we will not have stolen the milk of from here to Seamair Bhuaile'). I told this story to Thomas and he was satisfied that it rang true with his own intuitions, but unfortunately the story does not mention the coordinates of the place or anywhere that might be adjacent to it, so we were still as much in the dark about it as before.

The only category of story mentioned by Ó Catháin and Flanagan that Thomas did not tell on a regular basis was fairy lore, though like all countrymen he had an implicit belief in *an saol eile*, the 'otherworld', peopled by the souls of the dead, fairies, spirits, hags, pookas and those most redoubtable figures of all, *Aingil an Uaibhair*, the prideful fallen cohorts of Satan. When I was quite young he once started to tell me how he had seen a spirit by the road in Cill Mhic a' Domhnaigh, a huge giant sitting by the wayside with long skinny legs stretching across the road who pulled each leg up slowly to let him pass. At this point in the story he looked away in some distraction and I often wondered why. Later on I came across a story told about a similar personage encountered by someone else at that very same spot. Was it some lack of credence in the tale that stopped him, or a genuine dislike for passing off someone else's story as his own? I never got to the end of it, and he could never be prevailed upon to tell that story again.

But whether or not he ever saw that one, there is one spirit that he definitely saw. He was out ploughing the field called An Garraí Nua with a white gelding one fine day in May in 1927 when *The Spirit of St Louis* passed directly over the village, flying quite low. It had sighted land over An Baile Uachtarach in the parish of Ballyferriter, had flown down the gap of Mám na Gaoithe and straight over the village of Cahiratrant and down south-east over Dingle Bay and the Iveragh Peninsula on its way to landfall in Le Bourget airfield, Paris. Thomas's neighbour, Mike Long, was pulling up lobster pots just under the cliffs and nearly fell out of the boat with the fright the plane gave him when it passed directly above him. Another neighbour, John Shea, was herding yearling bullocks and they turned and nearly trampled him. Thomas was out ploughing and the white gelding bolted on him and it was with great difficulty that he managed to hold it back. 'Is that the first aeroplane you ever saw?' I asked him. Yes it was, he told me. 'And what did you think it was?' I asked, thinking back on the old man in my Granny's village who, when he saw his first motorcar, had rushed in to her swearing it was the devil incarnate, with huge lamps for eyes, trailing clouds of steam and sulphur behind it. 'What else would I think it was?' shot back Thomas in return. 'Sure and hadn't we been reading about it in the paper for a solid three days beforehand?' So much for my misguided apprehensions of a primeval state of mind, un-complicated by the clutter of modern conveniences.

And as I write this now I suddenly remember a similar occasion, an evening in October 1957 when Thomas rounded up the children of the village on his *buaile*, which had the best view of the whole village. He scanned the heavens for a while and then pointed to what seemed at first one small star amongst the myriad others. 'Féach ansan agaibh é,' he said, 'an sputnik' ('There you have it, that's the sputnik'), and our eyes followed the proof of the glories of modern science with almost as much wonder and admiration as his own. Of course the fate of the dog Laika later became a great topic of conversation in the village but no great source of regret to a generation adept at clifting stray animals and unwanted litters. It also got subsumed miraculously into the great ever-changing tapestry of *dinnsheanchas*.

From this you can perhaps get a necessarily cursory idea of the all-comprehensive and multi-dimensional qualities of just one man's repertoire of *dinnsheanchas*. Thomas Murphy's influence acts on my work at all levels, even where it is not ostensibly about *dinnsheanchas* or West Kerry. Witness, for instance, this new poem, in which he has metamorphosed into a stranded merman. This is based on a real incident, a time when I was a teenager and asked him for the name of a type of dogfish that I had found drying on the beach. For the first and only time in his life he mentioned to me his belief in merpeople. He was never to do so again, as later in his life he became rather coy and wary in speaking of mermaids or of fairy lore. The fact that I and my generation scoffed at him unmercifully from the heights of our newly acquired knowledge of biology and geology did nothing to recommend him to pass on his knowledge to us. Twenty-five years down along the line, much humbler and more dog-eared, I feel in no position to laugh at him. Actually I feel that his world-view has much to offer us as a middle ground between the severities of scientific abstraction and the loneliness of the individual in contemplation of them.

Admhail Shuaithinseach (in *Cead Aighnis*)

Aon uair amháin riamh im'shaol
a fuaireas oiread is an leide is lú ó bhéal
aon duine acu
go raibh saghas éigin cine-ghlanadh gafa tríd acu
is gur ó áit éigin eile ar fad, i bhfad i gcéin
a thánagadar.

A sé déag nó mar sin a bhíos nuair thárla sé seo.
Mé ag foghlaim bitheolaíochta
is teoiricí ceimice.
Bhíos faoi dhraíocht ag fiseolaíocht agus sláinteachas
is mé lán suas
de théarmaí staidéir gnó is ríomhaireachta.

Thángas de siúl cos lá trasna an Náth,
mo threabhsar fillte suas go dtí mo chromáin
is smut de bhrúscar cladaigh á tharrach im' dhiaidh agam.
Bhíos fiosrach faoi.
'Cé'n sórt bric í seo agam, a Thomáis?
Gadhar, ab ea ?'

Do leag an seanduine uaidh a rámhainn ar an dtráigh
mar a raibh na luganna á mbaint aige.
Buí, dubhghlas is crón is ea do ghlioscadar,
ag snámharnach de shíor sa chróca romhainn.
'Ní haon ghadhar é sin atá agat', ar sé,
'ach cat. Cat ceanainn'.
Do stop sé, thug catshúil thapaidh deas is clé
is cuir cogar-i-leith chugham.

'Níl aon ainmhí dá bhfuil ar an míntír', ar sé
'nach bhfuil a chomh'mhaith d'ainmhí
sa bhfarraige. An cat, an madra, an bhó , an mhuc;-
tá siad go léir ann.
Go dtí an duine féin, agus tá sé sin ann leis.
'Sé an t-ainm atá air siúd ná an mhurúch.'

Ghluais scamall dorcha thar a shúile ar dhath na dtonn
a dhein tiompáin mhara dhóibh.
N'fheadar cad a shnámhaigh anall is anonn
sna duibheagáin doimhne sin
mar sar a raibh am agam i gceart
é a bhodhradh lem' chuid cleatrála is lem' chaint
ar cheimic, fisic, is ar fhiosriúcháin muireolaíochta
do chas sé ar a shál is d'imigh uaim.

D'fhág sé ar snámh idir dhá uisce mé.

A Remarkable Admission

Only one time ever in my life
did I get as much as the slightest

inkling from any one of them
that they had gone through a sort of ethnic cleansing
and that some other place altogether, far away beyond
was where they really belonged.

I was sixteen or so when this happened.
Mad into biology and chemical equations.
I was enthralled by physiology and hygiene,
up to the gills
with accountancy and computer skills.

I came across the Náth one day on foot,
my jeans-legs turned up way beyond the knees,
trailing behind a bit of flotsam I had found.
I was curious about it.
'What class of a fish is this I've here,
Thomas,' I asked. 'Is it a dogfish?'

The old man laid his spade down on the strand
where he had been digging for lugworms. I remember how
they sparkled yellow, blackish-green and brown
as they slithered and seethed in the jam jar.
'That's no dogfish you have there,' he said
'but a specked catfish.' He lowered his voice,
glanced quickly left and right
and, in a whisper,
'There is no single animal up on dry land
that doesn't have its equivalent beast in the sea.
The cat, the dog, the cow, the sow —
they are all there.
Even to the human being himself, and he's there too.
The name they call him is the merman.'

A dark cloud passed over his sea-green eyes
that made them look like marine trenches.
I will never know what strange creatures swam
around in their great depths
because, just when I was about to pester the head

off him with chemistry, physics and the results
of the latest underwater explorations,
he turned on his heel and headed off

and left me stranded,
like a body floating between two layers of water.

Trans. Ní Dhomhnaill

Amongst the many belief systems that have been depotentated
and imploded in our time, I would argue, are Freudian and
Lacanian discourses. But if Freud has taught us anything, it is
about the return of the repressed, and so the level of mythmaking
present in something like *dinnsheanchas* should be admitted for
what it is, but not denigrated as such. In the face of our ultimate
mortality most things that we believe in are probably no more and
no less than enabling myths, without which it would be
impossible to get up in the morning. This mythic dimension
needs expression, and I think that *dinnsheanchas*, which though not
peculiar to Gaelic literature is a very prominent part of it, can be
considered a useful cultural container for our deeply held,
heartfelt need for both mythology and a homeland, another
compound word which puts together two of the most powerful
words in the whole vocabulary of human identity.

During the medieval heyday of *dinnsheanchas* Ireland was by no
manner of means a nation as we use the word today. It was a
mixum-gatherum of anything up to one hundred and sixty *tuaths*,
or petty kingdoms, divided on a clan system, and in many ways
like a rural version of the early stages of the Greek city states.
Most members of a particular clan ventured outside their own
territory very much at their peril; even saints had to be quite
circumspect about whose water it was they dipped any particular
big toe in. The only people welcome everywhere, in fact, were the
poets – the guardians, originators and constantly entertaining
purveyors of *dinnsheanchas* – since theirs was an art that surpassed
all petty boundaries, and cemented the society in a symbolic way,
however much that might be belied by the mundane and almost

gratuitous head-bashing which constituted the daily nitty-gritty of cattle-raiding. In its modern sense, it is epitomised for me in Thomas Murphy, whom I have chosen out of a large number of possible informants of his generation only because he was married to my aunt, and because I was therefore particularly fond of him, and had a long and easy acquaintance with him over a period of many years. I could as easily have chosen any of his neighbours, with slightly different results in emphasis: Mike Long, as much a seaman as Thomas was a landman, whose toponomical lore would have been speckled with the very sharply observed naturalistic details which were his particular specialty; Joeín Shea, who to this day is incapable of mentioning a place-name associated with Fionn Mac Cumhaill without launching into all sixty-seven verses of the Fenian lay on which that particular placename is based; Mike Shea, my own first and third cousin (his mother was my great-grandaunt), whose period of emigration to the States before his return in 1929 as a result of the Great Depression gave him a detachment and a certain modern streetwise slant of mind which was the source of a sly and very cynical sense of humour. To these and many others like them I owe a practical knowledge and sensible appreciation of *dinnsheanchas* as a lived dimension of life that has been enormously rewarding and enriching to me personally.

Although I am a writer, I think a lot of what Wendell Berry says in a recent interview, 'A Question a Day':

> It is not the written word that impairs memory, but dependence on the written word to the exclusion of the spoken. Some experience cannot be put wholly into writing. And so as dependence on writing grows, the communicated experience suffers a corresponding attenuation. The most complete speech is that of conversation in a settled community of some age, where what is said refers to and evokes things, people, places and events that are commonly known. In such a community, to speak and hear is to remember.

Particularly in the Irish-speaking communities of the western seaboard of Ireland, and to a lesser extent throughout the country-side, the collective memory of the community is enshrined in *dinnsheanchas*, which can function as that necessary psychic container

the French psychoanalytical critic Julia Kristeva considers absent in
our time. Through *dinnsheanchas* we can possess the land emotionally and imaginatively without any particular sense of or actual
need for titular ownership. Like, in a lesser way, the reading of the
future from tea-leaves, it gives us an 'objective correlative' on which
we can hang the powerful and ever-changing dimensions and
personages of our *paysage interieure*.

And *dinnsheanchas* can do more than this: it can also become a way
of uniting factions, of breaking barriers. In his classic study of rural
Fermanagh, *Passing the Time in Ballymenone*, the anthropologist Henry
Glassie describes his difficulty in finding the nucleus of a local
community divided along sectarian lines until he discovered that the
stories, the *dinnsheanchas*, were a material held in common, and were
the cement which kept the community together and distinct. The
geographer Estyn Evans, in a 1984 pamphlet 'Ulster: the Common
Ground', notes the varieties to be found in lore of place:

> I found that running through the whole there was a single theme
> with many variations – and this variety is in itself very appealing,
> although it is also a great source of dissension. I think we have
> somehow to live with that variety and exploit it rather than let it
> disturb our peace; because it is precious in that it stands in contrast
> to the almost universal monotony of modern culture, its dullness, its
> commercial exploitation and material values, its mass production.

I think that a sense of this imaginative stewardship of the land is
something that is increasing in leaps and bounds in Ireland.
President Mary Robinson's concept of 'The Fifth Province' is an
expression of this highly potent imaginative dimension. The
flurry of interest in local history and the plethora of clubs and
organisations that have grown up in the last five to ten years,
particularly in Northern Ireland, to cater for this interest bears
witness, perhaps, to the expression of a primary need. I believe
that a renewed interest in *dinnsheanchas* may enable us to share our
love and admiration and wonder of the land of Ireland, and can
cater in an imaginative way for the need of many for a place to
belong to so that we may love and cherish it rather than killing
each other over it.

An Bhanfhile Sa Traidisiun: The Woman Poet in the Irish Tradition

Irish poetry in the second half of the twentieth century has been forcefully changed by women's writing. The emergence of this writing has been gradual and often obstructed, hysterically fought against, condescended to and patronised. Eavan Boland has described her realisation, while facilitating women's writing workshops in the 1980s, that a new wellspring was being revealed in Irish poetry. These workshops were spoken of by other established poets, however, in a way that suggested they were full of second-class citizens, rather than writers of new themes, new approaches and new voices that would refresh the poetry. And yet despite this opposition, despite the talking behind backs, women's poetry in Ireland has slowly but surely built up the momentum of a tidal wave, inexorable, unstoppable: that's about the sum of it. What we are seeing are the white horses of surf on the top of the rolling wave about to break: we are talking here of a genuine watershed. Irish women's poetry offers a vital critique of what was going into the Irish poem in earlier days, and what was kept outside it.

What was going in and what was being kept out: this is for me a particularly telling notion, and one to which I will return later on. First let me go back a bit in time to when I first started writing poetry thirty years ago, in the late sixties and early seventies. At that time, to tell you the truth, it didn't matter a whit to me whether there were other women poets in my immediate environment or not. Put it down to youthful arrogance, if you like, and the first experiences of that exhilarating, heady feeling of going beyond the limits of one's conscious personality and in doing so producing poems. But maybe the fact that I was able to launch myself into poetry with such youthful and relative insouciance can be partly put down to the fact that there *were*, in fact, women poets in my immediate environment.

At my first ever reading – of 'Filí Éireann go hAonteach' at the first Cumann Merriman Winter School in my hometown of Nenagh in February, 1969 – I was congratulated and encouraged by no less a personage than Caitlín Maude herself. She was back from England, reciting poetry impromptu when she was not singing incredible 'sean-nós' songs like 'Dónal Og' or 'Liam O'Raghallaigh'. I was utterly enthralled: I had found my role model. And my sense of Irish women's poetry was undoubtably helped by the fact that, when Caitlín Maude encouraged me that winter, I had already had exposure to Máire Mhac an tSaoi, whose work was on the school curriculum. We had studied 'Oiche Nollag' – 'Le coinnle na n-aingeal tá an spéir amuigh breactha, tá fiacail an tseaca sa ghaoth ón gnoc' – for our Inter-Cert, and, even more significantly, 'Inquisitio 1584', on the Leaving Certificate course:

Sa bhliain sin d'aois Ar dTiarna
Chúig chéad déag ceithre fichid
nó blianta beaga ina dhiaidh sin
Seán Mac Éamoinn Mhic Uilig
láimh le Sionainn do chrochadh.

Probably because I was fortunate enough to have this double exposure to Maude and Mhac an tSaoi, women poets, so far as I was concerned, were a natural part of any poetic or scholarly inheritance. The Irish language itself has a term '*banfhile*', or 'woman poet', which is as neutral and non-judgmental a term as '*banaltra*' or 'female fosterer' (nurse) or '*ban-fheoirseach*', 'female weaver', unlike the term, say, in English, 'poetess', which is derogatory and reductive, especially nowadays. (Bringing this sort of gendering to its logical conclusion gets you the line from a children's book I saw recently: 'Two little ghostesses, sitting on postesses, eating their toastesses.') I had the term '*banfhile*' and the example of Maude and Mhac an tSaoi; the fact or lack of an active women's poetic tradition didn't bother me much then, which or whether, one way or the other. Now, though, thirty years down the road, it bothers me a great deal, since I have long realised just how fortunate and timely my own encounters were. The fact that the few women poets in the tradition appear to most as distant, ghostly islands in a great sea of indifference and a fog of unknowing disturbs me, because I know in my soul that such an appearance is not the whole picture, nor the true picture, but very much the result of the vagaries of canon-making: what is going in, and what is being left out.

A short historical recapitulation is perhaps in order, and demonstrates just this process of inclusion and exclusion in the Irish tradition. The first woman poet in Irish literature must be Fidelm Banfháidh (the prophetess) mentioned in the *Táin* as having just returned from Scotland, where she had been pursuing her studies. Maeve meets her as she is setting out on her great cattle raid to bring the Brown Bull of Cooley back to Connacht with her: she asks the prophetess to look into the future to see what will be the outcome of her hosting. Fidelm answers her in a runic poem, foretelling calamity and destruction – 'I see red, I see blood' – which doesn't please Maeve one bit, nor deter her either. She continues with her hosting, to disastrous consequences for the Connachtmen. Like the Trojan Cassandra, another prophetess who went unheeded, Fidelm was remarkably correct in her prophecy.

There are other examples of women poets mentioned in early Irish literature, such as Liadán of Corchaghuiney from the fragmentary epic of 'Liadán and Cuirithir', but there are also any number of poems attributed to famous women such as Déirdre and Derbhorghila, right back to the foremother of us all, 'Mé Éabha'. But here we have to make very important distinctions between (a) a woman poet producing a text, (b) a woman character described in a text produced by a man and (c) a woman described as a poet in a text produced by a man. We have no way of knowing at this point in time whether, for instance, Fidelm or Liadán or the Hag of Béara were ever in category (a), as women poets producing texts. All we can say with certainty is that they are in category (c), women described as poets in texts produced by men.

The first woman poet who might have an historical reality is

to be found in *Sanas Cormaic*, written about the year 900, where it
is mentioned that Seanchán Toirpéist, one of the earliest
historically documented poets, travelled to Oileán Mhanainn, the
Isle of Man, where he met a certain Iníon Uí Dushláine, a Miz
Delaney from Muscraí Liach, which the text informs us is in the
territory of the Uí Fidghenti. She had set out on her poetic *cuirt*,
a type of early Irish Grand Tour that poets used to make as a kind
of finishing school. While she was off on her *cuirt*, all her people
had been killed and her brother was frantically looking for her
through the length and breadth of Ireland and had not been able
to find her. She is described in the text as a '*bainlethcherd*', a woman-
lethcherd, a *lethcherd* being the second highest of the seven stages of
apprenticeship in poetry, second only to an *ollamh*, a sort of
professor of poetry. This Miz Delaney was a kind of Associate
Professor of poetry, then, in the terms we would use nowadays.

Another likely mention of an historical woman poet is in the
Corpus Iuris Hibernici, the great codifying of the Brehon Laws, where
we hear of Eithne, daughter of Amhalghaidh Mac Muireadaigh,
who was the lover of the king Eochaidh mac Feargusa. Eochaidh
had been beaten in battle by Cormac Ó Cuinn and was imprisoned
by him on Torey Island. Eithne knew this and wanted to make the
information as public as possible. She knew that Cormac Ó Cuinn
was obliged to inaugurate the great feast of Tara in three years' time,
and she wanted to go. There was only one snag. As the text says, 'ní
thigedh nech gan dán i dTemhair': nobody could come to Tara
without a poem. Nothing daunted, Eithne went off learning the art
of poetry under Firchirtne: 'Luidh Eithne do foghlaim éigsí la
Firchirtne i riocht giolla.' This last is the bit that bothers me
somewhat: seemingly to be allowed learn poetry necessitated a sex
change, for Eithne went off on her scholarly endeavors '*i riocht giolla*',
in the disguise of a gilly, or young man.

Besides these possible historical figures, we have others for
whom it is almost impossible to ascertain an actual existence –
even without the complications of cross-dressing. The question
of what category best befits a figure like Senteine Béarra, or the
Hag of Béarra, is a moot point. Seemingly the Senteine Béarra
was of the Corcha Dhuibhne, and was considered one of the best

women poets of that remarkably artistically gifted people. She thus belongs, possibly, alongside Brighid iníon Iustáin, Liadán ben Chuirithir and Uallach iníon Mhuineacháin, blessed by the saint Finín Cam, who foretold that the Corcha Dhuibhne would never be without a famous *cailleach* or old woman; and this blessing bore fruit, if storytellers like Peig Sayers and Máire Ruiséal are seen as their modern counterparts. Peig Sayers had an active vocabulary of about 30,000 words and knew how to use it, as did Máire Ruiséal, also known as Cú an Tobair, renowned as a wise woman and healer and consulted even by De Valera when he once toured the area. That some of their predecessors were actual historical personages is beyond possible; it is probable. That Uallach, the daughter of Muineachán, was indeed a historical personage is given some credence by the fact that her death is recorded in the annals of Innisfallen for the year 934. Her death is the only item recorded for that year, and she is described as '*príomh banfhiled Eireann*', the foremost of the woman poets of Ireland, leading one to believe that she was considered very important, and that there were a whole clatter of women poets following on after her. And it is true that whole groups of women weave in and out of Old Irish texts and are described as poets. Nevertheless, not one single line has come down to us that can be unambiguously proven to be from any one of their hands.

As a result, it has been the accepted wisdom that there were no literate women poets. But somehow this has always struck me as a little too pat. In his comprehensive book on the role of the poet in Irish culture, Daithi Ó hOgáin claims that there hasn't been a mention of as much as one woman poet in the Irish literary tradition for over a thousand years. Seán Ó Tuama, in an essay on my own work, remarks what little help the Irish literary tradition is to women poets. Gearóid Ó Crualaoich, in his controversial essay 'Dearcadh Dána', argues that the writing of poetry is considered a manly act in the Irish tradition. Indeed there is a consensus on this 'fact', which is expressed most succinctly, perhaps, by Seán Ó Ríordáin in his poem 'Banfhile', in which he repeats again and again with a sense of ever-increasing hysteria, 'Ní file ach filíocht í an bhean' ('Woman is not poet but poetry').

Although approximately twenty-five women from history are mentioned by name in Caerwyn Williams and Máirín Ní Mhuiríosa's 1979 *Tradisiún Liteartha na nGael*, 'our most substantial historical survey of the Irish literary tradition', as Máirín NicEoin describes it in a recent issue of *Graph*, most of these are the daughters or wives of famous men whose lives and work are discussed in the book. Williams and Ní Mhuiríosa themselves state quite baldly that 'Is beag rian a d'fhág na mná ar thraidisiún liteartha na Gaeilge' ('Women have left little mark on the Irish literary tradition'). Nowhere in the criticism of the Irish tradition, in other words, can I find anything but confirmation of Eavan Boland's claim that, until recently, women have been nothing else but 'fictive queens and national sibyls'.

In Ireland the myth of sovereignty envisaged as a woman (Éire, Banba, Fodhla and so on) sweeps through the ages from untold millennia. So glaringly obvious was this construct, in fact, that Freud's biographer, the English psychoanalyst Ernest Jones, gave a memorable address to the British Psychoanalytic Society in the late 1920s about the potency of the nationalist image of Ireland as a woman. Jones examined the image as an outsider, without any knowledge of the long line of cultural vehicles for this imagery that gathered momentum all the way through the 'aisling' poems and turn-of-the-century nationalist rhetoric:

'Did you see an old woman go down the path?'
'I did not, but I saw a young girl, and she had the walk of a queen'.

This image galvanised a whole population at the beginning of this century, and is still shockingly alive in the collective psyche, for all that an unholy alliance of Marxist-Freudian reductionist intellectuals may seek to deny it. Boland engages polemically with this image and is dead right to do so because, as Marina Warner has pointed out most comprehensively in her book *Monuments and Maidens*, the more the image of woman comes to stand for abstract concepts like justice, liberty or national sovereignty, the more real women are denigrated and consigned, most likely barefoot and pregnant, to the kitchen. We are all of us, men and women, as Eavan Boland points out, existing in 'a mesh, a web, a labyrinth of associations … We ourselves are constructed by the construct.'

You would think that when Ireland became an independent state that things would have changed, that the sovereignty myth would have been imaged differently. Actually, if anything, the situation worsened. In the pamphlet 'Sex and Nation', Geraldine Meaney discusses the difficulty in separating images of self-sacrificing Irish mother and suffering mother Ireland, demonstrating the mutual dependency of sexual and national identity in Ireland. Meaney situates her analysis in a wider post-colonial perspective, pointing out that the process by which a nation declares independence and sovereignty most often relies upon an assertion of 'masculine' authority:

> Anxiety about one's fitness for a (masculine) role of authority deriving from a history of defeat or helplessness is assuaged by the assumption of sexual dominance. Women in these conditions become guarantors of their men's status, bearers of national honour and the scapegoats of national identity. They are not merely transformed into symbols of the nation, they become the territory over which power is exercised. The Irish obsession with the control of women's bodies by Church, State, boards of ethics and judicial enquiries, has its roots in such anxieties.

These attitudes and ideas, Meaney concludes, are inscribed in the 1937 Irish Constitution. But I would argue that substantial damage to women's liberties and to civil liberties in general was done even before that, in the first eight years of the Free State, when draconian legislation such as the marriage ban and censorship laws were brought in. And these general social attitudes serve as an indicator of the ways in which women's writing was treated. Just as women were pushed out of work by virtue of Irish legislation, Irish women writers were kept out of print, out of the public sphere, by virtue of a widespread sexism.

But here we should return to the idea of what is being kept in, and what kept out: because the fact of the matter was that, though the literary canon was drawn up without them, there were women poets, even the few I have mentioned above. Maybe it just doesn't suit Daithí Ó hOgáin to hear mention of a woman poet in the literary tradition over the last thousand years, but there were definitely literate women in this period. After all, my own namesake, Nuala Ní Dhomnaill, sister of Red Hugh, an 'an bhean a fuair faill ar an bhfeart' as the poet called her, was a famous patron of poets to whom any amount of bardic poems were addressed. One would presume that for her to be able to appreciate their quality she must have been able to read them, and likewise the noble lady who is addressed in *Leabhar Clainne Suibhne*, to whom many poems in that book are addressed. A certain woman called Caitlín Dubh, probably of the O'Briens of Thomond, is mentioned in manuscripts from the second half of the seventeenth century, and at least five poems are attributed to her, the interesting thing being that they are in both the older bardic and the newer accentual metres, demonstrating a thorough knowledge of the larger bardic tradition. My attention has been also drawn by Liam Ó Murchú of University College Cork to the case of a certain Fionnghuala iníon Domhnaill uí Bhriain, who wrote a '*marbhna*' or literary lament for her husband, Uaithne Mór Ó Lochlainn, when he died in 1617. Ó Murchú argues that it is more than likely that very many poems of this sort were composed but never found their way into manuscripts simply because they were not entirely official. This one found its way into a manuscript written by Aindiras Mac Cruitín in 1727 because it was a special *duanaire*, commissioned by a certain 'Brian Ó Lochlainn', *doctúir leighis*, a medical doctor, and commemorated a noble person of his sept. Slightly further down the line we hear tell of a Máire Ní Chrualaoich, a frequenter of Éigse na Máighe, who not for nothing was known as 'Sappho na Mumhan', the Sappho of Munster, and on whose death Seán Ó Murchú na Ráithíneach composed a *marbhna*. Needless to say, unlike Sappho, of whose work we have at least a few fragments, not one single line of Máire Ní Chrualaoich's work has come down to us.

It is hard to say exactly what is going on here. Perhaps there were certain conventions in the relationship between the poets who composed the poems and the scribes who wrote them into the manuscripts. Perhaps it was considered something like bad form for a poet to write down his or her own poems. After all, we do not have a single line of Aodhagán Ó Rathaille's poetry in his own hand, although we have a manuscript of Seithrún Céitinn's *Foras Feasa Ar Éirinn* written down and transcribed by Ó Rathaille. A lot more scholarship is needed to clarify questions in this area. But whatever the outcome of such scholarship, it seems patently clear at this stage, to me at least, that whatever the actual literary status of women poets in the Irish tradition, they were in general not let near the ink and they were not allowed into the corpus of the canon: 'níor scaoileadh in aice an dúigh iad agus ní bhfuaireadar bheith istigh sna lámhscribhinní', but were consigned to the outer darkness.

From the twelfth century onwards through the seventeenth, bardic poetry flourished in Ireland; despite this, these centuries are even worse than the earlier period from the point of view of women poets. Apart from Isibeul Ní Mhic Cailín, Countess of Argyll, to whom at least one poem is attributed in *Dánta Grá*, there is no other woman mentioned as writing a poetic text of the time. (And she was Scottish anyway, writing before the common literary language of the two countries broke up along geographic lines, as the social fabric underlying the language imploded). There are no other women poets to be found; bardic poets were rigidly mindful of maintaining the status quo of their own position. As Donnchadh Ó Corráin describes it,

> this caste of hereditary quasi-hereditary scholars quite self-consciously held themselves in the highest esteem and discharged duties of very considerable political and social importance ... Their powers as arbiters of good custom, as provers of pedigree (and thus of claim to role and property), as panegyrists of the great and, above all, as makers of the past who reshaped it to accord with the pretensions and ambitions of the contemporary holders of power, were extensively and jealously guarded.

As we know from other professions – such as medicine, for instance – that have become positions of jealously guarded status and power, there was fat chance of women getting a look in. Out go the *banfhilí*, along with the *mná luibheanna* (herb women) and the *mná cabhartha* (midwives). In come the poets (male only) with the physicians and the obstetricians.

And things did not change rapidly. Even after the great shipwreck of the native tradition, when all that was left of

aboriginal literary activity was a few lonely scribes working by
rushlight in smoky cabins to transcribe the rather paltry oral
compositions of the day, women were not allowed into the canon.
This is evident when one considers the extensive tradition of the
caoineadh, or keen, which was a female oral and literary province,
with what Angela Bourke describes as the skill 'to express
powerful emotion with discipline and rhythm and to convey the
immediacy of grief without disintegrating into tears'. As Seán Ó
Coileán has pointed out in *The Irish Lament: An Oral Genre*, 'even
when the paper manuscripts which received it were poor affairs
indeed, transcribed by every common sort, the literary canon,
such as it was, still found no place for the keen'. The very
excellence of Eibhlín Dubh Ní Conaill's lament for her husband
in 'Caoineadh Airt Uí Laoghaire' is proof that this was a highly
intricate and extensive tradition, capable of producing
enormously affective poetic compositions. Eibhlín Dubh's
composition is not a once-off; it just happens to be one of the
very few (almost) complete keens which is extant. The fact that it
even survives at all is very much a fluke, and owes a lot to the
accident of the author's high birth, her youth and the keen's
appeal to Victorian romanticism rather than to any great effusion
of male generosity. There is no reason to believe that Eibhlín
Dubh was even literate in Irish, but that does not matter one whit
as she did not actually write this poem, but rather composed it in
a spontaneous oral performance on two separate occasions.

We owe the two most complete texts of her keen to tran-
scripts taken, with an interval of some seventy years between
them, from a single informant, a West Cork woman by the name
of Norry Singleton. Norry Singleton herself was a keener and,
unlike Eibhlín Dubh, is more typical of the traditional keener
described by Crofton Croker in *Researches in the South of Ireland* as
'poor, old and often living alone'. Angela Bourke has argued that

> Irish women lament-poets were doubly colonised; they belonged to
> a society and composed in a language considered inferior and
> barbarian to those in power, but even within their own society they
> were an underclass, not taught to write, not admitted to the academy
> of serious poets, rarely named as authors of their own compositions.

There may have been hundreds, even thousands, of them, and yet with the one exception of Eibhlín Dubh, none of them have made it into the canon.

The position of women poets in the oral tradition outside of the *caoineadh* is not much better. From scattered references throughout folklore collections we know that women poets existed, but that is about all. The very concept of a woman being a poet was inherently threatening. Indeed, I was brought up amid a welter of proverbs and formulaic phrases of the likes of

> na tri rudaí is measa i mbaile:
> tuíodóir fliuch,
> síoladóir tiubh
> file mná.

> The three worst curses that could befall a village: (to have)
> a wet thatcher (who lets the rain in)
> a heavy sower (who broadcasts seeds too densely)
> a woman poet (no reason given; none needed).

There was a widespread belief that if poetry which was a hereditary gift (*féith nó tréith dúchais*) fell into the female line then it was gone from that particular family for seven generations to come. There is a story about the poet Giúistí from An Leitriúch who, mindful that some such calamity had occurred, asked his daughter for a glass of ale in a spontaneous *leathrann* (half quatrain). When she equally spontaneously and deftly finished the quatrain while handing him back the beer, he knew that the poetry in the family was finished. Although it did not stop women being storytellers or *filiúil*, 'poetic' – though a better translation for this word might perhaps be 'witty' or 'quick at repartee' – a similar taboo existed against women telling Fenian tales – 'tráthaire circe nó Fiannaí mná' (a crowing hen or a woman telling Fenian tales).

The existence of such sayings mimics the goings on of the canon, which has consistently excluded women's writing – on the level of literary and oral composition. This situation I find totally unsatisfactory, and the downright unfairness of it bothers me no end. Women poets such as the ones I have mentioned here are like vocal ghosts haunting the tradition: now you hear them, now you don't. It is even more upsetting because their exclusion is not purely or merely an historic aberration, a relic of ancient barbarism put behind us now in days of better will. Oh no indeed: on the contrary, the great male bardic hierarchichal triumph still goes on. In as epochal a canon-making event as *The New Oxford Book of Irish Verse* (1986), the editor, Thomas Kinsella, didn't see fit to include contemporary women poets, though minor male talents such as Valentin Irmonger and Seamus Deane were given pride of place while major women authors were omitted. But no more than 'the leopard, he don't change his spots', you can't teach an old dog new tricks, and it looks as if we will have to put up with the final frenzy of patriarchal authority in its death throes before a more sane, considered attitude to the whole question of women and poetry can be expected.

The fact that *The Field Day Anthology* has acknowledged the unacceptable bias in its exclusion of women either as contributors, or, much more importantly, in my view, as editors may be the first crack in the male hegemonic poetic bastion. The all-woman fourth volume of *The Field Day Anthology* may go some way towards galvanising and publishing hitherto overlooked energies, but it is no guarantee that women can at last take their rightful and well-deserved place in poetry, no matter how profound their achievements. And that is because a much more fundamental fact than the mere exclusion of women must be fairly and squarely faced up to in the Irish poetic tradition, and that is that at its deepest level – you might say at the level of ontological underpinning – the Irish poetic tradition is sexist and masculinist to the core. Even as far back as the Old Irish period, as we have seen, it is only by undergoing a kind of sex-change, by disguising herself as a young man, that Eithne iníon Amhalghaidh Mhic Mhuireadaigh was able to go off and learn the art of poetry. The message is clear enough: to be properly accepted as a poet a woman has to unsex herself, play the men's game, usually better. And then, if she is lucky, she will be accepted amongst them, as one of them, a kind of honorary male.

Woman, as woman, has only been accepted in the literary tradition as either Muse or, if she refuses to play that dreary, boring and unpaid role, then as Bitch. Even the greatest of Irish poets like Yeats is not above this fundamental dualism. It is as if an evocation of the Archetypal Feminine in its most primitive form took the place of any real thought about women and many other things as well. So a sort of emotional shorthand has evolved where, amongst other similar equations, Woman=Ireland =Passive versus Man=England=Active. The especially debilitating form of male adult emotional infantalism which results from this rebounds to the credit of nobody on this island, male or female. A small but telling example: a few years ago a number of poets, mostly, as it happens, male, collaborated in a book of translation of my work called *Pharaoh's Daughter*. Immediately critics hailed me as a kind of Muse. Now let us get one thing quite clear. I was not the male poets' Muse: they were my translators. As it so happens, many of them were also translating other Irish-language poets such as Michael Davitt, Liam Ó Muithile and Cathal Ó Searcaigh, but did anyone have the temerity to suggest that Michael or Liam or Cathal was anybody's Muse? You bet your sweet life they didn't.

It seems to me that the hysteria with which the subject of women poets is broached in Ireland has all the hallmarks of not just the fear of loss of a privileged male vantage point; it goes much deeper than that. It cloaks a fundamental ontological terror. If the Archetypal Feminine, traditionally confined to hag or supine *spéirbhean* status, gets up off her butt and has a go writing about you, then, boy oh boy, have you had it. And signs on, the writing is on the wall, or rather in the hands of some fifty-odd good women poets who have either published collections already or have manuscripts together and will be published in the next few months, or even as I speak. The canon, 'hedged with taboos, mined with false meanings', in Adrienne Rich's words, will be greatly modified in the near future. I have no doubt about this, as Old Irish scholars such as Máirín Ní Dhonnchadha, Muirean Ní Bhrolcháin and Máire Herbert edit medieval texts that have as yet never seen the light, and as literary critics such as

Máirín Nic Eoin, Angela Bourke and Bríona Nic Dhiarmada bring a feminist perspective to bear on what is already available.

Eavan Boland and other of my peers have written about their difficulty in finding role models for the woman poet in Ireland. I was luckier than Eavan Boland, in that Caitlín Maude was already on the Leaving Certificate course and Máire Mhac an tSaoi already enshrined as one of the great trio of poets who had dragged Irish poetry, screaming and kicking, into the twentieth century by their stunning achievements back in the 1950s. There was no question about Mhac an tSaoi and Maude not being *banfhilí* or women poets, as their subject matter and technical strategies were very definitely different from the way men wrote poetry. There was also no question of their not being very good poets. But beyond these two role models, well, that was about it: and so I was left to my own poetic devices.

The usual catalogue of indignities dogged the steps of any poem I tried to see into print. Editors chipped and chopped with no by-your-leave. Totally outmoded ideas of '*an caighdeán*' (the standard) were brought to bear on what was purporting to be, after all, something other than civil-service jargon. One poem, 'An Cuairteoir', was refused publication because it was deemed to be blasphemous, although I meant it as a description of a possible female reaction to the presence of the Divine. When I first experimented with the long line it was deemed unprintable, and the poem 'An Casadh' was reorganised to suit the editor. It has been a long and tedious struggle for us women writing to get even a precarious toehold in visibility. Like the boy in the magic cloak in the fairy story, you've got to keep saying to the ship of culture 'seol seol, a bháidín, táimse leis ann' ('Sail sail, little boat, I'm there too').

And the tedium, the struggle, was made more intense by another aspect: that of language. The most unkind cut of all was the total lack of support or comprehension or even acknowledgement of the existence of women writing in Irish by women writing in English. Any of us who have chosen to write poetry in Irish have made our decision in full awareness of what it entails. Important work is, first and foremost, produced in solitude, far from the noise of the world. Work requires retreat, and is not easy: *ars est longissima via*. Thanks mostly to Ailbhe Smythe's inclusion of six women writing in Irish in her anthology *Wildish Things*, the long road has been shortened somewhat and the situation improved slightly, even if many of the reviews of that book left out the Irish altogether or took a rather arch and superior view of it. Many people are embarrassed by their own lack of Irish and are not woman enough to admit that it has a legitimate place on the cultural menu, and a significant role to play in the life of this country. If, as Máirín Nic Eoin suggests, the main post-colonial strategy that we Irish-language writers use – the use of the pre-colonial language as a creative medium – is beginning to be appreciated for the revolutionary and subversive act which it is, then who knows, we may be in for a brief period of being fashionable. That too will pass: these are all temporary aberrations. The long haul is what matters.

And part of the long haul is the patience that it takes to change traditions, to alter myths.

One of the strategies that I personally use to combat the sexist tendencies which are rampant in the nationalist tradition is to use the poems themselves to turn the tradition on its head. To counteract the hoary image of Mother Ireland, and to free myself of the sense that I as an individual woman am carrying a map of Ireland around on my back, I imagine the land as man, for a change; that has resulted in a poem like 'Oileán'. Another strategy I have used to ridicule the tradition is to pile up images taken from the canon of Gaelic patriotic verse, from Eoghan Rua Ó Súilleabhein in the eighteenth century to Padraig Pearse and beyond, throwing in for good measure examples of the native idiom as imagined by Revivalist writers. The overall effect is satirical, as the Kathleen Ní Houlihan theme collapses under the weight of its own rhetoric in a poem like 'Caitlín'.

Representation of Ireland as woman amounts to a form of cultural nationalism. And cultural nationalism, if not thoroughly laced with whatever egalitarian and humanitarian values are important at the time – women's suffrage and socialism at the turn of the century, or the continuing presence of feminism and ecology and gay rights in our time – can very easily turn into a deeply fascist, sectarian and sexist movement, as happened in Ireland in the twentieth century. Nevertheless, for all the difficulties it entails, and for all the contradictions and conflicts invited by being a *banfhile* or woman poet in the Irish language, I still put all my creative energy into the language, hoping against hope, and working towards a reinvention of myth, a new representation: towards, in effect, the establishment of a new canon, one that is not defined by what it keeps out.

I must be mad. It is a miserable day in late November and I am trudging round a windswept graveyard in the parish of Ventry, in the Dingle peninsula. This is, in fact, the most westerly point in Ireland, 'next parish America'. The weather is unspeakable: sudden squalls of wind mixed with hailstones batter the grave-stones, yet I am not alone. Ever since daybreak, which is late enough at this time of year, people have been coming here singly or in small groups, crouching down to pick up the small stones which will act as markers, and have been braving the elements to make the three, seven or nine clockwise rounds that are prescribed by the ritual of the *turus* or 'pattern'. They say a decade of the Rosary with each round, but also a special prayer for the occasion that begins 'Go mbeannaithear duit a Chaitlín Naofa' ('Hail to you Blessed Catherine'), which, intoned by so many poor wretches in these adverse weather conditions, is a veritable sup-plication out of the depths, *de profundis*.

Today, 25 November, is the feast of Saint Catherine of Alexandria in Egypt, who is also, due perhaps to local part-icipation in the crusades, the patron saint of the Parish of Ventry. Though not an official Church holiday anywhere else – three miles away in Dunquin life goes on as normal – today is a very special day in this parish. Apart from absolutely necessary duties such as giving winter forage to animals and milking the odd cow who has already calved, no normal work is permitted. There is a special mass for the feast day at ten o'clock, and the rest of the day is celebrated for all ostensible purposes like a Sabbath or Sunday, but an exceptional one at that. Old people and sick people and recluses who have not emerged from their houses from one end of the year to the other arise from their beds and make the supreme effort to perform the *turus*. They are later to be found in the nearby pub, greatly invigorated by the exercise and toasting each other's health and the health of the saint with Guinness and gusto. People will come from the surrounding parishes to do the rounds and to take part in the evening revelries. Expats like myself, forlorn in linguistic exile in Dublin, will have made the two hundred mile journey, daring life and limb on treacherous roads to get home for the pattern.

Linguistic exile? Yes, nothing less, because this is the Gaeltacht, or Irish-speaking area, of Corcha Dhuibhne, which comprises the seven ancient parishes on the westernmost tip of the Dingle Peninsula. One of the smallest of the surviving Gaeltachts, it remains one of the most important, one of the last strongholds of the Munster dialect. Of the three main Irish dialects, the Munster one is by far the most musical and resonant, as it was in Munster that the old literary and manuscript tradition was kept alive for longest. Many would say that I am biased, but if so it is with good reason, because it was here that I arrived, way back in the fifties, as a small child, to live with my aunt. Until then I had lived quite happily in a coal-mining town in Lancashire in England, and though Irish was spoken in the house, my knowledge of it was not alive. In Kerry this was to change radically.

To many people who have spent childhood or even adult holidays in the area learning Irish, the Gaeltacht is a magic place: long walks home from '*céilí*'-dances through tunnels of blood-red fuschia bushes, light still streaking the sky at one o'clock in the morning; the hilarious repartee and banter of good conversation in a pub; summer evenings spent swimming or walking the long beaches or clambering over rocks and cliffs, all 'through the medium' of Irish. Many good courses in the language are available for children and adults, as are introductory courses in local history, archaeology and botany, again all in Irish. Most Irish learners elect to stay in local homes where the *bean a' tí* – woman of the house – will chat away to you and even correct your grammatical mistakes with the same kindliness with which she will provide a hot-water bottle for your bed. Good food and lashings of drink are all part of the normal fare. The weather can be dicey, but with at least thirteen Irish words for different kinds of rain and showers, even the worst downpour can be a good excuse for sitting in the shelter of a stone wall or under an upturned *currach* and trying out the language with a local farmer.

I wasn't on holiday, of course, when I arrived at my aunt's home; I was there to live. I remember at first I refused to speak Irish. Why should I speak it? I had a perfectly good language of my own. But then one day at the table I was thirsty and, my cries of 'milk, milk' having produced no effect, I changed to the Irish word for milk, '*bainne*', and lo and behold the desired drink appeared before me as if by magic. This thing works, I decided. Six weeks later my father came to visit me, and I asked him in Irish, 'Why are you speaking English to me? Isn't this Ireland?' The metamorphosis was complete. I dare say it must have been painful enough at the time, and I remember some moments of distinct culture shock. It wasn't all perfect, but what I experienced in Corcha Dhuibhne then was a profound sense of fitting in, a making sense of myself that had not happened in England.

One of the events that provided even a child with the sense of the community's cohesion and its traditions was Cahiratrant's *turus* day, and the widespread respect and attention granted to St Catherine. The parish's devotion to St Catherine is remarkable, considering the fact that she never really existed. There is no ancient cult of this saint, no mention of her in early martyrologies and she inspired no early Christian works of art. Even Catholic scholars admit her legend is preposterous. Her cult began in the ninth century at Mount Sinai, where there still exists a monastery dedicated to her. The standard version has it that she was a learned young beauty dedicated to virginity, who with her great erudition made mincemeat out of her pagan philosopher opponents, rather in the manner of the Christ-child in the Temple. She refused the hand of the emperor Maxentius and was tortured on a fiery wheel (later to become 'the Catherine wheel'), but the wheel was miraculously destroyed and she was saved. She was finally beheaded, but from her severed head milk flowed rather than blood. Her divine bones, considered by many to rest in her monastery in Mount Sinai, exuded a healing unguent which was bottled and sold for considerable profit.

This last action is considered by the people of Ventry to be an example of typical foreign chicanery and sharp business practice, because everyone around here knows the truth of the matter: when the saint died, her coffin very conveniently drifted westwards the whole length of the Mediterranean, out through the Pillars of Hercules and northwards up through the Bay of Biscay, finding its way with unerring accuracy right into Ventry Bay, where it beached just under the present graveyard. Her body, found miraculously preserved, was buried in the *cill* or 'oratory' built here in her honour, where until recently she used to appear to favoured supplicants at sunrise, adorned, incongruously enough, in a red dress. As on Easter Sunday, a vision of the sun dancing was also vouchsafed on this day to specially graced devotees of the saint.

I have to admit that more imprecations than prayers have crossed my lips today as I stumble along blindly through lashing rain, slipping and slopping on the wet marram and couch grass that line the path. My father, not a native of this parish, has already given me short shrift: 'It would be much more in your line to stay in Dublin minding your children, and to say your prayers at home.' But that is missing the point. As the Japanese Zen masters knew, there are two ways to make an 'otherworld' voyage. One is by an act of will, where by fasting and other ascetic practices the spirit can be persuaded to temporarily slip off this mortal coil. The other equally valid method is where the 'otherworld' is projected by powerful symbolism onto the land-scape of the outer world. Thus as the pilgrim traverses the trans-ferred landscape in mind and body it is tantamount to his soul travelling to the 'otherworld' as in a vision. Thus the outer landscape and the chance encounters that occur as we journey in it become a mirror of our inner landscape and the personages that inhabit it.

Therefore when I look up from my rather perfunctory de-votions and let my eye dwell on the surrounding landscape I am not at all surprised that a whole pattern is revealed to me that connects even the remotest history to the present. This very graveyard witnessed Norman invaders: across from me, my aunt's village of Cahiratrant is, as its name implies, the site of the classic Norman manse of the invader 'De Terraunt'. The site of the towerhouse is still traceable in the centre of the village, and its well, with all of twenty-seven steps, was in use in my own time during spots of summer drought. Even the very rabbits which plague our existence in summer are direct descendants of the original rabbits introduced to Ireland as a source of protein by the Normans.

But beyond these direct connections with and reminders of medieval Irish history is something deeper and more unfathomable. Immediately south of me, as the crow flies, is the sheer cliff of Cuas Crom, called after an old pagan god. Although the advent of Christianity meant that this personage was demonised, it is still alive in the soul of the community: in my childhood, when an adult started a sentence by swearing in Crom's name – '*In ainm Chroim*' – it meant that they were about to fly off the handle and your best bet for safety was a quick scarper. The road leading from this cliff through the village and down to the strand is so old that at present it lies a good six feet beneath the level of the surrounding fields, impacted and compacted over the centuries by the weight of passing feet, both human and animal. At one point the road trails past a mound of clay covering over a huge fallen '*gallán*' or standing stone; I remember the very Sunday in November 1957 when, after surviving for four millennia, that great stone finally fell. A legendary queen is buried under it and it does not take too great a stretch of the imagination to suggest that, whoever she was, she preceded St Catherine as patron of this parish. St Catherine must have reminded our local crusaders of a very powerful earlier female pagan deity in this locale; and there must have been enough in common between the two presences for the substitution to have occurred seamlessly.

The name of this ancient road is significant. It is preserved in the local *dinnsheanchas* as 'Bothar Rí an Aonaigh' – the Road of the King of the Fair, which suggests a local *al fresco* version of Appian Way of Rome or the Divan Yolu of later Ottoman Istanbul, a *via sacra* down which the sacred king of the *tuath* or 'barony' proceeded ceremoniously on special occasions. The linguistic suggestion is born out by the fact that the spot where this road meets the strand called An Port Mór was until recently the site of the annual bonfire on St John's Eve. According to the folklore, this was the place and occasion for the summer races before they were moved, first to Miltown near Dingle, and later to their present site at the racefield of Ballintaggart. The Road of the King of the Fair did indeed lead to a place of importance.

This may be pure hypothesis on my part, but the pattern of the landscape leads me to an insight akin to that described for Greek sacred architecture by Vincent Scully. Viewed from Cuas Crom the whole parish functions as a 'Natural Megaron', or central hallway: directly north lies 'An Cnoc Breac' (the Speckled Hill), crowned with a megalithic tomb known as 'Leaba an Fhir Mhuimhnigh' (the Bed of the Munsterman), and some distance beyond the hill but on the same axis lies the double-peaked mountain of Brandon, functioning as horns of the goddess. This is a natural corridor of significant sites: is it purely accidental that just here you have the start of the great complex of beehive huts of Fán and Gleann Fán (from the Latin '*fanum*', holy place)? Peter Harbison has suggested that these were shelters used during medieval maritime pilgrimages which took in a visit to the Sceilg Rocks that sleep on the horizon and led, perhaps, as far west as America. Personally, I think it is no accident: there is some sort of ontological rhyme and reason to all of this 'chance'.

Later that evening I make my way over to the nearby pub of Páidi Ó Shea, the renowned Kerry footballer now turned publican, where the Catherine's Day festivities are in full swing. Local traditional musicians Seamus Beaglai and Steve Cooney are playing hornpipes and slides and reels and music for the Kerry version of the 'set', a fast and intricate dance descended from the quadrille. After years of being denigrated, set-dancing has swept the country in a mad craze recently: just shows you, you wait long enough and everything comes around. I am welcomed and made at home. Nods and salutes of recognition, offers of a drink in honour of the day that is in it. The repartee, in both Irish and English, is fast and furious; as they say around here, 'the craic is mighty'. I barely escape from Joeín Mháiread O'Shea, a neighbour from childhood who, knowing my interest in poetry, buttonholes me with a recitation of all seventy-seven verses of a Fenian Lay in Irish, 'Laoi na Mná Móire Thar Lear'. Joeín has a wealth of old-style 'recimitation' in both official languages of the state, his repertoire in English tending to Tennyson and Robert Service. Over the years I have listened with great pleasure to renditions of 'The Ballad of Sam McGrew' and 'The Green Eye of the Little Yellow God', but not tonight, thank you, Joeín. I am not so successful in evading the attentions of a Dunquin man, and a verbal altercation arises about the relative merits and demerits of our particular saint and her pattern versus the one held in his parish.

Later, taking a short-cut home across Ventry Strand, I have to admit to myself that they have a lot going for them also in Dunquin, though there wasn't a snowball's chance in hell that I was going to admit it earlier, because of the rivalry that has existed since time immemorial between the two parishes. Dunquin holds its pattern on 11 February, the feast of St Gobnait, which was concurrent with the ancient Celtic feast of 'Imbolg' before the calendar change brought in by Pope Gregory XIII in the seventeenth century, which 'disappeared' ten whole days from people's lives, to widespread consternation. Some more entrepreneurial saints like St Brigid moved with the new calendar, and so her feast is held on 1 February. But I find it delightful and reassuring that St Gobnait, being of older and more stubborn stock, stuck to her guns and would not be moved, even though it does mean that we now celebrate her feast ten days later than the present 'Imbolg'. Her pattern, like Catherine's, consists of a special mass in the morning, and then a ritual *deisal* or sunwise circling of a sacred site, which in her case includes a double cairn and a holy well. Strongly associated with bees, St Gobnait is the patron saint of many parishes in Munster, most notably Gabhlán, east of Dingle, and Ballyvourney in County Cork. Her name suggests an association with the Celtic smith-god 'Goibniú' and, like St Catherine in Ventry, she is without doubt a Christianised version of some much older female deity venerated in these parts since the dawn of time.

The goddess she may have replaced locally could be the eponymous mother goddess of sovereignty, Mór of Munster, who is associated with many local place-names: Faill Mhóire, the boat launch site for the Blasket Islands; Dún Mhóire or Dunmore Head, the most westerly headland in Europe; and Tigh Mhóire, or Mór's House, in Vicarstown, in the southernmost end of Dunquin, where she is reputed to be buried. Indeed all of Dunquin still goes under the popular name of 'bundún Mhóire' ('Mór's backside'), and people from the area still carry the name as a term of pride, notwithstanding the jibes from the people of Ventry.

Mór's House is an early Christian site, one of some sixty such sites to be found on the peninsula and the outlying islands. From here there is a clear view of Inis Tuaisceart, the most northerly of the Blasket Islands, looking for all the world like a giant lying on its back; indeed one of the popular local names in Irish for it is 'An Fear Marbh' (the Dead Man). Many stories are told locally about Mór, including one of how she fought with her husband Donncha Dí (a corrupted form of the male titular deity of the region) and how in desperation he wished to have the length and breadth of Ireland between him and her. As a god, he was immediately granted his wish: he was lifted through the air and landed down in Donaghadee, in County Antrim, just at the opposite end of Ireland. She set out to find him, but when she climbed up the pass and saw before her the wide expanse of Ventry she uttered the immortal words 'Nach fada fairsing í Éire' ('Isn't the land of Ireland great and extensive'), lost heart and headed back home. On the way, she was overtaken by a call of nature, and squatting down to relieve herself produced the two great ravines seen there to this day, much to the chagrin of unsuspecting motorists, and which give the road its name, 'An Clasach' (The Ravined Way).

Another tale tells how her two sons were abducted by a sailing ship crewed by a magic cat: and the tales are endless. Mór has survived many metamorphoses in the folk memory until she appears at last as Máire Ní Chinnéide, a legendary *bean luibheanna* or herb woman who, reputedly, was responsible for the fall that finally hospitalised the noted storyteller Peig Sayers. Seemingly some people visiting Peig had picked wild flowers from a favourite haunt of Máire's, amongst them the early purple field orchid *orchis mascula*, called in Irish 'an Magairlín Meidhreach', the merry testicle, and which was particularly efficacious in herb medicines. Peig swore that the reason she slipped was that Máire Ní Chinnéide, no less angry at the transgression for the fact that she was long since dead, had placed a corner of her shawl on the path and pulled it out from under Peig's plimsoll as she stepped on it, thereby causing her to fall. Whether or not such a ghostly visitation occurred or whether it was all just a figment of Peig's very fertile storyteller's imagination is beside the point. Indeed, like the other shadowy presences and personages who haunt the countryside, it is only in the narrative tradition in the Irish language that they have anything more than a shadowy half-life.

Anyone approaching Corcha Dhuibhne as a place of pilgrimage expecting to see great material landmarks will be severely disappointed. Unlike sites of pilgrimage on the continent, we can boast of no cathedrals or basilicas, not even the thronging crowds of such places of worship as Croagh Patrick or the Penitential Island of Lough Derg. Apart from the site at Riasc which has been excavated by the archaeologist Tom Fanning, the boat-shaped oratory at Gallorus or the Irish Romanesque Church at Cill Mhaolchéadair, even the early Christian sites are extremely simple and unpretentious, often no more than a small stone cross in a field as at Kilfountain or a tumble of broken-down huts as at Raingiléis. Their very ancientness and haphazard upkeep mitigates against them as typical tourist attractions. The holy wells are hidden and simple and, with two exceptions, built of undressed stone very different from, say, the Chalice Well of Joseph of Arimathea at Glastonbury in England with its pretty garden and its art nouveau brass cover. But the cultural continuity in this area due to the Irish-language narrative tradition is astonishing. The scholar Gerard Murphy remarked how 'many Irish folk-tale motifs are as old as the days of primitive Indo-European unity'; Professor Jan Filip has noted a significant degree of continuity into the Celtic world from the Late Stone Age in the matter of the Magna Mater. Is it any wonder, then, that when I started writing poetry seriously that these great personages from the oral tradition – Mór, the *cailleach* or hag and many others like them – walked unannounced into my work?

The next morning I am out on the road bright and early. The pilgrimage has worked; I am feeling earthed and invigorated, with a few more good stories to add to the inexhaustible and constantly renewable resource of *dinnsheanchas*. I stop at the top of the Connor Pass, which has reminded more than one traveller of the Khyber. Across from me rises the massive bulk of Mount Brandon, which, at 3,127 feet, is the second highest mountain in Ireland. This doesn't seem like any great shakes until you realise that the mountain rears to this height straight up from sea-level in a space of less than two miles. This is the site of the greatest pattern of them all at Cloghane, where the *turas* on Domhnach Chrom Dubh (our old friend Crom Dubh again!), the last Sunday in July, includes climbing the mountain to the very top. It is not a venture for the faint-hearted and yet local people of all ages and degrees of agility do it for reasons of their own: to do penance; for the craic; for the view; for a special intention; to give good example to the children, just as their forebears have done for millennia, celebrating the Festival of Lughnasa, the feast of the Celtic god Lugh. Though this is my father's ancestral stamping ground, to my eternal shame I have never done this particular pattern. I shiver as a huge storm cloud hides the top of the mountain and to myself I make a solemn and silent promise. Another time, when the weather is better, another day, perhaps.

A Ghostly Alhambra

The Famine, for me, embodies more than a specific series of years; more than a specific series of crop failures. I see it as the last and lethal body-blow to a distinct culture, world-view and way of life, epitomised by, while not purely confined to, the Irish language. This was the culture that produced not only a body of internationally famed textual material in Latin (such as the Book of Kells), but also an enormous corpus of medieval manuscript vernacular literature. The culture out of which both of these traditions arose has, in many ways, been elided from our present consciousness, and this seems to me to be one of the tragic consequences of the Famine: that we have been removed from the continuous sense of our own culture and, in particular, our literary and linguistic culture.

In an interview in *Poetry Ireland Review*, the literary historian Joep Leerssen comments on this phenomenon and argues that not only do we remain unaware of our distance from that medieval culture and its traditions; we are also all too often unaware of the ways in which our quite different approach to the world inhibits us from seeing and judging medieval Irish culture and literature in an appropriate way:

> All this ancient and alien material is rediscovered, re-appropriated, repossessed by minds that are trained in the universities that function on the basis of Humboldt and Matthew Arnold and Newman ... The only simile I can think of is the Alhambra destroyed and the same rubble used to rebuild a different building according to a different architecture.

Leerssen's image of the Alhambra is a striking one, and one that I return to time and again. In evoking this treasure of Moorish architecture he reminds us of the existence of other civilisations

NUALA NÍ DHOMHNAILL

and other ways of being in the world which are different to the global cultural hegemony which is now upon us. The image of the Alhambra also insists that we recognise the existence in Ireland until the Famine of a subterranean, native world-view as described by Robert Scally in *The End of Hidden Ireland*. It is our present, almost wilful, amnesia about that hidden way of life that I see as the Great Famine's most lasting scar.

I do not wish to appear heartless. The severe suffering and loss of life, the wretchedness and overwhelming despair of that time weighs terribly on my imagination, as it does on many of the people of Ireland. If, according to behavioural scientists, it takes seven generations for the overt behaviour patterns caused by deep emotional trauma to be bred out of a population, how long must it take for the covert ones to leave us? Overwhelmingly fixated as we have become by the vision of the people of the Famine as victims, do we not 'forget' something very important: that they are representatives of a culture as different to ours today as that of Brahmanic India?

It does seem true that the terrible imprint of the Famine and the trauma of colonisation is something that we in Ireland are finally coming to terms with. It is as if we are waking up from a state of zombification, of a waking death where we had no emotional memory of who it was that we were or what it was that happened – and so continued to happen – to us. Although this waking process is vitally important, I think that in some sense it will have been arrested mid-action if we do not allow ourselves to become aware of this ghostly Alhambra within, of another way of being still trembling at the edges of consciousness.

Surely the success of all colonial ideologies is predicated not only on the causing of material, physical and psychic trauma, but also on the prevention of that trauma from being expressed as it needs to be – in anger and in forgiveness – so that it remains impacted into the psyche of the colonised. Until we take proper cognisance of the non-Aristotelian psychic architecture of our ancestry, this inner Alhambra that remains to be recognised and expressed, we remain colonised. Imperialism has finally triumphed at the most important level of all: in the deepest recesses of our minds. Until we face this collective amnesia about who we are and where we come from, our existence will be at best highly fragmented, and at worst pathogenic.

This was all brought home to me most clearly last summer when I brought my children to the Famine Museum in Strokestown House in County Roscommon, a marvellous and heartening enterprise. It is a sign of our recovery from the collective trauma of the Famine that we can finally objectify it and put it outside our psyches, the better to study it. The paucity of the artefacts in the museum speaks for itself, powerfully revealing the lack of material possessions characteristic of the people who died in that catastrophe. These were people clothed only in rags; they had no furniture at all in their hovels; and even the basic useful implements of their trades and crafts, such as spinning wheels and fishing tackle, had already been sold in desperate attempts to procure at any price some of the precious little food that could be bought for love or money.

A scale-model of a typical *clachan* village, with its shared field patterns on the rundale system – with 'inner' fields devoted to intensive cultivation and 'outer' fields kept for the pasturage of animals – re-evaluates farming methods of the time, challenging previously held assumptions about the period. So-called 'lazy beds', for example, are shown to be highly efficient for the type of marginal lands involved, and reinforce my sense of the great intelligence, industriousness and other sterling qualities of the people involved. Far from their typical stereotyping by British and Anglo-Irish metropolitan travelers as shiftless and lazy, Irish people of the early and mid-nineteenth century were quite the opposite, as their back-breaking and tedious hand-cultivation of marginal land by spade evinces. These *clachan* dwellers knew what they were doing; this soul-destroying work was the most efficient way of ensuring a good harvest.

While the museum succeeds in challenging the stereotype of the nineteenth-century Irish farmer as feckless and lazy, nowhere in the museum do I get a sense of other significant aspects of these *clachan*-dwellers' lives. Nowhere is there an acknowledgement that ninety per cent of Famine victims were Irish speakers only;

nowhere is there an acknowledgement that a huge proportion (seventy to eighty per cent) of the people who left on the coffin-ships were Irish-speakers. They were the poorest section of the population, and their lack of English was part and parcel of the double-bind that kept them in such abject material poverty. Nowhere is there an acknowledgement of the fact that the reality of the people who died was experienced and expressed by them in the Irish language. Nowhere do I get a sense of their mental and cultural life, and the high development amongst them of such art forms as did not rely on material props: singing, dancing, extempore and spontaneous poetry and storytelling, the pounce and counter-pounce of quick banter and repartee, as well as their more formal, learned versions.

From my childhood in the West Kerry Gaeltacht, in what was still an Irish-speaking subsistence farming economy, I knew of the existence of these art forms. I knew also that, though poor in material terms, the daily round of the life of the ordinary people could be remarkably rich in verbal culture, in mental agility and emotional satisfaction. And, since my time in Kerry coincided with the late end of the phenomenon, I only got a faint taste of that cultural richness. What it must have been like in pre-Famine and right up to Famine times we can barely dream or imagine, but I know for sure that it was powerful and all-encompassing, and that even in the middle of considerable material distress the delight of word and song and story was mighty.

One example offers an illustration. As part of his enormous collection of over three thousand items of music, a near neighbour of my mother's family, the Reverend Canon James Goodman of Ballymore, Ventry, later Professor of Irish at Trinity College Dublin and a noted piper in his own right, took down over nine hundred tunes not otherwise extant. According to the late Breandán Breathnach, the noted musicologist who was working on this material before he died, up to 494 – one-sixth – of these otherwise unknown tunes were given to Canon Goodman by a single piper. Thomás Ó Cinnéide, originally from my aunt's townland of Cahiratrant, lived in Carraig during the Famine times, when he converted to Protestantism – took the soup, as it was called –

chiefly because the local parish priest, a Father Casey, had taken his livelihood from him by forbidding him from playing the pipes at weddings and at dances.

When Parson Goodman was sent as a clergyman to Ardgroom, near Skibereen in County Cork, he took his fellow-piper Thomás Ó Cinnéide with him. Breathnach describes them working together in a large attic room. Thomás was, at this stage, slightly paralysed down one side of his body as a result of a stroke that he got, he thought himself, from a fairy '*poc*' for playing fairy music at an inappropriate time and place, and without showing it the proper respect. Because of this he was unable to play the pipes himself, but used to walk up and down the attic room whistling the tunes and keeping proper time with his step, while Parson Goodman assiduously took down the music, and later played it back to his friend on the pipes. The tunes were written down in one notebook, and the name of each tune is, more often than not, the first line of the song. Whether or not the words of these songs were written down in another notebook and subsequently lost, or never written down at all, we cannot tell at this stage. Even as a child I used to dream of finding Goodman's mythical other notebook, the one with all the words: words of over four hundred songs that we know from no other source, and that were written down from one single piper from one small and terribly impoverished townland in a disadvantaged area on the extreme west coast of Kerry. The Goodman Collection is still relatively unknown in traditional-music circles in Ireland, and is unappreciated by the culture in general. That this extraordinary proof of the exuberance and cultural vitality of pre-Famine Ireland should be still such a closely guarded secret is proof to me that we have still a long way to go before we will have recovered from the long-term effects of the Famine.

None of this great cultural richness evident in the Goodman Collection is made clear to us in the Famine Museum. The very little evidence of even the existence of Irish is associated mostly with the dread diseases that carried off the victims: '*an fiabhras dubh*', '*an galar bhuí*'. Is it any wonder, therefore, that I leave the museum somewhat dissatisfied, overcome once again, as I always am when faced with memories of that time, by a sense of overwhelming and unaccountable loss? And ultimately this loss is also unconscionable: not only because the tunes and the songs and the poetry have been quite literally lost to consciousness, but also because the memory that they were all in Irish – that they are part of a reality which was not English – has been erased so totally from our minds. This seems to me to be part of the Famine trauma which is still not acknowledged by any post-colonial Irish political reality. This collective memory-loss, this convenient amnesia, is still one of the most deeply etched results of the Famine.

My family has one famine story, not particularly remarkable or memorable, but of direct concern to us. It was told to my mother by her grandmother, Léan Ní Chearna, who was from Gleann Fán, that precipitous and lonely glen on the seaward side of Mount Eagle, the most westerly mountain in Ireland. She came out of the highest of the only two houses in that glen, houses barely glimpsed from the road at the point where the water flows over a bridge, rather than the bridge going over the water. (This is called an 'Irish bridge' in some dictionaries, and I have yet to make up my mind whether or not I think this is a racial slur.) This story told by the woman from the high glen is not about the Great Famine of the 1840s, but about one of the many smaller famines that occurred in the more disadvantaged regions of Ireland right up to the end of the nineteenth century, and which are lumped together in Irish under the general euphemistic title of 'An Drochshaol', the Bad Times. There was a famine in 1879, during which Léan saw her father die of famine fever; her mother had died a few years previously, shortly after the birth of her youngest brother. Léan was seven the year her father died, and she told my mother years later that what she remembered most from that awful time was how long it took him to die. He was so weak in the bed that he couldn't pull himself into a sitting position, so the children had to let sheets down from the rafters of the house so that he could use them to pull himself up as he whispered to them his last feeble instructions. When he finally died five children were left orphaned, the oldest of them, Nellie Rinn Bhuí (called after the townland that she later married into) being at the time fourteen years old.

Today when I look up at that desolate glen with its small rocky fields running half-way up the mountain it seems amazing that even grown adults could have fed a family of five from its meagre soil and salt-blasted heaths, never mind it all being left to the devices of a mere fourteen-year-old. But feed them she did, even to the extent of managing to collect a dowry of sixty gold guineas not only for herself, but also for each of her three sisters. Thus they could marry into good farms to the east, the home farm being left to the only boy, Seán Dearthair, so that the Kearney name could stay on the land. This she managed, but the strain on both her and her younger siblings must have been incalculable. Léan remembered her sister Nellie as being uncommonly harsh on them all and never forgave her for this: so much so that she never once spoke to her after her own marriage, even when they met perchance by accident at the fair in Dingle. Léan, a soft woman in many respects, was deeply stubborn on this issue. She only relented at Nelly's death, and to everyone's surprise was present at her wake, family solidarity triumphing finally over deep hostility.

Each year as children we all took part in a family pilgrimage up the hill to Gleann Fán to visit Bríde Kearney, my mother's cousin and the last member of the family to live up in that wild spot. Bríde was always delighted to see us and welcomed us warmly. We children were regaled with tea and scones as this and other items of family history were rehearsed and retold: such as the time there was such an almighty storm that it blew the whole roof off the house, rafters and all, so that it landed, holus-bolus, out on the dung-heap in front of the cottage. Seán Dearthair got such a fright on that occasion that ever afterwards, whenever there was even the slightest hint of a gale in the air, he got up out of the bed and took his bedclothes out to the stable and bedded down under the donkey cart, in the hope that if the roof were to do another such somersault, the cart would save him. At which we all used to laugh mightily, thinking of the strange vagaries of those people of olden times. But it was a wry enough laughter, because we knew that we had all inherited a certain *eagla gaoithe*, or fear of high winds, which still keeps us without a wink of sleep on blustery nights.

Nearby was another, perhaps more poignant reminder of *An Drochshaol*, in the presence of a large out-cropping of rock called Cloch Shéamais Bháin. This rock had given shelter to a man of the Connors clan after he had been put out of his holding in the middle of the Great Famine by the notorious and ruthless female agent Bess Rice. At the time of the eviction, Seán's immediate family had been whittled by famine down to only himself and a nine-month infant daughter, Nance. At first his brother Thomás and then various neighbours took them in, but one by one they got a letter from Bess Rice warning them that they were to give him no help, on pain of eviction themselves. There was nothing else for poor Seán and the infant to do but to camp out under this rock, with a few sacks of wool stacked against the outside as their sole protection against the piercing elements. People still remember that when he had to go down the cliffs to collect seaweed and mussels to use as fertiliser for the few meagre potato drills that he planted on land loaned to him by neighbours he had no one to look after the infant, but had to take her down the cliffs with him on the creel on his back. He survived this ordeal and lived on and eventually was given some sort of hut or other in the townland of Kilvicadownaig, beyond Bess Rice's jurisdiction. The tiny infant Nance also survived, and went to the new National School that was soon opened near their home, where she excelled at the lessons and went on to become a 'monitor' or untrained teaching assistant in the same school. She married a tailor, Táiliúr a' Chlasaigh, a noted storyteller who was one of the chief informants of the American folklorist Jeremiah Curtin when he was collecting hero- and fairy-tales in the area in the late 1880s. Nance kept the teaching post until her son Tomáisín O'Shea was qualified as a National teacher under the new state, at which point she relinquished the position to him. Tomáisín O'Shea was a noted schoolmaster and more County Council and Gaeltacht scholarships were won by his pupils than by any other school in the area. It is my proud boast to have known him myself, as he was still the schoolmaster in Killvicadownaig when I went to school there back in the fifties.

There is a dark side to this story, though. Ironically enough, Nance was not very good to her own father at the end of his days; it is said that she banished him to an outhouse which he had to share with the yearling pigs. It is tempting to see her desire to excel at the lessons, her canny keeping of the good job for her son and her cruelty to her father all as a direct result of that famine. We have very long memories in this part of the world, and these memories can often rankle with bitterness and rancour. Right down until well into the last century a man of the Connors used to come down to St Catherine's graveyard in Ventry on Pattern day and do a triumphant hornpipe on the grave of Bess Rice, the erstwhile persecutor of his relations. It was, and remains, an eloquent gesture. In dead spite of her there are members of the Connors clan still alive and thriving and happy in the place, while her name, bereft of progeny, has long since died out.

Such things show me that a non-Aristotelian psychic space, the already adumbrated inner Alhambra, shimmers within us, just beyond the reaches of consciousness. Beyond the oral tales passed from generation to generation, another place this can still be found not only going strong but also winning the battle against Anglo-American blandness is in the musical tradition. As Fintan Vallely has written in *Graph*, 'Traditional music in Ireland touches the historically-conditioned dispossessed, rural, rebel or simply nonconformist strata that are never too far beneath the surface with a large number of us and define our difference from other nationalities.' The fact that traditional music is being incorporated into mainstream commodity pop music, a fact bemoaned by many, is seen by Vallely in a different light, as rather the proof that it has ridden out the storm and won. It has shaken off the 'top-down' sanitised view of music culture foisted on it by the parish priests and their efforts to 'improve' people according to the Victorian model, another direct result of the loss of cultural confidence caused by the Famine. One of the fall-outs of the Famine in my own family was the adoption two generations back of such a rigorous work-ethos that even singing and whistling were forbidden in the house, never mind dancing or wasting time or money on a musical instrument. In a short period of time, this had the net effect of producing from a reasonably musical family a whole generation who were and remain tone-deaf, and do not to this day possess a note in their heads.

One other area of real breakthrough is in the greatly renewed interest and outburst of creativity in the Irish language, especially in the oral tradition in general and in traditions such as *dinnsheanchas*, the special branch of area-specific placelore greatly revitalised, renewed and reappraised by writers such as Tim Robinson. *Dinnsheanchas* is a magnificent monument to the collective memory of the Irish people, and a source of great wonder and delight to me personally, because without the mediation of this dimension of the human imagination, rocks and grass and water are ultimately only rocks and grass and water. In this deeply resonant and highly articulated repertoire of myth, legend, folk-knowledge and local narrative we can find an imaginative impulse at work, a shadowy but nevertheless quite palpable imaginative delineation of that rose-red inner Alhambra.

Dinnsheanchas itself encodes the collective memory of the Famine in its pointing out of famine graves and its delineation of certain spots where famine victims died as 'hungry grass', which, if you walk on them, will provoke a sudden, overpowering hunger and weakness that might even be lethal. (Hence the good country habit of always carrying some item of food, be it only a crust of bread, in the pocket.) But at an even deeper level, *dinnsheanchas* encodes the collective trauma of the Famine. Again and again in the stories told about the landscape features of Corcha Dhuibhne, the Dingle Peninsula, which is the part of Ireland that I know most intimately, a certain pattern emerges.

Always and ever there is a submerged female principle or image just beneath the surface of the collective subconscious: whether like the *piast*, or 'monster', of Loch Crawley confined by the forces of Christianity under a cauldron in the depths of a lake; or like the ever-giving Magic Cow, an Ghlas Ghaibhneach, who was misused by being milked into a sieve and who as a result ran back into the sea from which she first came. Sometimes, like the legendary Carbuncle of Lough Geal on the Connor Pass, whose story entranced the otherwise doggedly empirical Praeger, she rises to the surface once every seven years and lights up the dark night through the brilliance of her shining. These stories point to a world-view that the tragedy of the Famine wiped from our consciousness, and it ill behooves us to leave it neglected if we want to try and overcome the trauma of that time.

Just like the legendary fairy islands that emerge in like fashion off our coastline, whether Hy Brasil or Little Arann or Cill Swithin or Dún-idir-dhá-Dhrol, all that this female presence is waiting for is a brave act of repossession. This is imaged in the stories in many different ways. Sometimes it is by throwing some of the clay of the real world on the mythical island that we recover it; other times it is through the planting of a lighting ember or the stealing of a magic cape from the guardian of the place that we finally force it up on to dry land. There it emerges into consciousness, and appears to all clothed in all the wonder and exuberance of an inner Alhambra.

Mis and Dubh Ruis: A Parable of Psychic Transformation

Let me begin by telling a little tale of West Kerry.

Mis was the daughter of Dáire Donn, who came in to Ventry at the head of the forces of the Eastern World, and who was promptly dispatched to eternity by Fionn Mac Cumhail and the Fianna in the Battle of Ventry, which some say lasted a year and a day. When Mis found her father's body lying decapitated on the sand, she sucked at the wounds, drank their blood and then fled in total insanity into the wilds, where she grew fur and killer claws with which she attacked and tore to pieces anyone she met. The intensity of her madness was such that she could run like the wind and no living thing was safe from her. She ate the meat and drank the blood of anything she caught, so that the whole barony of Clainne Mhuiris was turned into a wilderness bereft of people. In spite of all of this killing, because of who she had been, the king decreed that no one should kill her. Now the king, a smart man, thought that half a kingdom was better than no kingdom at all, and thereby he promised half of his own, and Mis's hand in marriage, to anyone who brought her down – alive, mind you, he said, mindful as ever of her former status. The best warriors went against her, all done up in armour, and had no luck. She made mincemeat of them, and soon there weren't many warriors left. The king was getting worried.

'If this is all right with you,' said Dubh Ruis, the harper, 'I'll have a go'.

'You!' laughed the king. 'With what?'

'With my harp.'

The king fell about the place laughing, but when Dubh Ruis said he would need a handful each of gold and silver to accomplish the task the king let him have them. So Dubh Ruis took the gold and the silver and went up the side of Slieve Mis to where he thought he might find her, and spreading his cloak out beneath him, he laid out the gold and silver all around the edges. Then he lay down on his back, placed the harp above him, opened up his trousers, exposed himself and started to play his harp. Suddenly there she was, perched on a tree above him. She hops down beside him. (As my friend and Old Irish scholar Máirín Ní Dhonnchú keeps pointing out to me, these last two lines are not in the original, but I can't help it — I can just picture her, holding on to a branch with her long claws, like a harpie.)

'Aren't you a human?' she asks.

'Yes,' sez he.

'What is this?' putting her hand on the harp.

'A harp,' sez he.

'Hmmmmm,' sez she. 'I remember the harp. My father had one of them. Play it for me.'

'I will,' sez he, 'only no harm to me or mine.'

'Done,' sez she, 'I'll not harm you.'

Then she sees the gold and silver.

'What are these?'

'Gold and silver.'

'I seem to remember them. My father used to have gold long ago, ochón ó.'

Then she glanced at his nakedness and his comely manliness and said, 'What are these?' to his balls, and he told her.

'And what is this?' said she, to the other thing she saw.

'A gaming stick,' sez he.

'Sfunny,' sez she, 'I don't remember that. I don't think my father had one of them. A gaming stick, is it now?' sez she. 'And what is the game?'

'Sit down here beside me,' sez he, 'and I'll play the game of stick with you.'

So she did and they did and …

'Ha-ba-ba,' sez she, 'that's a good game. Do it again.'

'I will,' sez he, 'but I'll play the harp for you a while first.'

'Throw away that bloody harp,' she said, 'and play the game instead.'

'I must eat something,' he said, 'I'm starving.'

'I'll catch you a deer,' she said.

'Do that,' sez he, 'I've got bread here with me.'

'Where is it?' she asked.

'Here.'

'Ha-ha,' she said. 'I remember bread. My father used to have it,' she said, and then, 'Don't leave me.'

'I won't leave you.'

The upshot of it all is that he cooks the deer that she delivers to him and she remembers that cooked meat is better than raw. Then he boils up the deer fat and bathes her in it and rubs her down until a lot of the fur comes away from her. He makes her a bed of moss, covers her with the deer skin and lies down beside her and next day builds a hut around her. She doesn't waken until afternoon, and thinking him gone, makes a lament which he overhears and which contains the immortal lines:

'It is not the gold that I miss, nor the sweet harp, nor the balls but the gaming stick of Dubh Ruis Mac Raghnaill.'

This idyll lasted for two months. Every day he bathed and scrubbed her down until all the fur fell away and her memory and reason returned to her. Then Dubh Ruis dressed her in splendid apparel and brought her home with him, returned to her former beauty and the same age that she had been before she went mad on the mountain. Dubh Ruis married her and she gave him four children and was accounted one of the most beautiful and accomplished women of Munster of her time ...

This is my favorite representation of a theme which has been called central to Irish literature since time immemorial: the idea of a loathly hag or *cailleach*, a *puella senilis* signifying the tribal land (or sometimes the whole island). The *cailleach*, however, when united with the rightful king in the conjugal act is transformed into her rightful form of *spéirbhean*, woman of great beauty or goddess. Such a tradition lies at the heart of the *aisling* genre, of Merriman's *Midnight Court*, and was even recycled with great aplomb by W.B. Yeats, encapsulating neatly the emotional nexus of turn-of-the-century Nationalism:

'Did you see an old woman go down the path?'
'No, but I saw a young girl, and she had the walk of a queen.'

To a visitor from another planet, or even from another island on this one, it must seem inconceivable that a whole generation of otherwise seemingly rational beings would shed blood and be prepared to lay down their own lives for what is after all at one level just an image in a poem or a play. But they did. And they do, and will continue to do so while the underlying mythic drama is kept from conscious evaluation and so fated, instead, to literal re-enactment.

What is the tremendous emotional appeal of the image?

The *cailleach-spéirbhean* transformation in lore and literature is immeasurably old, and would seem to reach back to pre-Celtic strata of Mother-Goddess worshippers. It is tempting to date it back to at least the age of Newgrange itself: the mid-winter penetration of that enormous womb by a ray of sunlight is an architectural marvel by which the central sacred image of the religion of the time, the penetration of the Earth-Mother by the Sky-God, the sacred marriage or '*Hieros gamos*', can take place – physically – before our eyes. This powerful image was naturally usurped by the invading Celts and pressed into play for their own political purposes. The Uí Néill dynasty would make their own of it with a superb sleight of hand in the story of how their eponymous ancestor, Niall Naoingiallach, unlike his over-fastidious brothers, not only kissed an ugly hag at a well in return for a drink of water, but actually slept with her. At this she was transformed into the *spéirbhean*, and announced that this was no mere water that she was giving him, but the drink of Sovereignty, which granted to him and his the right to rule. A related branch of the Celtic invaders, the East Eoghantacht, adapted the mytheme to even more blatant political effect, taking up the story of Lughaidh Laighde and his brothers at the well and adding their own difference. One of the brothers consents to peck the *cailleach* on the cheek, and when she is later revealed in all her resplendent splendour as the Goddess of Sovereignty ('Is mise an Fhlaigheas,' she says), he is rewarded with the promise of kingship to one of his descendants. Lughaidh, of course, being the hero, does everything right, and not only kisses the *cailleach* but sleeps with her, and so his heirs are prophesied as kings for several generations after him – with the one exception as repayment to his brother for the kiss. This is a formidable reworking of an ancient concept. Newspeak, how are you. The rewriting of history certainly did not begin with the Stalinist era, and discrepancies in the lists of kings throw light on a few interesting 'non-persons', among them a certain Dubh Ruis, of the Éireann, associated with Móir Mumhan, who flourished in the ninth century, and who may be, aptly enough, the hero of the tale with which I began.

The fact that the particular version of the theme in our tale is of late enough origin and shows signs of having been elaborated in a purely literary or para-literary manner to become a damn good story does not particularly matter: the basic material of 'Mis and Dubh Ruis' is ancient. It has been suggested that such madwoman tales, with their attendant motif of humans becoming animals who leap or fly, are older than the Suibhne Geilt story, which might, in fact, have been patterned after them. The main mytheme of our story, this issue of transformation, I take to have had cultic significance. In one form or another our story must have formed part of a liturgy: the very least we can say about it is that it is a sacred script in its description of a form of transubstantiation. This may not be quite as farfetched as it sounds: if all other documentation was lost now and all that was left of Christianity were a few snippets of literary classics, how could we ever piece together the ethos that was the major religion of the West, never mind try to reconstruct in detail the ceremony of the mass? Living religions are enacted totally and passionately, not described objectively.

Many have described the *cailleach* as the most potent image working subliminally on the collective psyche of this island. Why it should be the Negative Mother Archetype rather than another form of the Goddess that describes the underlying psychic reality of this island is not clear. Some say it is the result of the curse of Macha, a miasma or mother-curse. Others blame the climate. I have even heard it suggested that the Tooth-Mother is always overridingly prominent on the Western seaboards of continents due to the cultic use of the magic mushroom psylosybe, which grows naturally in this biozone. (The toothed monsters on the totem-poles of the Amerindians of the North-West Pacific coast have been cited as an instance of this.) Elsewhere I have seen it suggested that it is due to a strong male bias in the consciousness of the Celts which denies the deep Feminine and is thus 'rewarded' with a negative image from the repressed psychic contents. (This makes sense to me because if, as Anne Ross suggests, the head was the central icon of the Celts, being to their religious ethos what the cross is to Christianity, then long before the arrival of St Patrick and his cohorts our ancestors were already severely cut off – literally – from what the French feminist literary theorists call the 'language of the body'.) This is not to suggest that women did not have a relatively powerful role in Celtic society – there is enough evidence which suggests they had – but merely that the traits valued in women were 'masculine' ones like war-likeness, rather than the more nurturing virtues. We are in much the same dilemma today as women in this generation rush pell-mell to 'beat men at their own game', often at great psychological cost to themselves, without asking whether the 'real world' of male authority is really worth entering in the first place. While I don't wish to exonerate established Christianity from an unmistakable patriarchal bias, it may be that our head-hunting Celtic forebears played a role in perverting the moderately life-enhancing qualities of the message of Christ into the virulent life-denying force that has come to be Irish Catholicism. The Celts were already in their time too deeply patriarchal to attempt the inner transformation that is the *cailleach-spéirbhean* theme.

But a deeper stratum of consciousness can still be sensed on this island. Unlike most of the countries of Northern Europe, in Ireland the border between this world and the 'otherworld' was never drawn. The fact that a highly elaborate conceptual framework exists in Irish to describe and deal with the 'otherworld' is proof of that fact – a framework that, incidentally, is virtually untranslatable due to an inbuilt bias in the English language against the validity and tangibility of otherworldly experience. Put into English this perfectly serious and alternative state of consciousness is reduced to superstition or 'Pisroguery'.

And yet, happily, we live on an island in which large masses of people regularly see statues leaping about the place. Leaving the sometimes rather dubious orchestration of such phenomena aside, this is significant. In spite of the mass-media and an educational system which has vowed to destroy the imagination, we have proof that we have not yet entirely capitulated to purely rationalist empiricism. (If it moves, measure it!) Also, and what is even more to my point, the moving statues are all female statues. There has been no significant incidence of Jesus getting down from his cross à la *Marcelino* (a film which terrified many of us when hawked around the country in the fifties, for the benefit of what worthy cause nobody can rightly remember). Neither has St Joseph taken to tampering with anyone with his lily, nor, more surprisingly – given the propensity of his vicars for the exercise – never has the ubiquitous St Patrick delivered anyone a belt of his crozier. If an image is on the move within us, it is a female image, and we project outwards what is the reality within.

I take our story, like the central truths of many different religions, to be a gift from the subconscious that cannot be rationally explained. But it can be pondered, worried over, wondered at, told over and over again, and because of its deeply symbolic significance it never loses anything in the telling. Besides the fine psychological insight that it was the vulnerable man in all his nakedness who overcame the hag and not any of the conquering heroes, there is another level of the story that has deep significance for the times we live in. Given that such a story had a socio-political significance for its inventors, and that it was probably enacted publicly within the collective psyche of the *tuath* or tribe, it has still a very valid lesson to give to modern, almost post-psychological man. As the work of feminist theologians and literary theorists suggests, the only way forward is to somehow break out of the dominant patriarchal ethos of the age. For all of us, inwardly, the king must die. Then, as the work of Mary Daly would suggest, the Hag energy must erupt. The too-long repressed Feminine comes into its own, and, as we learn to come to terms with what is dark and frightening in ourselves, we can release others from the burden of carrying our resentment in one way or another. Then a new form of male energy asserts itself in the unconscious, and, challenging the hag, uniting with her, brings forth the conscious reality of the Goddess, as *spéirbhean*. Rosemary Radford Ruether ends her powerful critique *Sexism and Godtalk* with an epiphany, a powerful evocation of the Goddess. This is more than I can do with any honesty at present. I have to admit that I have not yet personally met the *spéirbhean*; I'm still working on that inner harper in all his powerful dream manifestations as Enemy, Sea-Horse or Minotaur, Bull of the Mothers. But there does seem to be a way forward, and I live in hope. It is only with the arrival of softer spring weather that inner transformation sometimes seems to take place, as happened, I think, when I wrote the poem 'Primavera' (in *The Water Horse*):

D'athraigh gach aon ní nuair a ghaibh sí féin thar bráid.
Bhainfeadh sí deora áthais as na clocha glasa, deirim leat.
Na héanlaithe beaga a bhí go dtí seo faoi smál,
d'osclaíodar a scórnaigh is thosnaigh ag pípeáil
ar chuma feadóige stáin i láimh gheochaigh, amhail
is gur chuma leó sa diabhal an raibh nó nach raibh nóta acu.
Bláthanna fiáine a bhí chomh cúthail, chomh h-umhal
ag lorg bheith istigh go faicheallach ar chiumhaiseanna
na gceapach mbláth, táid anois go rábach, féach an falcaire fiain
ag baint radharc na súl díom go hobann lena réilthínní craoracha.

Bhíos-sa, leis, ag caoi go ciúin ar ghéag,
i bhfolach faoi dhuilleóig fige, éalaithe i mo dhú dara,
ag cur suas stailce, púic orm chun an tsaoil.
Thógfach sé i bhfad níos mó ná meangadh gáire
ó aon spéirbhean chun mé a mhealladh as mo shliogán,
bhí an méid sin fógraithe thall is abhus agam roimhré.

Ach do dhein sí é, le haon searrach amháin dá taobh,
le haon sméideadh meidhreach, caithiseach, thar a gualainn
do chorraigh sí na rútaí ionnam, is d'fhág mé le miabhán
im'cheann, gan cos ná láimh fúm, ach mé corrathónach, guagach.

Everything changed as soon as her nibs passed this way,
she'd bring tears of joy to the very stones themselves, I'm
    telling you.
The little birds who were up to now in disgrace
have opened their throats and started piping it out
for all the world like a tinwhistle in the hands
of a teenage boy, as if they don't care a damn
whether they have or they haven't a note in them.
The wild flowers, once so shy and servile,
begging permission to lodge on the edges of flowerbeds,
are now unrestrained, look at the pimpernel
blinding my eyes with its sudden profusion of scarlet flowers.

I too was quietly weeping, far out on a limb,
gone to ground under a fig-leaf, become a grumpy old thing,
in a fit of the sulks, vexed generally with life.
I had announced beforehand, far and wide,
that it would take a lot more than a winsome smile
from a fair damsel to coax me out of my shell.
But she did it, with one shake of a milky thigh,
with a laughing, lascivious beam out over her shoulder
she wrenched up my roots, and left me addled, high and dry
footless, footloose, fanciful and fretful.

Trans. Ní Dhomhnaill, previously unpublished

The last time I visited Glendalough it was one of those gloriously crisp spring days: far and few-between clouds hovered motionlessly above the deeply glaciated valley in the massif of the Wicklow hills under a sky of clear cerulean blue. The grass was green as green, the sort of colour that gives Ireland its rather kitchy appellation of 'The Emerald Isle'. My sense of hyperreality was increased by the bright blaze of deep yellow on every hedge and ditch, sometimes covering whole hillsides, as the newly blossoming gorse (*ulex europeaus*) – called furze here in southern Ireland – shone brightly in the sunlight. This prickly bush, a former fodder plant especially beloved of horses and also used extensively in earlier times as a bedding material for other farm animals, used to be cultivated in small paddocks. By now it has long outstripped the boundaries once laid down for it, running riot throughout the countryside, colonising every acre of spare or waste land, and many a good field besides.

Apart from the farmers who consider furze a nuisance, everybody is grateful for its blossoming, for with its mild but unmistakable scent of peaches-and-cream and unforgettable colour, it is a blessing for the nose as well as a decided ornament to the Irish countryside. When the great naturalist Linneaus first set eyes on this glorious plant, he is reported to have knelt down and thanked God for its existence and riotous abundance. Seeing it now in the full blast of its first blooming, this story does not seem at all apocryphal, and in fact is particularly suited to Glendalough.

The monastic settlement of Glendalough flourished for six centuries after the death of the founding father St Kevin in 622

AD. It attracted a large population for its time, with at least one thousand monks and over three thousand lay-people or students under them. This was the equivalent at least of our modern universities, at a time when the rest of Europe was experiencing the Dark Ages and still reeling from the effects of barbarian invasions and the fall of the Roman Empire. A contemporary text, the early ninth century *Martyrology of Oengus* (the latest possible date for which is 810 AD), describes the significance of Glendalough in no uncertain terms:

> Emain's burgh, it hath vanished
> Save that its stones remain:
> The ruam of the west of the world
> is multitudinous Glendalough.

'Emain' is of course Emain Mhaca, the capital of Ulster in pre-Christian times, and the setting of the saga material dealing with the goings-on of King Conor Mac Neasa and his Red Branch Knights, including, notably, his nephew Cúchulainn. The writer's evident satisfaction at the disappearance of the world of Cúchulainn would no doubt increase today, when much of that world and history remains veiled to us. While we are well used to the idea of the demise of pagan Ireland, however, we are not well used to the suggestion made in the last two lines of this verse. The word '*ruam*', used to describe a great city, comes from 'Roma', the Latin for Rome. And we might find the writer's belief in the city status of Glendalough slightly premature, as this settlement in the remote 'Glen of the Two Lakes' has long been superseded and supplanted as a metropolis by many other civic centres, not least by the upstart Dublin, which in the writer's time was nothing more than a ford across the river Liffey.

But all that comes later, with the arrival of the Anglo-Normans and the impact of the feudal system which they brought with them. Before destruction by English forces in 1398 left it the ruin it still remains, Glendalough was, in both ecclesiastical and political terms, one of the most important settlements in pre-Norman Leinster, and control of its bishopric and abbacy was a bone of great contention between rival kings. It is accorded many references in the Irish Annals, and was subjected to frequent plundering, burning and rebuilding. Many future saints and scions of noble families from across Europe are mentioned as being educated there. The traffic was not just one way, either; a certain Gilla na Naem Laighneach, having retired from being bishop of Glendalough, went to Wurzburg where he died as head of the Schottencloster c.1160.

Even Glendalough's ruins are impressive. They consist of a double-arched gatehouse, a cathedral, a round tower and a number of other churches. All of these were originally surrounded by both an inner and an outer enclosure, which was once also chok-a-block with smaller wooden structures, long perished, where the inhabitants lived and where extensive artistic, educational and commercial activities flourished. Beside the gatehouse, the only one of its kind preserved in Ireland, a large cross etched on a wall proclaimed the rule of monastic law and the right of sanctuary to all who obeyed the monks' rule, whatever their status in the law of the land outside.

Not far away is a hundred-foot high and extremely well-preserved round tower. These structures, originally built as bell-towers, also served as landmarks for approaching visitors and as places of refuge and watch-towers in times of attack, especially from the Vikings, who by the tenth century had established permanent bases in nearby Wicklow, Arklow and Dublin. Close to the tower is also a small building called 'the Priest's House', whose original use remains unknown, but which may have served as a mortuary or as a reliquary for the display of holy items in times of pilgrimage. This is not far from a large early cross of local granite with an unpierced ring, of the type commonly known as Celtic crosses. Unlike crosses from other notable Irish sites like Clonmacnoise, Monasterboice and Moone, which have Celtic designs and Biblical scenes, this cross is simple and unadorned.

Only a few metres away is the most important church in the complex, the cathedral, which stands on a plateau of rising ground in the centre of the valley. It is built in Irish Romanesque style, and the nave is one of the widest of early Christian churches in Ireland. Large stones of mica-schist are laid on edge in what is known for good reason as Cyclopean masonry. Inside a very early gravestone laid on a wall urges us to pray for the souls of two lost to time, Diarmaid and Maccois. A much later gravestone on the opposite wall proclaims the death of one Walter Byrne, who died 6 March 1750, aged 106 years. A visitor with more than a drop of Byrne blood in her veins announces with evident satisfaction that 'It must be the good mountain air and diet' that kept her ancestor alive so long.

These ruins and the lower Trinity and St Saviour's Churches are left behind as I set out on the four kilometre Miner's Road that hugs the Upper Lake in Glendalough, and which is one of several marked nature walks in the Glendalough National Park. Walking through the Scots pines – not native trees, but planted by the Mining Company of Ireland around 1850 – it is impossible not to notice the variety and abundance of small birds round about. Great, blue, long-tailed and coal tits shoot by like streak lightning. A robin redbreast sits unconcernedly close by on a nearby rock. And was that a jenny wren, the smallest bird in the Irish fauna, that I spied just now up a tree? A mistle thrush trills its heart out from a holly-bush. There are, however, no larks. Popular tradition has it that no larks ever sing in Glendalough: Saint Kevin banished them because they caused the builders of his cathedral to rise too early in the morning and thus feel tired and listless at their work. Who am I to demur at such local wisdom?

Directly across the lake is the site of this very cathedral, with a ruined church, Temple-na-Skellig or the Church of the Rock, built (in the tenth or eleventh century) on the site of a church dating from St Kevin's time. It is surrounded by steep cliffs, and only accessible with any ease to middle-aged hikers by boat, though at various times my teenaged children have clambered over the rocks to it, and managed to come back safe. Near it on the right is the raised area which probably contained simple huts which were lived in by the first monks.

To the left is the small man-made cave called 'St Kevin's Bed', which is the oldest Christian relic in the valley, used as a hermit's cell by the eponymous saint 1,400 years ago. It is probably a much older cave, for it is similar to Bronze Age rock tombs known in Normandy and Sicily: it may have been cut for the burial of an important member of a Bronze Age community which lived in this valley over 3,500 years ago. Either way, its useful recycling is typical of how early Christianity made its peace with an earlier pagan substratum on this island.

The story of Glendalough, founded in a remote valley by an ascetic hermit and later developed into a great monastic *civitas* or city of over three thousand students and a thousand monks, is surely, by any standards, a remarkable one. Its founder, St Kevin (in Irish Caoimhghin, which means 'beautifully born' or 'gentle conception'), died in 622 AD. His surviving biographies, written in Latin and Irish, date from several centuries after his death and credit him with having reached the great age of one hundred and twenty. Assuming that he lived to a less remarkable ripe old age of about eighty, we may surmise that he was born circa 540 AD.

Twelve angels with golden lamps were said to have attended his baptism, and the fort in which he was reared was never subject to frost or snow. A mysterious white cow used to come to give its milk voluntarily for the child's sustenance. An angel told him to study for the priesthood, and on receiving holy orders he was instructed by the same angel to cross the mountains and seek out his retreat in the lonely and remote Glendalough, where he wore only the skins of wild animals and would lie by night on bare stones doing penance.

Kevin banished a great monster from the lesser to the greater of the two lakes, and as a result various sicknesses of men and beasts were healed by a visit to the lesser (and lower) lake. The healing qualities of the lower lake are still widely credited locally, the rationale being that the monster in the other lake takes the illnesses upon itself and is thereby too weak to inflict them on anyone. Every few years the monster turns on her side and the water is said to rise as high as the peaks of the surrounding mountains. Anyone who sees this happen is destined to die within a week, I am told, but by a local with a gleam of mischief in her eye. 'Fat chance of that happening today,' I reply, looking at the huge cliffs towering over the dark waters.

St Kevin became renowned for great holiness. He was alone in the wilderness for seven years and at peace with all nature. When he prayed, in the fashion of the time, with arms outstretched, little birds would often perch on his hands and shoulders. An anecdote tells us that once, when he was fasting during Lent, a blackbird landed on one of his outstretched palms and made its nest there. Rather than disturb the nesting bird, the saint kept his hand in the same position until the blackbird's young were hatched. Maybe that explains the prolific bird-life to this very day: a distant echo, perhaps, of the saint's benevolence.

St Kevin's fame for holiness spread rapidly and many flocked to join the small monastic community that grew up around him. What he himself must have thought of this enforced sociability is not recorded. He seemed to have been unwilling enough to leave the narrow site of his original monastery for a more spacious and commodious site at the mouth of the Upper Lake. Once again an angel did the necessaries, and following its orders a second monastery was established in what are now the ruins of Reefert Church, in Irish Rí-feart, 'the burial place of the Kings', and an indication of how important Glendalough had already become by the early medieval period.

On the wall beside the path, stones are overgrown with masses of moss and studded with lichens. This gladdens my heart, as it is proof that the air above is still clean. When air pollution or acid rain occurs, the lichens, tough enough organisms in other ways, are always the first to go. Their variety here is therefore extremely reassuring. In between the stones are the round succulent leaves of pennyworth (*umbilicus rupestris*), one of whose Irish names is *arán glas* or 'green bread'. It was one of seven different plants known as 'bread' because of their widespread use as a famine food. I look over at the bleak spot where the hermit Kevin practised his great feats of self-mortification, and wonder if he ever used this plant to vary the diet of sorrel and nettles on which he subsisted for seven years.

Growing amongst the heather beside the path I also find the first new green shoots of the low-lying bushes (*vaccinium myrtillius*) which later in the year will produce bilberries or whortleberries, known locally as 'whorts' or 'fraughans' (from the Irish '*fraocháin*'), and which are a smaller and sharper-tasting cousin of North American wild blueberries. These are quite delicious; I'm sure St Kevin himself did not disdain them. Collecting them was, in fact, the main activity of Fraughan Sunday, the last Sunday in July, part of the old Celtic harvest festival of Lughnasa, made more widely known by the success of Brian Friel's play *Dancing at Lughnasa*. There were a lot of superstitions attached to fraughan-picking, I am told. For one thing, it was a communal activity: going off to pick them alone was frowned upon. Stories were told about girls who went picking them on their own and were later found not quite in their right minds with their mouths and hands blue from the berries. I shiver involuntarily at this, whether from an atavistic memory or just from the cold I cannot tell.

By now I have reached the end of this particular trail, the ruins of a lead-mining village from the last century. The path gives out onto a desolate wilderness of bare rock, where a wild stream tumbles down the head of the glen. On the other side graze some of the wild goats and deer which are the curse of local home-steaders. It is quite extraordinary that such a genuine wilderness can exist within one hour's drive of homes in Dublin. This ease of access to nature is one of the things that makes Dublin very special as a capital city, and it is what I have missed most of all when I have lived for any time abroad.

Beneath me the upper lake glitters, shining and dark between the trees. There was, a local tells me, a sort of bad feeling about the lake; children were never allowed swim in it, as the feeling was that if anyone drowned in it the bodies were never recovered and would be gone forever. Again an involuntary shiver, though it must surely be from the sharp breeze blowing off the lake. I think of St Kevin praying waist-deep in its icy waters as he recited his vespers, a classic example of early Celtic asceticism. Rather him than me, I think, and turn to go back.

Long after Kevin's death a third and even more extensive monastery was established beside the smaller, lower lake, and it is this which preserves the most extensive ruins, including an imposing double gateway, a 200-foot tall round tower or bell-tower, an eighth century monumental High Cross and St Kevin's

Church with its unusual stone roof. There is also a Romanesque cathedral boasting trimming in an oolitic limestone which comes from as far away as the Dundry quarries near Bristol in England, a sign of the extensive commercial networks of Glendalough.

And it is to this, the lowest and most extensive of Glendalough's three monastic sites, that I return. I enter the visitors' centre to watch for what must be the umpteenth time the short video 'Ireland of the Monasteries', scripted by the medieval historian Peter Harbison, which is a classic of its kind. It imparts a lot of knowledge without the slightest trace of pedantry, and places Glendalough in its historic context, showing the enormous effect that it and other Irish places of learning had in rescuing Europe from the Dark Ages.

Outside, the day is still clear and bright. On the guided tour that follows I play truant and stop to read the names on the modern gravestones that fill what is so obviously most hallowed ground. O'Toole, O'Byrne, Kavanagh, Kinsella: these are the modern versions of the names of the once kingly septs of Leinster who were always buried here. May they rest in peace. It must have been of a quietly epiphanic moment such as this that W.B. Yeats wrote in his late poem on Glendalough:

> What motion of the sun or stream
> Or eyelid shot the gleam
> That pierced my body through?
> What made me live like these that seem
> Self-born, born anew?

One late summer day when I was five, I was walking up the village of Cahiratrant in Ventry parish, where I had been recently fostered out to my Aunt May to learn Irish. Wrenched unceremoniously from my middle-class existence in Lancashire, I was coping rather dubiously with cows, dusty roads, no running water or electricity. More importantly, I was also coping with Irish, and the fact that nobody could understand my Scouse English – no more than I could understand their Kerry accents. I met an old man, Jacsaí Shea, coming down the road toward me. 'Cé leis tú?' he asked me – 'Who do you belong to?' – which was the usual local way of asking children their name. Taking the phrase at its most literal meaning, I drew myself bristling to my great height of all three-foot nothing and stoutly replied, 'Ní le héinne mé. Is liom féin mé féin' ('I don't belong to anyone. I belong only to myself'). Chuckling mightily, Jacsaí continued down the road to the house of Peats Mhic Ó Cinnéide, which was the village *Dáil*, or parliament, where the older men were wont to gather in the evening to discuss the affairs of the world, great and small. My encounter with Jacsaí was obviously part of the evening's entertainment, because the story went around the village like wildfire, and even now, almost fifty years later, it is occasionally thrown in my face, especially when I have done or said something that is considered a bit 'bold' or 'too independent'.

Such sauciness is inevitably put down to *dúchas*, or genetic heritage – but from 'the other side', my father's bloodlines to the north of the peninsula beyond the Connor Pass, 'i dtaobh thíos de chnoc' ('below the hill'). It is put down especially to my Great-Aunt Elly, of whom I am supposed to be the temperamental dead spit. I knew Elly slightly as a child and was rather fond of her, perhaps because she seemed to take a special interest in me and liked what others considered my 'cheeky' ways. As an adult, I have often felt she was a woman before her time who was given a bad press for being independent and strong-willed, and I have sought to correct the story somewhat by writing a poem about her. Elly was no angel, but I try to explain some of her more cantankerous behaviour as the natural consequence of the historical ill-treatment of the local people, who were used worse than wild animals from the time of the Elizabethans onward.

In Memoriam Elly Ní Dhomhnaill (1884–1963)
(in *An Dealg Droighin; Pharaoh's Daughter*)

Fuair sí céim onórach
sa bhitheolaíocht
i míle naoi gcéad is a ceathair.
Ansin chuaigh abhaile
chun a baile fearainn
tóin le gaoith,
taobh thíos de chnoc,
is d'fhan ann faid a marthain.

Níor phós sí riamh.
Ní raibh éinne timpeall maith a dhóthain di.
Nuair a phós a deartháir
ní raibh an bhean a phós sé
maith a dhóthain dó, shíl sí,
agus do dhíol sí an talamh orthu.

Do throid sí a hathair.
Do throid sí a deartháir.
Do throid sí an sagart paróiste.
Dar léi, níor chóir
na síntiús a bheith á léamh amach os ard
i lár an Aifrinn.
Thuig sí an t-uaibhreas
a chuirfeadh ar dhaoine bochta

íoc thar a gcumas don Eaglais
ag fágáil a leanaí ocrach.
Dá réir sin,
shuíodh sí ina piú féin go sásta
a lámh ar a bata draighneáin
is ar a ceann hata,
fad nglaoití amach ón altóir
'Elly Ní Dhomhnaill – dada'.

M'athair an t-aon duine
a théadh á féachaint
pius Aeaneas na clainne –
is nuair a cailleadh í
d'fhág sí an tigh aige
a dhíolamar de bharr taise.
Gheallas-sa go scríobhfainn litir chúichi
rud nár dheineas.
B'fhéidir gur litreacha
a bhfuil scríofa ó shin agam
a seoladh chuig an spiorad uaibhreach
nár chall di luí
le fear a diongbhála.

Cuireadh m'fhear céile
ar a aire im choinne
ar eagla an drochbhraoin chéanna,
á rá go rabhas-sa mar í féin,
cúl le cine,
is nach raibh aon oidhre eile uirthi.

Fadó
bhí binib sa bhfeochán gaoithe ag séideadh ó Bhinn os Gaoith
is ár sinsear ag dul le heallach isteach go Macha na Bó.

In Memoriam Elly Ní Dhomhnaill (1884–1963)
(in *Pharaoh's Daughter*)

She got an honours degree
in biology in nineteen-four,
then went back to her homeland
at the butt of the hill,
its backside to the wind,
and stopped there all her days.

She never married.
No one around was good enough for her.
When her brother married,
his bride wasn't good enough for him,
in Elly's view, and
she sold their land.

She fought with her father.
She fought with her brother.
She fought with the P.P.
To her it was all wrong
that dues were read out aloud
in the middle of Mass.
She saw right well the cheek –
imposing on the poor
to pay the Church beyond their means
and leave their children hungry.
On that account, she'd sit
satisfied in her pew,
hand on her blackthorn,
hat on her head,
awaiting the call from the altar,
"Elly O'Donnell – nothing".

The only one to visit her
was my father
– the family's pious Aeneas –

and when she went
she left him the house,
which we sold – too damp.
I promised to write to her
but didn't.
Maybe everything I've written since
has addressed itself to that proud spirit,
who had no call to lie
with a man her match.

My own man was warned off
when he met me
for fear of the same bad drop,
saying I was just like her,
a loner,
her sole heir.

In olden times
there was venom in the withering wind from Binn ós Baoith
as our people were herded like cattle into Macha na Bó.

Trans. George O'Brien

Even if my character was sometimes put down to a Ní
Dhomhnaill inheritance, my youthful encounter with old Jacsaí
remains a crux of a matter that has determined much of my life.
Based on a semantic misunderstanding, it sums up inescapably my
relationship with West Kerry. Of the Gaeltacht, I am not from the
Gaeltacht; the existence of an Irish diaspora had made that
impossible. Inexorably drawn to the Irish-speaking communities of
the Western seaboard, and knowing them intimately, I am still
always an outsider, the little *cailín Sasanach* or English girl that I was
then. This fact has cultivated in me what Seamus Heaney, in an
article a few years ago in *The Irish Times*, called 'a doubleness of
focus, a capacity to live in two places at the one time and in two
times at the one place, a capacity to acknowledge the claims of
contradictory truths without having to choose between them'. It
has also led to a capacity to be genuinely bilingual, to live in two
languages, in very different mind-sets.

I wonder: is this always, or necessarily, a good thing? Does a bilingual existence really, as many claim, lead to a genuinely stereoscopic and enriched view of life, or is it the cause of mental astigmatism and blurred vision, a sense of displacement, a deep anxiety? I have found at times that the inner contradictions bilingualism entails cause psychic pain: sometimes it is as if a civil war were going on inside me, and the sheer effort of maintaining a standoff of the warring parties is deeply exhausting. All my energies get sucked down into the subconscious, with a depression characterised by overwhelming lethargy as its most obvious physical manifestation. Even in better times there is a constant restlessness. Is this feeling of being unsettled, vaguely in exile from somewhere I know not where or something I know not what, connected with the sheer complexity of Irish history – or is it just an ineradicable part of the modern condition? There is no Ithaca to return to. The cancerous spread of global 'pop' monoculture has seen to that.

If Jacsaí had asked me the more usual 'Cad is ainm duit?' ('What is your name?'), there would have been no initial misunderstanding. Ask a simple question and you will get a simple answer. But Jacsaí was of an older generation, with a completely different *Weltanschauung* – which could no more imagine an unattached human being than it could identify a star without its surrounding constellations. The modern concept of an 'individual' with inalienable 'rights' had not yet emerged out of the seething and teeming collective amoeba that was the local Irish-speaking community. His was a relational imagination; it could go back at least seven generations on all sides, through all of the combinations and permutations, in what was a community of very small farmers, in a subsistence economy so poor that many might ask, Why bother? Why bother remembering such things? All of these people lived and married and had so many children and died, but none of them was rich or important. But to think in this way would be to entirely misunderstand the case. The people of Cahiratrant in the 1950s may have been materially poor, but linguistically and spiritually they were heirs not only to an oral culture going back millennia, but also, because of the vagaries of history, to the literary and manuscript culture of medieval Irish. A line from a Fenian lay or an Old Irish saga was as apt to trip off their tongues as a remark on the difficulty of scuffling mangolds.

George Thomson hits upon a fitting analogy in *Island Home: The Blasket Heritage* — 'Every educated Greek is familiar with Homeric tales of the Trojan War, but only from literary sources; for after the introduction of Christianity the pagan stories were forgotten by the common people. In Ireland, too, many were lost in this way, but others have survived in oral tradition down to our time.' What Thomson found to be true of the Blasket Islanders was equally true of the parishioners of Ventry, from which many of the Islanders had come originally. (Though they have lived in Dunquin since their evacuation to the mainland in the early 1950s, many of the last of the ex-Islanders are buried in St Catherine's Graveyard in Ventry, for this is their *fód dúchais*, or ancestral sod.) The generation of adults I knew in Cahiratrant when I was a small child was no different from their Island relatives. Jacsaí, Joeín Shea (no relation), Mike Long, Joe Keevane, Moss and Paddy Martin, John Shea (whose mother was my great-grand aunt), or Thomas Murphy (married to my Aunt May) — they and many others like them were willy-nilly tradition-bearers.

For them, and therefore for us children listening to them, the surrounding landscape was steeped in legendary memories of the past. One of the best-loved of the Fenian tales, 'The Battle of Ventry', was set on the very strand that met our eyes every day. This battle, which lasted for the mythical year and a day, pitched the Fianna, guardians of Ireland, against the forces of Dáire Donn, the King of the Eastern World. A medieval manuscript tale written down by a monk in Regensberg in Germany in the thirteenth century, it was assimilated into the local tales and traditions. Wasn't Dáire Donn's grave in the field behind the local National School, Scoil Chaitlíona, at Cill Mhic an Domhnaigh? And the big rock called Lic Caoil off Thomas Murphy's land at Barr na hAille, wasn't that the petrified body of the giant Caol Mac Criomhthain, the last of the Fianna to be brought down? When he was drowned while preventing the last surviving invader Fiannachtach Fiaclach from escaping, didn't his body come in on the strand called to this day after him Tráigh Chaoil? That large standing stone or *gallán* in Sheehy's field that we passed every day, wasn't that the spot where the great queen, his wife, was buried when she dropped dead on the spot, after pouring out her grief in the great lament for her husband, 'Géisid cuan'?

> The harbor roars out
> over the fierce flow of Rinn Dá Bharc.
> The hero from Loch Dá Chonn drowned:
> The wave mourns it against the shore.

Trans. Thomas Kinsella

One day, while sitting in his favorite spot at the south-facing corner in the middle of the village, Mike Long told me how as a boy he had seen the main fleet of the British Navy, on manoeuvres before World War I, sail into safe anchor in Ventry Bay. He and the other young lads of the village had rowed out to meet them and had been aboard many of the great vessels, including the flagships HMS *Dartmouth* and HMS *Falmouth* (on which, we always believed, my grand-uncle from Cork was subsequently drowned when it went down with all hands in the Battle of Jutland). As Mike recounted it, 'the masts of the ships were so thick in the bay you'd swear they were trees of the forest', and they 'walked from the farthest out boat in onto the strand, going from deck to deck, without as much as wetting their feet once'. My heart gave a little leap of joy: I recognised both phrases as straight out of the medieval text of *The Battle of Ventry*. World War I, the mythical Battle of Ventry, what difference? – they were all grist to the great mill of local and popular imagination. They fuelled a conversational art of enormous elasticity and wide-ranging mythological reference, and of a stylistic and syntactical elegance that was breathtaking.

And herein lies a point crucial to my considerations. In Ireland, everything, including personal and collective history, gets subsumed into the mythological. Our unconscious is still by far our most creative side. For one reason or another, on this island the door between the rational and the irrational has never been locked tight shut. There was always someone – the bard in the hall, the *seanchaí* by the fireside or the balladeer in the pub – who kept his foot in the door. Walter Ong would deem this a result of our 'high degree of residual orality'. And the spoken word, by its very nature and spontaneity, has a plumb-line into the sub-conscious, which, except for the very best fiction and poetry, literary activity very rarely has.

I love this aspect of our culture. It is one of the main things that drew me back to live here, after years on the 'shaughraun'. It is infinitely more exciting and much more of a human challenge to live in a country that is intermittently in touch with the irrational than in one that has set its face resolutely against it. It is one of the reasons, I think, that the arts are in such a wonderfully creative state in Ireland at the moment. Art necessitates a holistic approach to life – at the very least a strong neck that is the necessary bridge between the head and the rest of the body – and no artistic creation that has been approached in a purely rational or logical manner is going to satisfy us aesthetically. Nevertheless, this great gift of ours is not without its drawbacks and its inherent dangers, one of which is that, like children, we are so overwhelmed by our inner scenarios that we can act them out in a public manner, without any awareness of the Reality Principle, or of the fact of other people's necessarily different realties. Collective hysteria is an example of this psychic state, and God knows this country has had more than enough of the likes even recently, as with the moving-statues phenomenon a few years ago, when thousands saw the Blessed Mother or the Virgin Mary (take your pick) in various grottoes throughout the island come to life and bless their supplicants. Another problem with this compression of history and myth is that it can lead to an idealistic culture of sacrifice, which has been a part of Ireland's tragedies in the twentieth century. A generous dollop in our educational system of the twentieth-century discovery of the operating mechanisms of the subconscious's great continent would be of enormous benefit to everyone. It would help us achieve a certain detachment from our unconscious mentation and, instead of repressing it, help us to incorporate it into our lives.

The world-view of the oral tradition is ahistoric in that it 'telescopes' the events of history into mythological time. This 'telescoping' of time and events was identified by Ó Catháin and

Flanagan in *The Living Landscape* as characteristic of *dinnsheanchas* in a Mayo village: 'Events are often telescoped in a bewildering fashion and it seems almost as if Kilgalligan people, as can be seen from the lore, do not feel the heyday of the Vikings, for example, to extend much further back than the famine itself.' This notion was brought home to me most strikingly on one particular occasion in my early teens. I had noticed from the perusal of some map or other that the townland of Cahiratrant was completely surrounded by another townland called 'Na Ráithíneacha', or 'Rawheens' in English, where it seems to mean 'Little Raths'. I had never seen a townland so cut off before and so I questioned my aunt's husband, Thomas Murphy, about how this might have come about. In his typical mode of mock exasperation he shot back at me: 'Ná fuil a fhios ag an saol go raibh an Treanntach ró-mhaith d'Fhionn Mac Cumhaill' ('Doesn't the whole world know that de Terraunt was too strong for Fionn Mac Cumhaill'). This was the first inkling that I had ever had that 'Rawheens' could be as easily, and probably more properly, construed as the plural of 'Ráth Fhinn', or 'the Rath of Fionn'. And so the historical drama of the Norman invasion and the erection of a manse by the conquering knight de Terraunt, which thereby displaced the former Gaelic order, still shows up most succinctly in the townland names on a map – and the entirety of this history can be summed up by a local farmer in one sentence: '*Ná fuil a fhios ag an saol go raibh an Treanntach ró-mhaith d'Fhionn Mac Cumhaill*'.

For me this wonderful heterogeneity of material is an advantage rather than a disadvantage and one of its main attractions for a poet, speaking as it does of a spontaneous eruption of unconscious material, an associative mode of thought that lends itself very easily to poetry. Thus many poems of mine grow naturally from the stories that I had heard in Cahiratrant as a child, and encompass these traditions:

An Bóithrín Caol (in *An Dealg Droighin; Pharaoh's Daughter*)

Laistiar de thigh mo mháthar,
anuas an Bóithrín Caol,
i leith ó Bhóthar na Carraige,

trí thalamh chlann Uí Chíobháin,
do thagadh muintir Fhána
le húmacha ar chapaill,
glan trí mhíle ó bhaile
anuas ar an tráigh
ag triall ar ghaineamh.

Gaineamh le leathadh
ar urlár thithe
is i dtithe ba,
chun go meascfaí é
le haoileach
is go gcuirfí ina dhiaidh san
amach ar ghoirt é,
chun go bhfásfadh bleaist seaimpíní
ó thalamh bocht
nach raibh puinn críche air.

Do théadh na mná scafána
anuas na failltreacha
ag dul ag baint iascán
is cliabh ar a ndroim acu.
Bádh ceathrar cailín óg
ar Leacacha an Ré,
— 'triúr Máire agus Máiréad Bán
a chráigh mo chroí —
is chonaic na daoine
fear an chaipín deirg,
ina shuí sa tonn a bháigh iad.

Uaireanta ar an tráigh
chím i mboghaisín
na dtonntracha ag briseadh
i gcoinne na gaoithe aniar
fear an chaipín chéanna.
Go hobann
tá píobaire ar an gcarraig

faoi bhun na faille
ag seimint
is gan aon fhocal as,
is nuair a fhilleann na capaill istoíche
faoi na húmacha lán de ghaineamh
ní bhíonn fir a dtiomána
ag portaireacht a thuilleadh.

The Narrow Path (in *Pharaoh's Daughter*)

Behind my mother's house
down Bóithrín Caol,
over from Bóthar na Carraige,
through the lands of the Kavanaghs
the people of Fán would journey
three miles to the strand
with horses bearing panniers
for sand to dress
their kitchen floors and byres;

sand trodden into dung
and then laid out at last
on thin potato fields
to grow prodigious Champions
conjured out of famished land
too lean to bed such promise.

With creels lashed
to their backs
women
used to clamber
down these cliffs
for sustenance of mussels.
Four young girls were lost
at Leacacha an Ré –
Three Marys and fair Margaret
who set my heart astray

and people saw
a red-capped man
astride the wave
that took them under.

Sometimes from the strand
I seem to glimpse
that red cap
lustrous in the spume
flayed off the waves,
and then,
without a word
a piper from the cliff
releases drone
and chanter.
When horses
turn at nightfall,
swaying under sand,
the men who lead them home
chatter no longer.

Trans. Michael Coady

But there is another side to this idea of, as Michael Coady
translates it, 'chattering no longer'. I sit here at my desk in Dublin,
wondering why I am writing this. What is it I am trying to
explain, and to whom? I have just got back from the local
supermarket, where there was not a single word of Irish in sight.
I turn on the Irish-language radio station, Radio na Gaeltachta, a
sort of lifeline. It is sometimes banal enough: a black-and-white
dog has gone missing in Connemara, the results of last night's
bingo in Na Doire Beaga are as follows. But I keep feeling there
is something very important I have to say, and that it has to do
with Irish. Just because Irish is almost invisible in suburban
Dublin doesn't mean that it doesn't exist. Like yeast in bread, it is
invisible, but it is what makes the culture rise. This is a difficult
enough point to make in modern Ireland, where for many people
it is the acme of sophistication and a kind of badge of modernity

to deny any knowledge of Irish. Predatory capitalism, a sort of cultural law of the jungle, reigns supreme, and in such a schema Irish is superfluous, to stay the least, if not downright retrograde. Love Irish as I may, I live in a maelstrom of other people's ambivalence and indifference to it, and it is a constant struggle to put it on the cultural menu.

An instance from a few yeas ago, when a journalist came to interview me, illustrates this struggle. An editor had heard me on some radio programme or other, and thought I might produce good copy. The journalist was female, smart and young, with a particular blond 'gamine' haircut that I have subsequently always hated on sight. The first question she asked me when she came into my house was, 'Are you a fascist?' My jaw dropped. Apart from the utter ludicrousness of such a question – as impossible to answer with any credibility as 'When did you stop beating your wife?' – there was the downright cheek and bad manners of it. This woman felt she had the right to waltz into my house and ask me such a question for the sole and simple reason that I write poetry in Irish. If I had had my wits about me I would have said 'Out out out'. As it was, I back-pedalled furiously and said, 'I am a poet. I think in images. I don't know what '-ist' words mean – 'leftist', 'rightist', 'fascist', 'tourist', they are all the same to me.' Thus I bought myself some time, but my answer hardly elucidated the proceedings. The question I ask myself now is how a woman of my generation, about my own age, who like me grew up in Ireland, about the same time – how on earth we could be so totally different? How is it that all of us living as we do in Ireland can be living in worlds that are so totally different? And all of this makes me return to Jacsaí Shea and his innocent question: Cé leis tú?

My mother's people, Muinntir Fhiannachta, came originally from Beaufort, in South Kerry. They were brought west by Lord Ventry to look after his horses on a farm appropriately called 'the Paddock', which he carved out of the townland of Ballameetrant in the Dingle Gaeltacht. Signs on they were horse-mad and still are. But not all of them remained in Ballameetrant or in the Gaeltacht; 'Muinntir Fhiannachta' was subsequently Anglicised at

Ellis Island as 'Fenton'. The first of my forebears we know to have emigrated was my great-grandfather, Eoghainín Fenton. A heavily built man, or *balcaire*, almost as wide as he was tall, his *leas-ainm*, or pet-name, was 'The Giant Goliath'. Like most of the people of the Dingle Gaeltacht he went to the area around Springfield, Massachusetts. In 1872, at the inauguration of the newly built St Patrick's Church in nearby Chicopee Falls, 'The Giant Goliath' was given a golden fob watch for winning a dancing competition. The family legend had it that he did the long dance called 'The Blackbird' 'on a polished table'. We have a photo of him taken during his time in America: a handsome man, with clean, open features and jet-black straight hair.

When his elder half-brother died, Eoghainín was brought home to be given the land. He was glad to be home, and hadn't really liked America, dance prizes or no. He liked the good life, as the phrase about him prevalent in the family goes: 'D'íosfadh sé an Mhuclach; d'ólfadh sé an t-Iarthar; chaithfeadh sé an Stát' ('He would eat the Muclach [a large rock out in Tralee Bay]; he would drink all the West; and he would spend all the money in the State'). Once home, he promptly sold the gold watch and bought a racehorse, reverting to his horse-mad roots. How he expected to be able to feed the poor animal on ninety-six acres of bog and hill nobody knows, and I have never found out what became of it in the end.

He was a generous man, with the locally admired virtue of *mórchroí*: a spirit of humanity uninhibited by calculations of self-interest. A few years ago when I was collecting folklore in the area, I was told to visit an old man in Baile Bhoithín, Eoghan 'ac Loingsigh. When I called to the house he wouldn't let me in at all, but told me to come back another day. When I called again the contrast couldn't have been greater. I was very welcome, and he couldn't do enough for me. In the meantime he had made some enquiries about who I was and that was why he was now particularly good to me. It seems that when his father was a young man he used to have to go once a year and do a spell of work for the landlord, the Reverend Goodman, over near our farm, and Eoghainín – whom he took to be my grandfather – had been particularly good to him. As the old man now said with great seriousness: 'Is mór an ní fear muinteartha in áit dheoranta' ('It's a great thing to meet a friendly man in a foreign place') – the foreign place in question being just two miles down the road.

Eoghainín liked nothing better than a good story and in this he was joined by his wife, Léan Ní Chearna, who did not have a single word of English. Léan could not read or write in any language, and was ignorant in the way that the poet Michael Hartnett has spoken of his own grandmother:

> ignorant, in the sense
> she ate monotonous food
> and thought the world was flat.

Yet she too was an active tradition-bearer with a wide oral repertoire. A story I recently came across in the Department of Folklore in University College Dublin will give an idea of her sometimes recondite knowledge. The story is told in Irish by a neighbour, Séan 'Touhy' Ó Ciabháin, and it is in his own words. In it he is explaining to the folklore collector one of the strangest things that had happened to him during his life. I have made a rough translation of the original Irish.

The Three Souls of the Human Being

I was inside in the bed down south in Ballymore when whatever it was took Eoghainín Fenton out, he saw me go out of the house. He called over to his wife, Léan Ní Chearna. 'My soul from the devil, Léan,' said he, 'but there must be a fairy stroke or something on Séan Touhy. Look at him going down the side of the house. Go out,' he said, 'and call him in.' Then he saw me turning up the way again and going into the house. Léan did not call out to me at all. The next day they were telling me this and I wouldn't have believed Eoghainín at all if Léan hadn't [been] saying the very same thing too. I swore that I had not left the bed from the moment I got into it until I rose up out again in the morning, but instead that I had slept soundly all night. 'Such things are known to happen,' said Léan, 'and I thought of that last night. If I had called out to him that time,' said Léan, 'he would have stayed out there forever. I have always heard tell that the human being has three parts: the breathing soul, the feeling soul and the immortal soul. The immortal soul is the one that remains with you until you die.' 'I wonder,' says Séan

Touhy reflectively, 'was it my breathing soul or my feeling soul that was outside that night when I was lying fast asleep. That is the one thing that I still do not know.'

What seems most remarkable to me about this story is how a supposedly uneducated West Kerry countrywoman who had no English was privy to the knowledge of the ancients, which at some stage or other had been shot-through with a dose of the intellectual Gnostic tradition, in which these concepts were maintained long after they had disappeared from the dominant European discourse.

Léan and Eoghainín had thirteen children. Nine survived into adulthood, and most of them emigrated to America. Four of the girls left home on the same day; two of them made their dowries working as servant girls in big houses, then came home and married locally, Auntie Mary in the next townland, Ballymore West, and Joan in the next parish, Márthan. The other two married in America, and lived to be on average twenty years older than their sisters who had returned to Ireland. A few years ago I went to see them. Aunt Nellie, now a widow, still spoke Irish and named out fields in the old farmstead: Gort na Spoinnce, Cuaisín na gCaorach. She kept in touch by frequent letters and telephone calls and knew more about what was going on in the parish of Ventry than most of the people living there. Auntie Bridie was more remote and did not speak Irish. Needless to say, none of their children had a word of Irish, as, unlike with the dancing or musical traditions, emigration has brought nothing but destruction to the memory of the old language.

My grandfather, Séan, had also emigrated and spent some years in the States before being called back to the land on the death of his elder brother. In this he was preferred over his half-twin Maidhc, who was five minutes older than himself and who had also emigrated, as the latter was a bit of a drunkard and a rake. Maidhc later became a recluse, cutting all ties with the family, except for an occasional note in response to the yearly letters of my Aunt May, his godchild. He was one of the casualties of emigration, neither fish nor fowl, lost between two worlds, like the bodies of drowned fisherman '*ar snámh idir dhá uisce'* ('floating between two waters'), nearly drowned and nearly saved. Though the American dream is trumpeted in emigrants' letters home, who knows how many men and women like Maidhc were lost in every generation?

As George Thomson remarks about the exiled Irish-speakers in general:

> to these exiled America offered an escape from the poverty of their home life, but only on condition that they surrendered their cultural values. Some of them paid the price without regret, others only with a lifelong sense of loss. For a few the price was too heavy, and they came home.

If they could come home. My grandfather was lucky – he was given the land and he was glad to be back. Just as it hadn't really suited his father, America hadn't really suited him either; and so there was a push-pull mechanism at work now for two generations. He was intelligent and had some knowledge of English – though nothing more than compulsory primary education – but his health gave out young under the hard regimen of subsistence farming, and he died in his forties.

My mother's generation, born into the new order, was the first to go beyond primary school. Under the aegis of the new state, she gained one of the first ever Gaeltacht Scholarships to Secondary School. Eoghainín, her grandfather, could hardly contain his pride. 'Our Eileen is gone to Dingle to buy a parasol,' he announced to a disbelieving village when she went to buy the regulation uniform, which included an umbrella. Her grandmother, Léan, was equally insistent on the importance of further education: 'Lean leis an léann, is ní bheidh cac ar do bhróga' ('Persevere with the learning, and you won't have cowshit on your shoes') was her shrewd assessment of the new development. My mother went to Coláiste Íde, the new preparatory school that had been set up in Burnham, Lord Ventry's former residence. The schooling was in Irish, but still the ethos was very different to that of her life until then, aping a way of life that was at best neo-colonial. Education really meant learning English and preparing for a way of life that would cut her off from her own past and people. Ngugi wa Thiong'o warns about the dangers of such alienation, no less colonial for the fact that it was taking place in Ireland rather than in Africa and under the auspices of a native elected government rather than the preceding British rule:

> Colonial alienation takes two interlinked forms: an active (or passive) distancing of oneself from the reality around; and an active (or passive) identification with that which is most external to one's environment. It starts with a deliberate disassociation of the language of conceptualization, of thinking, of formal education, of mental development, from the language of daily interaction in the home and in the community. It is like separating the mind from the body so that they are occupying two unrelated linguistic spheres in the same person. On a larger social scale it is like producing a society of bodiless heads and headless bodies.

This sense of physical dislocation, almost akin to mutilation, is something played out in the work of many modern Irish poets, including Seamus Heaney, John Montague and Paul Muldoon.

And this alienation, a psychic fault-line, a personality cleavage along two different language-lines, will return to plague us later. It is something that is denied and glossed over much too easily. There seems to be an idea abroad that all languages aspire to the condition of English and that only backwardness and lack of development stop them from becoming it. I doubt this greatly. I also doubt that the acquisition of English, by emigrants abroad or our own people at home, was ever as easy as it has been made to seem in retrospect. The question of language-change exercises my imagination considerably. But how to dramatise this issue? I found myself toying with a rather dangerous opposition of the amniotic fluid of the local Irish-speaking community as being akin to the sea, while the lonely, because perforcedly individualised, reaches of the professional middle classes might be akin to dry land. So I began to imagine a tribe of merpeople who have, for reasons which become evident as the poems progress, come up on dry land. This framing metaphor is dangerous, I admit, because the sea/land, Irish/English contrast could be accused of being reductive and essentialist. The poems themselves, however, seemed to me to overcome such idiocy, and attempt to capture a past, a loss, a bemingled present, intrusive, oppressive and depriving, yet not without beneficence either.

Because the more I thought about it, the more it seemed that to be educated out of one's mother tongue, to have to change language, must be as deep a shock to one's sense of identity as a radical change in body image. Just about this time I happened to be reading a story in Oliver Sack's book *The Man Who Mistook His Wife for a Hat* about someone who had a severe brain lesion that left him unable to recognise parts of his body as his own. He woke up in hospital with what he took to be a strange leg in the bed with him. Thinking it was a practical joke on the part of the hospital staff, he threw it out of the bed, only to discover, to his amazement, that he fell out of the bed after it, that somehow it was attached to him. 'There, now I have it,' I thought, 'that's my mermaid.'

An Mhurúch san Ospidéal (in *Cead Aighnis*)

Dhúisigh sí
agus ní ribh a heireaball éisc ann
níos mó
ach ispigh sa leaba léi
bhi an dá rud fada fuar seo.
Ba dhóigh leat gur gaid mhara iad
nó slaimicí feola.

'Mar mhagadh atá siad
ní foláir , Oiche na Coda Móire.
Tá leath na foirne as a meabhair
le deoch
is an leath eile acu
róthugtha do jokeanna.
Mar sin féin is leor
an méid seo'
is do chaith sí an dá rud
amach as an seomra.

Ach seo í an chuid
ná tuigeann sí: –
conas a thit sí fein ina ndiadh
'cocs-um-bo-chead'.

Cén bhaint a bhí
ag an dá rud léi
nó cén bhaint a bhí aici
leosan?

An bhanaltra a thug an nod di
is a chuir í i dtreo an eolais –
'Cos í seo atá ceangailte díot
agus ceann eile acu anseo thíos fút.
Cos, cos eile
a haon, a dó.
Caithfídh tú foghlaim
conas siúl leo'.

Ins na míosa fada
a lean
n'fheadar ar thit a croí
de réir mar a thit trácht na coise uirthi,
a háirsí?

The Mermaid in the Labour Ward (in *Southern Review* 31, 1995)

Something stirred in her;
not the swishing meteor of her fin,
but in the pit of the bed
a body-long split of ice,
languid as dulse tentacles,
flaccid as fishbait.

'Lord bless us isn't this a hoot –
some kind of Night of the Long Knives –
half the staff as pissed as a newt,
and the rest of them you couldn't trust
as far as you could throw them.
I've had it up to here.'
As she upped and yanked the sea-legs
out the door.

The crunch came
when she found herself head over heels in their wake
were these creatures joined to her,
or was she hinged to them?

It took the nurse
to give her the low-down
and put her in the picture:
'What you have there, dear,
is called a leg,
and another one to boot.
First leg,
second leg,
left, right,
one goes in front of the other.'
It's little wonder
in the long months that followed
as her instep flattened
and her arches dropped
if her mind went with them.

Trans. Medbh McGuckian

Coláiste Íde was a sort of forcing ground for National teachers, and a more radical, or comprehensive, concept of education was not within its remit. Too much ambition was not encouraged, especially in girls. My mother speaks with indignation of the time she was filling in the form for the Gaeltacht Scholarship to university. 'Whatever you do, don't fill in "Medicine"', advised the appropriately named Sister Borgia. 'Why not?' asked my mother. 'Because the son of "an Seabhac" [a local writer] is doing it and finding it very difficult.' '*Ní mise Mac an tSeabhaic*' ('I am not the Seabhac's son'), shot back my mother – and out of sheer spite put down MEDICINE as her proposed area of study. Is it any wonder, then, that 'medicine' and all it implied became for her a lifeline out of what she considered to be the poverty and backwardness associated with Irish and its world-view? She espoused what might be called an analytico-referential attitude with a vengeance: the

language and empiricism pioneered by Bacon became her inner
lodestar, the highest good under the firmament.

I have tried to dramatise this situation in another mermaid
poem, equating the rejection and denial of Irish with as radical an
action as for the mermaid on dry land to deny the existence of water.

An Mhurúch agus Focail Áirithe (in *Cead Aighnis*)

Ná luaigh an focal 'uisce' léi
nó aon ní a bhaineann le cúrsaí farraige: –
'tonn', 'taoide', 'bóchna', 'muir', nó 'sáile'.
Ní lú léi an sioc samhraidh ná trácht a chlos
ar iascach, báid, saighní trá nó traimile, potaí gliomach.
Tá's aici go maith go bhfuil a leithéidí ann
is go mbíonn gíotáil éigin a bhaineas leo
ar siúl ag daoine eile.

Ceapann sí má dhúnann sí a cluasa is má chasann a ceann
go mbeidh sí saor orthu
is ná cloisfidh sí búir dhúr an eich uisce
ag fógairt gaoil shíoraí léi go doimhin san oíche,
ag cur gráinníní ar a craiceann is brat allais
amach trí lár a codladh uirthi.

Níl aon namhaid eile aici
ach an saol fo-thoinn a chleacht sí
sarar iontaigh sí ar a hathshaol ar an míntír
a chur i gcuimhne dhi. Séanann sí ó bhonn
go raibh oiread is cac snioga de bhaint aici leis
aon am – 'Ní raibh aon tsuim riamh agam
sna piseoga sin, nó in aon sórt seanaimsireachta.
Aer, eolas, solas gléineach na heolaíochta
is ea a shantaíos-sa'.

Ba chuma liom ach go bhfuireas-sa amach
san éitheach í.
Istigh sa Roinn le Béaloideas Éireann,
tá lámhscríbhinn iomlán de Bhailiúchán na scol

breactha óna láimh,
scríte in uisce, le clipe de sciathán rotha,
ar scothóg feamainne mar phár.

Tá trí cinn déag de scéalta fada
agus smutaíocha de chinn eile, i dteannta le
horthaí, seanphaidreacha, tomhaiseanna agus aroile
le tabhairt faoi ndeara ann. Ón a hathair is ón a máthair
chrionna is mó
a thóg sí síos iad.

Diúltaíonn sí glan dó: – 'An máistir
a thug mar obair bhaile dhúinn é fadó
thiar sa bhunscoil. Chaitheamair é a dhéanamh.
Ní raibh aon dul as againn'.
Cháithfeadh sí fuil shróine
sara mbéadh sí riamh admhálach ina thionscnamh.

The Mer-lady's Lexicon (in *Southern Review* 31, 1995)

To her you must not mention the word 'water'
nor any other omen of the ocean;
'wave', 'tide', 'deep blue', 'sea' nor 'salty main'.
Well she knows how landfolk 'fish' in 'boats',
drop their 'pots to trap the lobster'
and drag 'nets that trawl and strand.'
Yet she'd prefer to thole a summer frost
than speak of such.

To 'hear or see
no evil'
is her guard against the coast, while a deaf ear
tries to
drown the kelpie's constant drone
sighing for a lifelong love from the night's dark depths,
a slumber-piercing wail that saturates in sheets of
sweat
that goose-pimpled scaly veil called flesh.

Thoughts of life below the wave —
her only haunt —
but a span long spurned
for life upon the shore.
Denying all knowledge of her ocean-home,
'In the guiding air-filled light of science'
she now puts all store, scorning
'superstition and taboo.'

But in the Schools Collection
of the Folklore vaults in UCD
I have found the evidence to indict her —
a weighty seaweed parchment
penned, through the quilled nib of a ray's fin,
in ink of brine.

Thirteen sagas, ranging and roaming,
with other sea-tale clippings rounded off,
incantations, mermaid rites and riddles —
recited by her father and grand-mère.
A text she now dismisses as a distant,
childhood homework, wrenched in the west
by a cane-wielding master
in the National School.
She would rather now her blood were spilt
than admit to having hand nor part in it.

Trans. Art Hughes

With her education finished, newly qualified as a doctor, my mother was not particularly surprised to find that there were no jobs available. After all, her educational experience was predicated on being uprooted. She went to England, where after a few short stints as a doctor working for ICI (Imperial Chemical Industries) and in a mental hospital in Berkinhead, she landed a job as a junior partner in a private practice in St Helens, South Lancashire. Within a few years she was senior partner in a practice of some seven thousand souls, going to all and sundry, in good Gaeltacht fashion, by her maiden name, Dr Eileen Fenton, even long after she had married my father.

My father's background was slightly different in that his family had made the jump from West Kerry subsistence farming a generation or two earlier. His grandfather, Séan 'Caol' Ó Domhnaill, being the second son, like many young men in his position, joined the Royal Irish Constabulary. But not finding it to his liking – the family mythology has it he couldn't bear taking orders – he left after nine months, managed to do teacher-training in Marlborough Street College and returned to West Kerry as principal of the local school, first in Fearanacille, and later at Ballyduff. A noted disciplinarian, he terrified the local children into good English and the rudiments of science and mathematics. He taught them parsing and mental arithmetic, algebra and the roots of verbs. Although he taught Irish in school on a voluntary basis (even though, or probably because, the school manager, the local priest, was against it), he made sure that his charges were well versed in English, as he knew they had been bred merely for export. Almost a hundred years after his heyday, my mother heard one of her own relations in the States say about someone who was acting a bit thick, 'It's easily known he didn't spend a week with Caol.' When she asked about the phrase, they said they didn't know anything about who Caol might be, or who his people were, that it was just a phrase used locally about someone who didn't have his wits about him. My mother knew all about Caol and his people. After all, hadn't she married into them?

If he was tyrannical to the children in his care, Caol, it seems, was equally so to his wife and son. In the morning he was said to be particularly monosyllabic: 'shirt, studs, shaving-brush', 'breakfast at eight' and 'polish me boots' being the only words he ever addressed to his wife before he went out to school in the morning. Graindeá rebelled against his father's martinet ways, and, taking his mother's side, espoused the rights of Irish with total commitment. When his father and the local parish priest conspired to send him to study for the priesthood at the Irish College in Paris, he went along for the lark, thinking it was a good way to get a good education. When he left *ad saecularia sua sponte*, he could not go home again as 'a spoilt priest', but registered at University College Cork, where he took an MA in Celtic Studies under de Hindeberg. He got caught up in the revolutionary fervour of the times, joined the Irish Republican Brotherhood, was seen training Volunteers in the streets of Cork city, taught in a well-known secondary school and organised a strike in the city for the teachers in the Cork Workers Union against the pedagogic malpractices of the religious teaching orders. When the strike was over, all staff members were taken back again except himself, and he was blackballed throughout Munster as a miscreant and trouble-maker. After eking out an existence for a few years as a travelling Irish Language Organiser, he eventually became a primary school inspector in 1928, when the first open competition for such a position was held under the auspices of the new state. In his autobiography, *Vive Moi*, Seán Ó Faoláin calls Graindeá the one real revolutionary among his teachers, crediting him for having had such a large influence as to turn the hitherto John Whelan into Seán Ó Faoláin.

Graindeá was so utterly disgusted with the events of the Civil War, especially brutal in Kerry, that he never breathed a word of his youthful exploits to any of his four sons. Henceforward cultural nationalism was the sole aim of his revolutionary zeal. He wrote handbooks for Irish learners and an algebra textbook in Irish. It has always been understood, in our family at least, that it was he who translated the parts of the bicycle into Irish, making of the handlebars *na cluasa*, or ears, in a term redolent of small boys and donkeys. He was one of those responsible for the establishment of Irish at the core of the primary school curriculum, and so if one million Irish people say in the last census report that they have some knowledge of Irish, then a lot of the responsibility for this state of affairs can be laid at the door of a handful of language enthusiasts like himself. A man of sterling qualities and idealism, and yet ...

My father adored him and still thinks that the sun and the moon shone out of a particular part of his nether anatomy, yet an older brother is not so sure, calling him 'a cantankerous old so-and-so'. As is often the case in such family disputes, they are probably both right. In many ways he was grave and innovative and ahead of his time. Already in 1916 he had written an article for *An Claidheamh Solais* on the value of the new-fangled medium of film for resuscitating ancient Irish myth and legend. In 1919 he produced a booklet entitled *Comhacht Uisce in Éirinn*, which was a harbinger of the hydroelectric schemes of the twenties and one of the few success stories of the early state. He translated the plays of Daniel Corkery into Irish, and even acted in some of them. He wrote at least one pleasant ditty, and many deeply melancholy original poems. He did a series of translations from Old into Modern Irish, and had a passionate love for the old language and a deep and abiding conviction that writers of today should steep themselves in both its poetry and prose. The older I get and the more immersed I become in the art and discipline of writing poetry in Irish, the more I come to acknowledge his intellectual flair and intelligence. And yet ...

He was also a member of the Cork Irish-language 'mafia', a bunch of misogynist elitists who looked down their noses at the rest of the country as some form of Yahoos. He never spoke anything but Irish to his children, though his wife did not have a single word of the language. One of his Irish-language cronies used to come to high tea without fail every Sunday evening at five o'clock, and though he accepted tea and sponge cake from the lady of the house every week, he never once deigned to address as much as a single word to her, as this would have meant breaking into the abhorred and dreaded *Sacsbhéarla* or Saxon tongue. The very same crony is said to have corrected the Irish grammar of his own wife on her deathbed. She asked for the bedpan, calling it *an áras*. 'An t-áras, a bhean, an t-áras,' he snapped back at her. They were the last words ever said to have passed between them.

My mother, a healthily self-regarding, independent-minded Gaeltacht girl, was horrified by such 'carry-on'. The natural good manners and courtesy of Gaeltacht people often won out over any considerations of linguistic integrity, so much so that when someone without Irish came among them, a whole company might lapse into broken English rather than have the stranger feel left out. I have inherited her disgust with such churlishness and for the rather dubious pleasure that some people evince in striding around speaking in loud voices the kind of revivalist Irish that has been practised over the backs of silenced women and children. I hate it with a terrible hate. One of the things that makes me get up on dark wintry mornings and sit at my desk and work at my poetry is the desire to take Irish back from these linguistic 'gauleiters', those grey-haired, grey-suited, grey-minded greybeards who have attempted to make the language into their personal fiefdom. Only the Freudian notion that you are in danger of becoming what you hate gives me cause to pause or let up in this matter.

It is often hard for people of my generation to realise that a hundred years ago, when Conradh na Gaeilge was founded, learning Irish was an empowering act for ordinary Irish people. Hundreds of thousands enrolled in evening classes and studied the language through Father O'Growney's primers and textbooks. Writers like Seán Ó Faoláin wax lyrical about what it was like to go off to the Gaeltacht in the summer to Irish courses, and some of his most poignant short stories are enacted in this setting. Nevertheless, by the time my generation came round, something had gone wrong.

For many of the main social commentators of our time the existence of Irish is not an issue at all. It is a total non-runner, accepted as moribund at best, and the sooner dead and buried the better. This is the attitude of Dubliner Fintan O'Toole, a popular newspaper columnist and essayist. Another influential commentator, Vincent Browne (originally from Munster, where a certain high enough water-table of Irish is commonplace), is so ignorant of the language that he thinks the word for sex in Irish is '*uinscinn*', which actually means 'gender', but then only in the grammatical sense of a noun having a masculine or feminine gender. No less an authority than the poet Thomas Kinsella, in his book-long cultural essay *The Dual Tradition: An Essay on Poetry and Politics in Ireland*, can write: 'Irish literature exists as a dual tradition. It *was* composed in two languages' (my emphasis), thus by a subtle sleight of hand consigning to outer darkness the large corpus of literary work being composed at present in the language and which is of as high a standard any day as its equivalent in English.

This happens because the only form of the language he and

many others have been exposed to is the sanitised, bowdlerised, air-brushed version taught in schools, with its emphasis on an idealised rural myth of peasant life in the West, a myth seen through by most of the children subjected to it as the ridiculous hogwash that it is. Loath as I am to accept it, this form of Irish, as represented in such works of fiction as Roddy Doyle's Booker Prize-winning *Paddy Clarke Ha Ha Ha*, is punitive and soul-destroying, consisting only of peremptory orders given by sad and sometimes sadistic teachers, one more stick with which to beat small children. Novelist Pat McCabe represents this violence in *The Dead School*, in which the two generations that have come to maturity since the establishment of a separate state are pitted against each other. No accommodation is made by either side, no mercy given or expected. If the first generation was Catholic and Irish-speaking, idealistically austere, clean-living and authoritarian in the extreme, then the next (my) generation, whatever else about it, has a positive and understandable dislike for this archaic language called Irish which has been rammed down its throat. The emotional realities depicted in this and other novels are salutary and compelling: it is obvious that in Ireland the language revival movement has lost steam, or gone sadly awry. I know that teenagers in every country in the world nowadays are caught up in a global, pop MTV culture which is not interested in minority languages. The dominant language of this global culture is English, and yet in spite of all of this young people in Finland speak Finnish, in Israel speak Hebrew and even as near to us as just across the sea an awful lot of young people in Wales speak Welsh. Something has gone wrong in Ireland, but what, and why?

I blame a lot of it on De Valera and his cohorts of the 1950s Irish state, geriatric and sclerotic, with its severe poverty and its solemn national ceremonies. My husband reminds me that the fifties were awful everywhere, and definitely no less so in Turkey in his time than in Ireland in mine. But I feel that the general and unprecedented despair that hung over the land in those times was like a miasma, or a modern-day Curse of Macha. The country was ruled by a gerontocracy, with De Valera, blind and unbending, at the fore. To compare the presidency of Ireland during his time with what it has become in ours under Mary Robinson and Mary McAleese is to see how far the country has come. But the damage has already been done, and the language is still for many inescapably linked with a shibbollethic, ritualistic, mind-numbing outreach of extreme authoritarian paternalism which dates from that time.

But beyond the governmental, there were other mistakes, not least of which was the cultural festishisation of the *cainnteoir dúchas* or 'native speaker'. This amazing and historically documented development forgot completely that language is basically a form of communication, and that there can be no meaningful language without people to speak it to. So fetishised was the native speaker that nobody, it was felt, but such a mythical or legendary beast could speak the language properly, let alone write it. Such an attitude was lambasted satirically by Myles na gCopaleen in *An Béal Bocht*. In one memorable scene a litter of bonamhs dressed up in jackets are successfully passed off to a Governmental Inspector as a large family of children, their indecipherable grunting being proof positive of the excellence of their dialect of Irish. Again and again in this marvellous book the outlandish behaviour of some language enthusiasts is mocked and brought to nought. And not without good reason, because many of their attitudes fostered an amazing elitism amongst the few legendary beasts called 'native speakers' that did exist, while reducing the rest of the country to the great unwashed and uncouth 'lumpen' to whom the very best that could fall would be crumbs from the master's table. If they could not actually be trusted to speak the language, then let them get on with the other, albeit minor, trappings of 'Irishness' like dancing or playing music or, most popular of all, the playing of Irish games. Perhaps as overcompensation for a sense of lack of authenticity, bodies like An Comisiún le Rinncí Gaelacha, Comhaltas Ceoltóirí Éireann and the Gaelic Athletic Association enacted practices of the most extreme nationalistic sort, like the GAA ban on any of their players participating in or even attending 'foreign' games. Such fringe lunacies were common; in *Over the Bar*, an autobiography that masquerades as a partial history of the GAA, the star reporter Breandán Ó hÉithir describes 'the animosity towards Irish shown by some of the most vehement supporters of the Ban when they lost their tempers and the thin skin of pretence came off – like so many tomatoes dipped in boiling water'. Somehow, somewhere, amidst all the kerfuffle, sight was lost of the ball. The Irish-promoting bodies became like sub-chapters of a giant 'Neurotics Anonymous', attracting people who had severe personality problems rather than a genuine love of the language. No wonder Irish became a cultural non-starter and lost out amongst the next generation, through no fault of its own.

Irish was important, however, to my parents. They married in St Helens, Lancashire, where my mother's practice continued to flourish; my father was the registrar in the nearby Providence Hospital. The wedding was all in Irish, with an tAthair Tadhg Ó Murchú, the Irish-speaking priest who had first introduced them, brought over specially to officiate at the ceremony. They set up house in a newly built red-brick residence at 406 Leach Lane. At my father's wish, it was called, rather incongruously, 'Banba', one of the three mythical names for Ireland, which would lead one to the supposition that if the Englishman's home is his castle, then for the exiled Irishman his home takes the place of his homeland. The house had been built to my mother's specifications, and never again was she to have a house she liked; even now, fifty years later, it still stands out as her ideal home. That time as a doctor in England, after she had recovered from the tuberculosis for which she was hospitalised after my birth, she still counts as the happiest time in her whole life.

Irish was spoken in the house, and we even had a relation of my mother's by marriage, Noirín Keevane, staying with us as an Irish-speaking nanny. A few years ago, on a visit to see her in Springfield, Massachusetts, I discovered to my great amazement that she was only twelve years older than myself. 'So, how did you do the housework in England, and you so young?' I asked in surprise. 'Nuala,' she declared, 'I never had to lift a finger in that house. All I ever had to do was to speak Irish to you kids.' So much speaking went on, in fact, that my sister Neasa finally left England at the age of four without a single world of English except for 'Mammy's car', the term '*gluaisteán*' in Irish being too much of a mouthful for one so young. Ironically, she is the only one of all of us who later changed her name by deed poll from the Irish version on her birth certificate to the English version 'Nessa O'Donnell', because of the hassle she received as a medical student in the wards of teaching hospitals in Dublin for having her name in Irish. I, on the other hand, who left England with much less Irish and much more English, am the self-avowed language fanatic.

Though my mother was absolutely in her element in England, my father was much less happy. He was disturbed by the sheer racism he encountered because of being Irish. Not, I must add, from the ordinary people of Lancashire, but from his colleagues, who should have known better. There was resistance to the fact that he had his name in Irish, Séamus Ó Domhnaill, and constant stupid jokes about his name (Séamus = Shame us, ha-ha-ha). After eight years he had had enough. He was going to give it two more years, ten being a good round number, and then he was either going to change his name to its English equivalent, James O'Donnell, or somehow, by hook or by crook, go back to Ireland. When a position as County Surgeon came up in Nenagh, County Tipperary, he jumped at it. The whole idea was initially greeted by others with some incredulity. Nenagh, where on earth was it, for starters? My mother, who had done her geography through Irish, could not be persuaded that it was even in Munster. It seemed to her like the back of beyond: somewhere in the dreaded Midlands. The Doldrums of Ireland. The Horse Latitudes. A Valley of the Squinting Windows sort of place. And she was right.

The house was north-facing and dark, most of the rooms painted bottle green. It did boast what had once been a meticulously kept garden; but abandoned over the summer while the house lay empty, it was now stupendously and promiscuously overgrown. At age six you could get as easily lost in the herbaceous border as in any upstairs room, where monumental furniture had the uncanny habit of falling over on passing children. Stalking through the elephant grass, we fell upon Damask roses with no less avidity than hunters in India on tigers. Years later in seed catalogues I was gradually to learn the names of some of the flowers – lupins, columbines, delphiniums, cosmos, aquilegia – but at that time we stared at them like beings from another planet. They were deliciously dangerous and exotic. And poisonous, of course: one of them wasn't called 'anemone' – an enemy – for nothing. If you ate one you would surely die. The only 'good' flowers were the peony roses, which were in great demand for petal-strewing on Corpus Christi. And there were also trees. Never in my short personal history – in our Lancashire mining town or the wind-swept seaboard of West Kerry – had I seen the likes of the trees of the rich farmlands of North Tipperary. Huge, climbable trees, trees you would never ever want to come down from.

But it was not all trees and peonies. Most of the time I had to go to school, to nuns: Sister Agnes, in first class, who sewed ignominious lengths of brown paper on the dress of any unfortunate seven-year-old whose skirts were high enough to expose the kneecaps; Miss Maguire, in second class, a lay teacher at least, but constantly chewing lozenges and giving out slobbery wet kisses; Sister Paul who boxed ears; Sister Pius who got us reading by the then innovatory pedagogical brainwave of starting a class library; Sister Peter, in sixth class, who had a flat, well-seasoned stick that stung the skin like bees.

And so started the second chapter of my rather complex relationship with the southern state of the Republic of Ireland. We lived in Nenagh for fifteen years, but I for one never settled there. I was made constantly aware of the fact that we were 'blow-ins'. Earlier, in Kerry, I had already been aware that I was somehow 'different'. I remember trying to explain to the village children once what television was. This was a time in Cahiratrant of dirt roads and no piped water or electricity, when women and girls went to the toilet in the cowhouse, and men and boys went somewhere up the fields. We kids were busy all afternoon racing snails on the pavement up from the *geata beag* or 'small gate'. Did I race snails over in England, they asked? Well no … Why not?

Well, I dunno, maybe there were no snails, or maybe no one to race them with. So what did we play over in England? Well, we looked at television. And what was that? Well, it was a sort of box in the corner and you could see all sorts of things in it, Snow White and the Seven Dwarfs, and Robin Hood Robin Hood Riding-through-the-Glen, and there was the Cisco Kid and Pancho, and the Lone Ranger, who always beat the baddies and then rode away on a white horse, and then, of course, there was Mr Ed, a horse who talked ... That did it: with a talking horse I had overstepped the limits, and severely strained their capacity for suspension of disbelief. They ignored me and went back to the serious business of racing snails, their total silence speaking volumes of their disgust at the arrant liar in their midst.

But it was in Nenagh that my relationship with my surroundings slid from this level of some discomfort down into the nether reaches of horror and melodrama. There was a palpable sense of a barely contained religious hysteria and violence, which now seems to me to have been largely ruled by sexual repression. In school the pedagogical input was minimal, the discipline extreme. But in retrospect, I can see that much of the unspeakable misery that I associate with that time and place was that, as the eldest girl, I picked up in no uncertain manner on my mother's deep unhappiness. There was then in place a condition of service, if not an actual law, known as the marriage ban, by which once a woman got married she was forced to give up any salaried position she might have: whether as a bank clerk, a civil servant, a doctor or a teacher. I have searched the 1937 Irish Constitution high up and low down for the exact wording that led to this cultural occurrence, but have been unable to find it, as such. As she had identified so totally with her role as a doctor and dearly loved her profession, the ban was a terrible blow to my mother. At one stage she volunteered to help the diocesan pilgrimage to Lourdes in her medical capacity. When she went down to the Garda station to get a passport, a policeman told her that she would have to get her husband's permission to leave the country. To an independent-minded woman in her late thirties who had previously run a large medical practice almost on her own, this was the last straw. Though no one described it in so many terms at the time, in losing her profession she lost her sense of identity, and slowly but surely sank into a dreadful depression which lasted about fifteen years.

If my mother's sudden loss of her life's work hung over me, the fact that we spoke Irish didn't exactly help either. When any school pals I might have had came around to our house my father met them at the door, spouting Irish at them. They ran off and that was often the last I saw of them. Know your friends, indeed. Then my granny came to live with us. She was of the spare-the-rod-and-spoil-the-child persuasion and I soon found out that in any dispute that might arise between us, I invariably came off second best, as, no matter what evidence to the contrary, my mother always took her side. She also hated my father, and so we children immediately rallied to his defence, causing more ructions. I soon learned to keep my big mouth shut and my nose stuck in a book instead.

On Sundays we went to eleven o'clock mass. To avoid the inevitable traffic jam afterwards, we often took a back road home, around by the ruins of the old Franciscan Priory. There, at a place called Sherlock's Field, was a large sign proclaiming to my barely lettered eye: 'Trespassers will be Persecuted'. Now I knew all about persecution – wasn't that the Christians being thrown to the lions? And you mean to tell me that just by stepping on that land, putting your big toe in, maybe, that you would be thrown to the lions? It did seem awfully strict. But then such was the emotional minefield that we tiptoed through at the time that nothing seemed impossible. And after all, wasn't this the selfsame field that a man was working in on a Sunday with his *seisreach* – his plough team – and plough when the first bell went for mass in the Priory behind him? Then the second bell went and the third and still he paid no heed. Then what do you know but didn't the ground open up and swallow him, horses and plough and all. 'Obair Dhomhnaigh, Ní maith í' ('Sunday work is not a good thing'), as my granny would pronounce from the corner, nodding more violently than ever to make up for the understatement of the proverb.

The only place I really felt at home was up in the mountains:

the Silvermines, up Step and Glen Coloo, by the side of Keeper Hill or beyond in Templederry where my father leased the shooting rights on half of a hill named Cooneen, right across from a slightly higher one which rejoiced in the much more unlikely name of Bolingbroke. Here we trained gun dogs, burned heather in strips to encourage the young growth beloved of grouse, built quare fangled traps for scaldcrows. So much time did we spend in those hills that even now I know every inch of them, could walk them barefoot and blindfolded.

An elaborate code of reciprocity soon developed with the upland people. The odd goitre or hernia got patched up in return for cups of tea and bottles of a more potent brew innocently presented as 'holy water', which was the world's own power for flaming the Christmas pudding. Once even the Garda super-intendent himself asked my father if he knew where you could get good poteen thereabouts. Naturally, my father never let on. Still, even in the mountains you were never unobserved. My mother was in the habit of bringing along the Sunday newspaper on those upland jaunts, and used to sit down on a ditch when the endless quartering back and forth after dogs became too much for her. One day a man accosted her. From his rig-out it was obvious that he was a countryman taking a short-cut home over the hill after staying on a mite too long in the pub after mass. He approached her warily, but he was very inquisitive. The more he asked what she considered personal questions, the more she spun him a tissue of lies, to put him off the scent. He bade her farewell most courteously, then turned tail and ran pell-mell down to Maddens', the nearest house. 'Quick quick,' he shouted, 'send for the guards. There's a madwoman escaped from the madhouse in Clonmel, didn't I hear it on the radio this morning, and she's up there on the hill, I just met her.' It was with great difficulty that they managed to persuade him that the woman he saw on the hill wasn't stark raving mad. After all, what grown woman in her sound mind would travel half-way up a hill in order to find a ditch to read her paper on?

While episodes like this one seemed comic even then, there was also a serious undercurrent to them. I have read Heinrich

Böll's *Irische Tagebuch* in amazement, wondering how the same country at around the same time could have seemed so different to two people. Beyond the time in the hills, it was for me a time of unnameable horror, constructed out of a heady mixture of religious mania, physical violence and a deep dislocation of power between the sexes. Women's psychic and spiritual power was, as usual in Ireland, enormous, but it had absolutely no institutional outlet. This enormous repressed feminine energy, lacking any useful arena in which to play out its natural dynamism, turned fetid and inward. My most vivid memory of that period is of waiting at the gate of the erstwhile Nenagh Gaol for the Corpus Christi Procession to begin. We little girls in white dresses were drawn up beside a throng of middle-aged women – many of them grandmothers and often formidable matriarchs – who seemed happy to don the infantilising garb of white veil and blue cloak which marked them in the doubly dependent role of 'Children of Mary'. As the rain clouds rolled over us, threatening to destroy the procession, these women used to intone in an act of sympathetic magic a kind of mantra, an address to St Thérèse of Lisieux, which was a sort of rain-prayer in reverse: 'Little flower, in this hour, show your power.' This went on for hours. What with the smell of incense, the constant singing of hymns and chants, the wavy movement of religious insignia and brancarts through the streets of the small town, the radiant glory of the monstrance held on high, the strewing of rose-petals … is it any wonder that when I looked up at the sky and saw the still-looming clouds turn deepest blue I convinced myself I had seen 'Brat na Maighdine Muire' ('Our Lady Mary's Mantle'), a genuine miracle, and not the fairly common meteorological phenomenon that it really was?

Boarding school wasn't much better, because I was not good boarding material. Already by twelve I was a loner, well on my way to becoming a full-fledged recluse, and the forced proximity of a hundred other girls, not to mention forty nuns, was more than my nerves could stand. I got around the problem as best I could by developing a reasonably personable extroverted personality that has stood me in good stead ever since. I hesitate to say that it is a false personality, because it has grown on me like a kind of second skin. Deep down in me, though, there was a pool of pure vitriol, a seething anger that nothing could touch. I tried to dispel it by keeping a diary, but given the total lack of privacy in the place, this was a chancy business. Girls had been expelled in dire ignominy for less, sometimes just for things they wrote in letters. I countered by keeping the diary in code, and in Irish, counting on the fact that the one nun who could be calculated to snoop in it had no Irish, and the only nun who had enough Irish to be able to read it was a lady to her fingertips, incapable of stooping to something so low. This journal became my lifeline, and with it began the lifelong habit of writing something every day, even if only a snippet of the previous night's dream. In a sense this coded diary was the perfect apprenticeship for a poet: a way of using words to express something deeply personal, yet in a veiled way, the deepest core of meaning often remaining inscrutable. Seeing as I was so often distraught or emotionally overwrought, writing developed naturally as a coping mechanism, and the poems gradually grew out of this writing habit.

Another habit I had acquired by then, through my schooling but also through a process of symbiosis, was the studying of Irish as a literary language. I learned by heart hundreds of songs and poems that had nothing at all to do with the Leaving course. My first literary love affair, and still my deepest source of artistic satisfaction, were the Munster poets of the seventeenth and eighteenth centuries, and the song tradition – what Sorely MacLean, talking about their Scottish Gaelic equivalents, called 'those ineffable melodies that rise like exhalations from the rhythms and resonances of the words, the songs that alone make the thought that the Gaelic language is going to die so intolerable to anyone who knows Gaelic, and has in the least degree the sensibility that responds to the marriage, or rather the simultaneous creation, of words and music'. Thus it seemed a natural enough thing to do, when my first attempts at poems seemed so awkward in English, to try them out in Irish instead, where it was obvious, even to me, that they were infinitely better. And so the die was cast, for better or worse, and at seventeen I was a bit of a poetaster, with the aim of being a poet, in Irish. I often think that this more than anything else is what growing up in Ireland gave me: Irish at the level of a literary language. Definitely the 'doppelgänger' that peeps over my shoulder when I travel through the North of England, the person I would have been if we had stayed on in England, doesn't have it.

University, in the beginning, brought me a much-needed sense of freedom after the rigors of boarding school. And then the catastrophe happened, though it didn't seem like a catastrophe at first: I fell in love. It just so happened that the man I fell in love with was a Turkish geologist. Muslim, not Irish. Deciding that for once I had something worth fighting for, I went for broke, and the whole card-house of middle-class respectability my family had been playing at came tumbling about my ears. In a short, sharp lesson I discovered that my deepest fears were not unfounded, that the intimation of boundless horror that had been my strongest memory of childhood was in fact based on a closely intuited sense of reality, that human relationships are just a rickety rope bridge thrown across the fuming abyss of the human soul. I fell through the meshes of the patriarchal mindset that underlies Western discourse and its civic structures. The whole concentrated power of the State, the Church, the Family was brought to bear on me in a way that would seem to many as absolutely incredible in the last quarter of the twentieth century were it not for the reality of the X-case recently, or the sectarian murders that are still dogging us, if not in Northern Ireland, then in Sarajevo and Srebrenice. To prevent my love affair from continuing, I was made a Ward-of-Court under the Guardianship of Infants Act of 1964; after reading my father's depositions, the then president of the High Court, a certain Aindrias Ó Caoimh (Irishspeaker!), signed away all my civil liberties without a cavil. At the age of nineteen and a half, I was considered an infant in law, and not even allowed to give my side of the story. Not once was the fact that I might have a personal opinion on my fate as much as taken into account.

In the aftermath, I wandered in an inner wilderness of reactive depression that had no signposts or markers. The mellifluousness of the great Munster poets, until then my greatest literary joy, meant nothing to me. All the tenets that had underpinned my previous existence were shown up to be an utter sham, and so I dragged myself around, in free-fall through some private abyss. I was a shadow of my former self, a spectre, a spooky kid, for all the world like the Life-in-Death and Death-in-Life character from 'The Ancient Mariner'. People had never much got through to me much before that, but books had; I tried to concentrate on my studies, but now even this last solace was gone, and anything I read seemed hollow and empty, 'words, words, words'. Then one day in the 'Rest', the student canteen, my friend Greg O'Donaghue handed me a book, saying, 'Take a look at this!' It was John Berryman's *77 Dream Songs*, which Greg had gotten from America on the recommendation of John Montague. I opened it at random and read Song 46: 'I am, outside. Incredible panic rules.' I was hooked: this place of utter darkness where I was had been experienced by somebody else, and this somebody was crying to me, wringing his hands and gnashing his teeth. I read another, Song 67:

> I am obliged to perform in complete darkness
> operations of great delicacy
> on my self.
> — Mr Bones, you terrifies me.
> No wonder they don't pay you. Will you die?
> — My friend,
> I succeeded. Later.

To his immortal credit and my immeasurable thanks Greg let me have a loan of his *Dream Songs*, though not without some misgivings. Soon I had ordered my own copy, and also one of *His Toy, His Dream, His Rest*. It and other books circulated amongst the students; volumes like Suzanne Langer's *Form and Feeling* and Jerzy Grotowski's *Towards a Poor Theatre*, along with Shakespeare's tragedies and Sonnets, became my sacred texts. It was these sacred texts that helped me cobble together an epistemological safety net, including a theory of suffering and art which I wrote out in countless letters to my boyfriend (now husband) and then promptly forgot. But the experience of finding such texts and writing out my response to them did save my life; and what

literally staved off the inner and outer demons was the learning
off by heart of reams of Shakespeare and John Berryman. Their
poetry was entwined in my mind:

> Let us not to the marriage of true minds
> Admit impediment. Love is not love
> Which alters when it alteration finds
> Or bends with the remover to remove.
> Oh no, it is an ever-fixed mark
> That looks on tempest and is never shaken;
> It is the star to every wandering bark
> Whose worth's unknown, although his height be taken …

This was juxtaposed with the likes of:

> Life, friends, is boring. We must not say so.
> After all, the sky flashes, the great sea yearns,
> we ourselves flash and yearn,
> and moreover my mother told me as a boy
> (repeatingly) 'Ever to confess you're bored
> means you have no
>
> Inner Resources'. I conclude now I have no
> inner resources, because I am heavy bored.
> Peoples bore me,
> literature bores me, especially great literature,
> Henry bores me, with his plights & gripes
> as bad as achilles,
>
> who loves people and valiant art, which bores me.
> And the tranquil hills, & gin, look like a drag
> and somehow a dog
> has taken itself & its tail considerably away
> into mountains or sea or sky, leaving
> behind: me, wag. (Song 14)

This was the only stuff that got near me; that heady mixture
of Shakespeare and John Berryman brought me back from the

abyss. I drank in the poems like a lamp drinks paraffin. They touched a chord, a need, which nothing else came near to fulfilling. At that moment in my life, it was more than a general tonic to be studying English literature; it was a lifeline.

Mind you, I would have known the Shakespeare if I had not been doing English at university. Even a secondary-school education would have given me what Seán Ó Ríordáin calls '*srathar sibhialtachta an Bhéarla*'; but Berryman? If I hadn't been studying English, it is unlikely that I would have made his acquaintance in print in those days in Ireland. And it's not as if he was on the course of study. John Montague's presence in the English Department, though, meant new exposures. Though John was ostensibly teaching the Romantics – I remember particularly interesting lectures on Blake's 'Songs of Innocence and Experience' and on Wordsworth's 'Nutting' – he was also disseminating modern American poetry amongst the students.

Among modern American poets, John Berryman spoke to me from the brink of the ontological abyss that had been dared by few, and survived by less. What moved me above all was his description of a sheer terror rarely experienced in our time in the West. This level of terror is reached by others, notably Emily Dickinson, as well as Sylvia Plath in the last poems in *Ariel*, but for me to this day Berryman's description and inscription of what the French feminist theoretician Julia Kristeva calls 'abjection' is bettered by nobody.

Still, more than a mere theme or voice, what I ultimately went on to learn from John Berryman was a technique. Central to that technique was Berryman's creation – amongst other voices – of 'Henry', an invented character not to be confused with John Berryman, author and poet. As Denis Donoghue has put it, 'The poet, living in various degrees of chaos, dissociates himself; allowing each fragment its corresponding voice. The fragments scream; that is sing.' These different fragments interact in kaleidoscopic combinations in a way that makes the whole much greater than the parts. Thus what the poet does in the process of bringing a poem together is akin to the work that a shaman does in other societies; Berryman himself described the poet's process as one 'In constant danger of breakdown, of ceasing to function, or of functioning fantastically, in ways that were too private to elicit a public response.' Thus Berryman transforms a minstrel show into an imitation of a sacred action designed to purge fear, and in doing so produces a poem. This is an act that takes the place of psychotherapy, that modern religion for the over-literal. Berryman himself knew this. In a review-article in 1959 he speculated that the motive for writing poetry may be 'complex beyond analysis. Poetry is a terminal activity, taking place out near the end of things, where the poet's soul addresses one other soul only, never mind when. And it aims, never mind at either communication or expression – at the reformation of the poet, as prayer does.' Berryman was somehow my ur-poet or medicine-man, the soul addressing me.

The ability to hold different parts of the poem in opposed tension while simultaneously keeping the poet at his desk and the arrangement of the words on the page as poetry in full view – all this is, of course, a Berryman permutation of the Yeatsian Mask: Henry/Mr Bones is, in many ways, an updated version of Yeats's 'Ribh' or 'wild old wicked man'. Oddly, I never thought of taking the technique from Yeats directly. I daresay a certain inverted snobbery was at work here; as an Irish speaker I was intensely aware that a lot of Yeats's Celtic credentials were at second hand. But there must have been more to it than that; whereas Yeats's antithetical selves – Crazy Jane, Ribh, Hanrahan and so on – are clearly defined and distinct, in Berryman, something else happens. The voices are fragmentary, and it is the relationship between them that is important, rather than what they are actually saying. Berryman's stanzaic method allows for deliberate disjunctions of normal syntax and sentence structure, with multiple shifts from standard to colloquial to vulgate, and registers ranging from archaic and precious 'recherché' terms to baby-talk. The fragmentation and disjunction in Berryman's poetry had a particular appeal for me: early on Berryman said that he was 'less impressed than [he] used to be by the universal notion of a continuity of individual personality', and this is what probably drew me to him at a time when my own personality was so shattered as to be totally fragmented.

In 'This Sex Which Is Not One', Luce Irigiray describes the phenomenon of fragmentation as typical of women's writing. Men and women's desires are strangers to each other, she argues, and to presume a symmetry between women's ontological position and men's is a mistake. Instead of taking account of both the masculine and feminine, Western culture is predicated on the masculine as 'norm'. The rejection – indeed exclusion – of a female imaginary puts woman in the position of experiencing herself only fragmentally in the little-structured margins of the dominant ideology. According to Irigiray, *écriture féminine*, or 'feminine writing', tends 'to put the torch to fetish words, proper terms, well-constructed forms'. This could easily be a description of the *Dream Songs* of John Berryman. The character Henry is quite cavalier in his attitude to women, dividing them either into those he has slept with or those he hasn't and whom he consequently idealises in medieval, pseudo-Spenserian terms. The poet John Berryman, however, *is* witness to a feminine imagination, in that he never posits the most tacit assumption of those with phallic power – that of a 'self' which is distinct and separate. Berryman taught me not only about technique or voice; he also provided an example of a male poet utilising feminine energy.

When I read Berryman, the heyday of poetry in the Cork English department was yet to come. By 1974 I myself would be long gone, married and pregnant in Holland and setting out for Turkey by train, which granted the probably not unique but definitely memorable experience of vomiting through every country in Eastern Europe, and arriving in Istanbul to another life. I do have, though, a particularly vivid 'literary' memory from my time in Cork of John Montague pontificating in Starry's – The Western Star on Western Road which was then, as now, a major student haunt – to the effect that you couldn't have a woman muse poet, because that would be tantamount to a woman being in love with a woman, and that wouldn't do now, would it? Not having read Marina Tsvetaeva at the time, I wasn't in a position to carry that particular argument, but I already knew it was wrong, because by this stage I was already a poet, and a muse-poet at that.

After Berryman, after the interaction with fellow writers and thinkers, the event that rose to save my sanity *in extremis*, a spontaneous gift of the subconscious, was that after about nine months of a strange gestation, during a few days of high winds – as if the external elements had whipped up an internal storm – I produced out of my turmoil a series of poems in Irish subsequently called the 'Mór' poems. They were a mustering of remnants of folk-memories of the Goddess of Sovereignty, Mór of Munster, but put by me in a modern setting. This series of poems was published in 1973, in *INNTI 3*; these were the first real poems I had ever written. They are also clearly indebted to the nervous, jazzy rhythms of the Berryman *Dream Songs*. The Mór character as I describe her has a lot of the frequent, wry self-depreciation ascribable to Henry. There was something wonderfully zany, off-the-wall and also terribly bleak about Henry:

> and God has many surprises, like
> when the man you fear most in the world marries your mother
> and chilling other,
> men from far tribes armed in the dark, the dike-
> hole, the sudden gash of an old friend's betrayal,
> words that leave one pale. (Song 168)

This sort of thing, suitably leavened with the *dinnsheanchas* stories about Mór Mumhan that I knew from West Kerry, these were the ingredients of the particular 'objective correlative' that gave me the lens through which I could begin to see the experience I had been through, though darkly, and then begin to express it, though obliquely. And the two completely disparate language registers of West Kerry *dinnsheanchas* and the *Dream Songs* of John Berryman were equally important to that process.

Years later I managed to track down the reasonably obscure early medieval text that deals with Mór, but at the time I was working purely from the folk, or oral, tradition, and the last twitches of the old tale surviving in it. No one was more surprised by these poems at the time than me, and it has taken me until now, almost thirty years later, to be able to deal analytically with the themes that I set down in them through sheer artistic intuition. One of these themes was that of the transformation of the despised and rejected feminine from *cailleach*, horrible hag, to her rightful state of *spéirbhean*. Quite unknown to myself, I had hit upon one of the motherlodes of Irish literature from medieval times until now. Characteristically enough also, I inverted the normal mytheme, as in our time the discovery of the inner reality of the *cailleach*, a repressed energy that images itself as female, is news enough in itself. Years later, I still feel that these poems are important, and that in them I had intuited what I feel is one of the greatest psychic realities of our times: the need to express these repressed energies. It may be that the collapse of established ideologies, the intertwining of different forms of art and the breaking open of fixed cultures are only the symptoms or superficial signs of something much more significant on the move: some deep emotional realities of consciousness – the literally unthinkable and until now unspeakable – knocking at the door and asking to be integrated into our modern frame of reference.

In her book *Strangers to Ourselves*, Julia Kristeva suggests that one of the greatest problems of our time is an implosion of psychic space. Christianity, Kristeva argues, has been dis-empowered as a belief system, as have other, competing systems been equally unsuccessful at staying the course. As a result, there is no longer a cultural container for fantasy, a kind of anteroom where the contents of the subconscious can be transformed and mediated before they enter the world outside. Therefore, symbolic material – whether utopian fantasies or those con-stellations of energy that are the gods themselves – is forced to be acted out in a childish, literalistic manner, and so enters the world in a way that was never meant to be.

The practice and discipline of poetry has taught me that there is a psychosexual, emotio-imagistic level of human nature – maybe you could call it the soul – that we deny individually or collectively only at our peril. It is a mythopoeic function natural to the human being which has particular difficulty achieving expression in Western civilisation, where it has fallen foul of the dominant mind-spirit duality and disappeared into the chasm between them. This mythic dimension needs to be expressed, but that does not necessarily mean that it needs to be acted out literalistically. On the contrary, the literalistic acting out is a wholly inappropriate and uncalled for response to this dimension. It would be like acting out a dream without taking into consideration the difference that exists between dream reality and outside reality. As to whether I think the mythic represents a greater or lesser truth, suffice it to say that it is a different way of knowing. Because of the strictly rational bias of Western society, it has, however, been denigrated and repressed. What we need to do is to find some room for it in our lives, so that it can play itself out and dance its dance on its own terms, which are imaginative ones.

For me the medium for this dance – by some accident of genetic predisposition and upbringing – is poetry, and I believe that it is only in a very simplistic and reductionist form that Auden's dictum that poetry does not make things happen is true. The very articulation in the all-so-human terms of image, metre, and words of these messages and intuitions from the 'otherworld' beyond rational consciousness actually changes them as it crystallises them. It is an inner alchemy in which disparate entities, put under great pressure in the retort of the individual human personality, actually change in the process – as coal under such circumstances in the intense heat of the bowels of the earth turns into diamond. It is an actual spinning of straw into gold, and every poet worthy of the name dares the challenge of Rumpelstiltskin. As I once heard the French poet Yves Bonnfoy saying to an Irish poet who had made a facetious remark about surrealism being the chance meeting of a lobster and a sewing machine on an ironing board, 'It is metamorphosis that we are speaking about, Monsieur, not metaphor.' This is by no means an easy process; in fact it often happens at a terrible cost to the individual poets involved. We have each to undergo a breakdown of ego-boundaries: it is all very well to talk blithely of the Sumerian myth 'The Descent of Inanna' as a metaphor for this transformation process, but myth itself shows us how the reality is no joke, and it has been a harder reality for women, and women poets, for a long time.

In 'The Descent of Inanna', the Goddess of the Morning

Star, Inanna, chooses of her own free will to divest herself of her power in this world and to pass through the seven gates of Hell, the realm of her banished sister Erishkigal. In willingly undertaking this journey, Inanna seems to have underestimated the power and malice of her sister and ends up in a dire predicament:

> Inanna was turned into a corpse.
> A piece of rotting meat,
> and was hung from a hook on the wall.

Trans. Wolkstein and Kramer

The myth shows the way. Out of the forgotten nothings of our lives, in a place akin to Yeats's 'foul rag and bone shop of the heart', we, as Father Enki did in the myth, create the *kurgurra* and the *galatur*, small creatures who travel to the Underworld, commiserate with its queen Erishkigal in her great pain and suffering and receive in return the corpse of Inanna, which they bring to life again. This myth enacts for me a way to correct the enormous imbalance in the Western human heart, created when the Attic Greeks refused women the right to the *polis* and the *agora*, and thus the right to contribute to intellectual citizenship. This was a time when male heroic ideologies, as exemplified by Theseus, smote the dark side of the Mother-Goddess in the guise of Medusa and consigned her, like Erishkigal, to the outer darkness, where she sits wailing and gnashing her teeth. It seems to me that, at last, this imbalance is in the act of being corrected. Certain male symbols *par excellence* are receding, while female energy and imagery is literally leppin' out of the woodwork, or stonework, as in Eiléan Ní Chuilleanáin's fine poem 'Pygmalion's Image', where

> Not only her stone face, laid back staring in the ferns,
> But everything the scoop of the valley contains begins to
>   move …
> The crisp hair is real, wriggling like snakes;
> A rustle of veins, tick of blood in the throat;
> The lines of the face tangle and catch, and
> A green leaf of language comes twisting out of her mouth.

Such considerations being beyond me at the time, I could only write the poem:

Teist Dhonncha Di Ar Mhór (in *An Dealg Droighin*; *Selected Poems/Rogha Danta*)

Do sheas sí lomnocht
sa doircheacht.
a basa fuara – iasc gealúr –
ar mo ghuailne
a cromáin – tine ghealáin
faoi dhá ré a bruinne.

Thumas mo cheann
i bhfeamnach a gruaige;
bhí tonn ghoirt na sáile
am' bualadh, am' shuathadh;
ár gcapaill bhána ag donnú
ina bhfrancaigh mhóra,
gach aon ní ina chorcra.

Nuair a dhúisíos ar maidin bhí tinneas cinn orm.
Thugas fé ndeara
go raibh gainnní an liathbhuí ag clúdach a colainne.
Bhí fiacla lofa an duibheagáin
ag drannadh orm.
Sea, thógas mo chip is mo mheanaithe
is theitheas liom.

Donncha Di's Testimony (in *Selected Poems/Rogha Danta*)

She stood naked
in the dark,
her palms cold
like luminous fish
on my shoulders;
her hips
flashing fire
beneath the two moons
of her breasts.

I sank my head
in her sea-weed hair
and bitter waves of sea
bruised and battered me,
our white-horse waves
rusted to rats;
all became empurpled.

In the morning waking
my head aching
I saw sallow scales encrusted her
and rotten teeth from the abyss
snarled at me and hissed.
I took my awl and last
and left the place fast.

Trans. Michael Hartnett

And I took the good advice of my own poem and got out of
Ireland as soon as I was legally able to.

The two years spent in Holland were formative, giving me
something to define myself against. I saw the riches of that
tradition of high material culture, a strain lacking in Irish
history, the 'Golden Age' of Dutch and Flemish art occurring at
the very stage when we 'mere Irish' were being reduced almost to
oblivion by the Penal Laws. Five years in Turkey then gave me an
entirely different, non-Eurocentric perspective on reality. Still
and all, in some ways we were unfortunate in the timing of our
return to Turkey. As the seventies progressed, the country was
gradually destabilised politically, a small party led by Alpaslan
Turkes creating a position of power for itself with acts of
unremitting terror and political assassination totally out of
proportion with its percentage of support from the voting
population. This tyranny was answered by the mobilisation of
the Left, and very soon the country was being diametrically
polarised, just as has happened in the North of Ireland, only on
a much larger scale. If sectarian violence led to the death of three
people per week in the North, then in Turkey at least thirty were
being killed each week in politically motivated murders. The

country was on the brink of civil war, and I did not see it as a place in which to bring up my children.

Towards the end of the five years I had also, as a result once more of an emotional crisis, begun to write poetry in Irish again, discovering that this was what I wanted to do more than anything else for the rest of my life. I submitted an extensive portfolio to the Arts Council/An Chomhairle Ealaíon, and won a bursary to come back to the Gaeltacht for a year to write full-time. I threw up my university job, sold the furniture to buy the tickets home and, telling my husband that he could follow me if he wanted to, headed for West Kerry. There I learned that my memories had been tinted somewhat by the rose-coloured spectacles of distance. The Scarlet Woman who had run off with a Turk was back now with two children in tow and no husband in sight – and was definitely *non-grata*. The re-entry syndrome was like the disease that deep-sea divers call the bends, and more painful by far than the so-called culture shock I had experienced in Turkey. It was like being back snail-racing in the *geata beag* of my childhood: there was a great big world out there that I wanted to tell everyone about, but the silence was deafening. No one was interested. I was 'home', and it still wasn't easy.

Ultimately, the complications of my relationship with Ireland have to do with language. Unable to live permanently in Turkey, I was equally unable to remain permanently in the Gaeltacht, and there are times when I feel as much in linguistic exile in Dublin as I ever did among the wide whistling wastes of the Anatolian plateau. I have a basic allegiance to a sense of 'Irishness' that is all-inclusive, but I find precious little of it in the psychic wilderness of the South Dublin suburbs, with their proliferation of housing estates with ever more grandiose names and titles – a growing agglomeration of Richmond Downs, Westbury Heights and such likes, aping the mock-grandeur of places from Southeast England in a way that no self-respecting Northern English person would, being secure enough in their own local culture in a way that many Irish are not. Still and all, in Dublin I have Radio na Gaeltachta, Radio na Life, and a widespread Irish-speaking network of about five hundred people, many of whom I have never heard speak English, though when I stop to think of it they obviously must have it, too.

I can also go into University College Dublin and read the material that people I know and love gave to the Folklore Department back in the 1930s and '40s. This material at both the more superficial level of vocabulary and the deeper level of syntax and theme feeds naturally into my writing of poetry. For reasons I still cannot fathom, in moments of impossible crisis, poetry in Irish is what pours out of the recesses of my being, and helps me structure a personality that is maybe so deeply fractured that otherwise it might not survive as a thinking entity. There have been times of deep depression – when, as Máire Mhac an tSaoi, another exponent of multilingualism, has expressed it: 'Bím balbh i dhá theanga' ('I am speechless in two languages') – but Irish has, again and again, saved me from madness.

In my attempt to escape what Tom Paine called 'the dead hand of dead generations', I had tried the Joycean expedient of 'silence, exile, and cunning', and it did not work. One of the things I learned from this attempt, however, was the utterly masculinist bias implicit in the dominant literary ethos in Ireland. So blinded had we all been by the brilliance of Joyce, and so entranced by the need to 'fly by those nets' of nationality, language and religion, that we had never stopped to think that the title of the *Bildungsroman* that had affected us so deeply was *A Portrait of the Artist as a Young Man*. Not as a young woman. Or even as a young person.

Being the rather solitary, bookish child I was, I filtered my personal hurts to a large extent through the metaphors and analogies of the arts, especially those of literature. Inasmuch as I have been able to associate the 'slings and arrows of outrageous fortune' that have befallen me with precedents in a text or piece of literature, I have always been able to protect myself from the raw immensity of any stimulus, to sample it in small quantities, to get a handle on the overwhelming event. In other words, I have always, to some extent, lived through a book. Picture my chagrin in my late twenties, therefore, to discover that all the time I had been

living through the wrong book. Rather than living out the very
letter of the Joycean *Bildungsroman*, I would have profited by taking
a page instead from Kate O'Brien's novel *The Land of Spices*, doubly
so indeed, in that it was set in the same boarding school I attended,
but sixty years earlier. For all that Kate O'Brien loved her Joyce and
in many ways set out to emulate him, what she ends up with is
actually something very different altogether from his austere
philosophy of cut-and-run. The plot of her novel entails the very
opposite: a nun named Helen Archer who had gone into religion
'with a merciless heart' after a major trauma in late adolescence
learns, through her care for the young Anna Murphy, to break out
of her frigid loneliness into warmth and human entanglement. A
high point of the novel is a scene of momentous emotional
bargaining where the nun, now Reverend Mother, forestalls the
petty puppeteering instincts of Anna's appalling grandmother,
who disapproves of wasting money on the academic education of
a girl. By a subtle piece of emotional blackmail, ironically 'Irish' in
its way, Reverend Mother bests the granny, and Anna gets to take
up her scholarship and go to college and therefore buy time for
growth. The Reverend Mother, by dint of involving herself so
passionately in the affairs of another, also breaks free from her
inner permafrost into almost a state of Grace, and is finally
capable of understanding and forgiveness.

Unlike Joyce's *Portrait* with its image of nets as things that tie
you down, its horror of Ireland as the sow that eats her own
farrow, O'Brien's *The Land of Spices* contains a very different image
of what constitutes freedom. Anna realises that 'In fact if a girl
sees liberty as the greatest of all desirables, she will have to spin
it out herself as the spider its web, her self-made snare in which
to catch Anna did not yet know what.' Here the threads that bind
us to life, to family, to community are not to be cut, but instead
to be spun, always and everywhere out of ourselves. Ariadne and
her thread lead into, and out of, the labyrinth of the self. A
different mytheme is at work here from that of the conquering
male hero. O'Brien's alternative provides a marvellous antidote to
the worse excesses of the rampant ego-as-hero fiction that underlies all of modern Western risk-capital production.

I had spun out those nets of friendship and mutual aid and respect in Turkey, and in many ways it was a terrible source of grief to leave them. Often when we go back to Turkey, I meet people with whom I used to teach at the university and wonder what would have happened if I had stayed on there. Would I, like them, have become a middle-aged Turkish lady, a *hanim hanim*, well-groomed, happy and fulfilled in my home and my children? Probably not. I carried too many demons within me, and a lot of those demons were place-specific and had to do with my relationship with Ireland. I discovered that no matter how you cut and run, you end up carrying all of your demons with you. Sometime or other, I had to turn back and face the music. I am glad I was young enough and strong enough to do so when I did.

It wasn't easy. The eighties in Ireland were very difficult for women. Many notorious incidents rocked the country and polarised the population. In one incident, the so-called 'Kerry Babies' case, a young woman called Joanne Hayes gave birth alone to a baby who did not survive the night. The following day a newborn baby was found amidst rocks on the coast fifty miles away, dead from multiple stab wounds. Joanne and the members of her family were brought into police headquarters in Tralee for questioning. Such was the pressure brought to bear on them that they signed statements as a result of which Joanne Hayes was charged with murder. Subsequent blood tests showed that Hayes was not the mother of the baby found on the rocks. A public tribunal was called for, ostensibly to ascertain by what methods, lawful or unlawful, the Hayes family had been brought to admit to a murder they did not commit. Instead of investigating the police methods used, the tribunal turned into a public inquisition into the sex life of Hayes, what poet Brendan Kennelly called 'some medieval witch-hunt with the victims burning at the stake and the crowd dancing around the fire'. Evidence was heard for five months, one lawyer alone asking Hayes 2,216 incredibly personal questions. The detective's lurid speculations about Hayes included the notion that she had been 'carrying on' with multiple partners and had conceived twins by two different fathers on the same night. Before long there were three, rather than two, babies involved. Incredibly, in his report the judge exonerated the Gardaí, whose behavior was regarded as merely 'gilding the lily'. A greater demonstration of the hysterical prurience of Irish males concerning female sexuality could not have been found; in time, a proper sociological analysis of the whole case will, I'm sure, view it as indicative of many deep-seated fault lines in the collective psyche. Another noted case at the time involved the death of a teenager named Ann Lovett and her newborn baby, delivered without assistance beside a grotto of the Blessed Virgin. And in another part of Ireland a teacher, Eileen Flynn, lost her job in a secondary school run by nuns for becoming pregnant with the child of a married man with whom she was living and whose other children she was raising. (She could not marry him because there was then no divorce in Ireland.)

The traumas of the cases of the Kerry Babies, Ann Lovett, Eileen Flynn and other social scandals only highlighted the utter contempt in which the lives of ordinary women were held by an unholy alliance of clerics and lay bigots who still ran the show in the Republic of Ireland. The decade's two controversial referenda, one on divorce and the other on writing into the Irish Constitution a specific clause dealing with the right to life of the unborn, were utterly depressing. Right-wing power groups with their specific agenda swept the boards.

But it might have been the 'hour of the wolf' mechanism at work, the last mustering of darkness just before dawn. The election of Mary Robinson as president was the first faint glimmer of light. I felt vindicated: for the first time since returning home ten years before, I had voted with the winning side in a major political contest. The infamous 'X Case', in which we saw an attempt at the forced internment in Ireland of a fourteen-year-old rape victim so that she could not travel to England for an abortion, was the last stand of the mastodons. The whole country reacted. The ribbons tied in protest on the railings of the Dáil were not put there by liberals, or 'Lefties', or any such group easily marginalised and disempowered. They were put there by whole groups of ordinary families – fathers, mothers and children all protesting together at the deep inhumanity involved. They won, and the Supreme Court decision in this case was, for the many right-wing groups that had dominated Irish politics in the previous decade, the beginning of the beginning of the end.

Though the struggle still continues and the price of democracy is eternal vigilance, for the first time since my arrival in Ireland at the age of five, I feel that I live in a country characterised by positive and optimistic feelings, rather than the self-hating obsequiousness I had witnessed as a child. All is not won, of course, as the recent case of the double life of one Michael Cleary has shown. After Cleary's death it emerged that this well-known right-wing priest had been living with his 'housekeeper', Phyllis Hamilton, as husband and wife for going on twenty years – and even had a teenage son in residence. The lived realities of the woman's existence were totally denied, denigrated and calumniated by Cleary's siblings and so-called close clerical friends. The schizophrenic existence whereby his public, priestly self could not own up to his other, private self was condoned by all and sundry. It is a sign of a deep ambivalence that is still with us. Maybe if Phyllis Hamilton had had the American panache of Annie Murphy, the woman who forced Bishop Casey of Galway to own up to being the father of her son, she might have been treated differently. That the punitive streak in the Irish psyche is one-sided and highly gendered is proven by a recent case in which there was a complicitous and ominous delay by officials in the Department of Public Prosecution in bringing to court the clerical culprit in a case involving the sexual abuse of children. But case after case of what seems to be public psychotherapy for the whole nation is finally having an effect, and this last injustice brought down a government. Maybe as a nation we are growing up emotionally after all.

The cessation of violence in the North after a period of twenty-five years is not unrelated to this upsurge of hope and optimism. A major change is occurring in Ireland, North and South. It is as if we are all coming out of a very dark tunnel in the middle of the night. Because it was dark outside anyway, we hadn't realised we were in a tunnel. Only now, as we come out the other end, and the echoes of the past which were deafening us and precluding any attempts at conversation come to an end – only now do we realise how long we have been in that tunnel. The imprint of the traumas of colonisation and the Great Famine is beginning to fade from Ireland's collective psyche at last. One of the proofs of this supposition is that finally, one hundred and fifty years after the event, we are able to externalise and describe the catastrophe of the Great Hunger by measures such as the establishment of The Famine Museum in Strokestown House in County Roscommon. After a visit to this museum, as I drive down the main road from Longford to Dublin, my mind is miles away. I am already working the museum into a mermaid poem. After one hundred and fifty years of being up on land, the merpeople finally get their act together and erect a museum to the basic trauma of their existence: their having to come up on land. They have extensive reconstructions of their former marine existence, and specimens of fish, shell and seaweed in all their varieties abound. The one thing failing them is water. At one stage they had an exhibit of just three drops of the precious liquid, but one day a few summers ago, in the middle of the hottest summer in living memory, didn't the cooling system break down, and the three precious drops evaporate? Unlike the corpse in the Turin Shroud – a medieval forgery for starters – the precious liquid left no mark at all on the material surrounding it. Gone for good …

… and not a soul knew
what it is they were missing.

Years later, the children of the merpeople
dream of water.
At the weekly therapy session
they find it very hard
to describe this thing
of which they dream.
They lack the vocabulary
and terminology to describe 'water'.
They do not anymore possess
the suitable conceptual apparatus.

'A transparent liquid' one of them says
doing her damnest. 'Yes,'
murmurs the psychiatrist, 'keep it coming.'
She tries again, – 'A thin flowing mass,'
she calls it, searching carefully through
her word-hoard. 'A shining covering,
a dripping material, wet stuff.'

Trans. Ní Dhomhnaill, based on version of
'Cuimhne an Uisce' in *Cead Aighnis*

Yes, that is how it should go ... something like that, anyway.
I must work on it, and then maybe I can send it to the curator
of the museum, when I finally have it finished. He might even
put it into the museum, as an exhibit. At least it would be
something in Irish.

When Jacsaí asked that question all those years ago, he couldn't
have been aware of the implications it would have for me; neither
could I. I think back on the child I was then and the woman I am
now and I know that there are many, many people to whom I
belong, and who belong to me. And I know now too that for all the
confusion that such a question might bring on in the recesses of my
own and many others' psyches, there are moments of clarity,
moments when the answer is as clear as water, as clear as day, as
clear as the light that was sinking into the sea that childhood
evening as I strolled 'home'.

Dinnsheanchas: *Holy Wells and Psychic Depths*

There is a small well that I am particularly fond of in the west of Ireland, in the parish of Minard on the Dingle Peninsula. It is a holy well dedicated to St John the Baptist, one of the approximately sixty such sites on the peninsula which have been documented by the noted folklorist Dr Kevin Danagher. Like many of the other sacred monuments in the area, it is small and unpretentious – just a circle of mossy stones with a simple inscribed cross at its head. A whitethorn tree grows above it and most of the year white and purple candles of pennyworth and foxglove sprout between its stones, while in the well itself grows a mat of pondweed, called in Irish *luibh gan athair gan mháthair* ('fatherless motherless plant') because of its seeming lack of roots. I love this well for its sheer simplicity, its grace, and the way it seems to nestle into the scoop of the surrounding natural hollow and just lie there quietly without fanfare.

I was so overwhelmed by the sheer numinosity of the place the first time I visited it that I immediately wrote a poem, imagining the scene through the passage of the year as seen through the plastic eye of a doll which had been thrown into the well:

From An Bhábóg Bhriste (in *Féar Suaithinseach, Pharaoh's Daughter*)

A bhábóigín bhriste ins an tobar,
caite isteach ag leanbh ar bhogshodar
anuas le fánaidh, isteach faoi chótaí a mháthar.
Ghlac sé preab in uaigneas an chlapsholais
nuair a léim caipíní na bpúcaí peill chun a bhéil,

nuair a chrap na méaracáin a gceannaigh ina threo
is nuair a chuala sé uaill chiúin ón gceann cait ins an dair.
Ba dhóbair nó go dtitfeadh an t-anam beag as nuair a ghaibh
easóg thar bráid is pataire coinín aici ina béal,
na putóga ar sileadh leis ar fuaid an bhaill
is nuair a dh'eitil an sciathán leathair ins an spéir …

From The Broken Doll (in *Pharaoh's Daughter*)

O little broken doll, dropped in the well,
thrown aside by a child, scampering downhill
to hide under the skirts of his mother!
In twilight's quiet he took sudden fright
as toadstool caps snatched at his tongue,
foxgloves crooked their fingers at him
and from the oak, he heard the owl's low call.
His little heart almost stopped when a weasel
went by, with a fat young rabbit in its jaws,
loose guts spilling over the grass while
a bat wing flicked across the evening sky …

Trans. John Montague

Even after the poem was written, this place remained and remains for me a place of a deeper reality – known in Irish as *an saol eile*, the 'otherworld'. Inaccessible most of the time, and never easy to reach, the 'otherworld' makes a liminal appearance in our world through places such as this well. That this has been so for many other people before me is evidenced by the myriad stories and folktales about this site. One of these stories tells about the *breac beannaithe* ('blessed golden trout') that is said to reside in the depths of the well, a glimpse of which presaged happiness and was a good omen:

There once was a married couple with no children who lived beside the well. One day the woman of the house went out to the well to get a bucket of water, which she brought home and poured into a large pot hanging over the fire. She had a great turf fire blazing away under it, and yet even after an hour the pot had not yet begun to boil. She took the cover off the pot, and lo and behold, in the bottom of the pot was this tiny little trout from the well. She said nothing, but poured the water back into the bucket, trout and all, and brought it back to the well, and carefully emptied the fish into it. She then filled her bucket with well-water again, but more carefully this time, making damn-well sure that there was no fish in it, and when she brought it home and set it on the fire, it boiled almost in no time. Nine months later exactly, she was delivered of a child.

This simple story, which has many variants, is not attached specifically to this well; I have heard it told about many other holy wells in the area too. The tale thus seems representative or indicative of Irish lore connecting the physical landscape to the 'otherworld', through places like the well, and so when several years ago a group of us were making a series of television programmes about local antiquities for the then brand-new Irish-language channel Teilifís na Gaeilge I wanted to use it. The commissioning editor had real trouble with the story, though, since according to him 'it had a huge cringe-factor'. I was dumbfounded, but maybe should not have been so. After all, an outsider (originally from Dublin and therefore quite unspeakably foreign!), he was in no position to understand the tradition of *dinnsheanchas* or local placelore from which this story and myriad other stories like it emerge. A product of the Cartesian, Appolonian, 'civilised' perspective of those educated in cities, he was armed with what has been conveniently oversimplified as 'the Western Gaze', which flattens all obstacles to linear progress, notably the natural 'lie of the land' and any aboriginal understanding of it such as is evidenced in *dinnsheanchas*. And *dinnsheanchas* has been from time immemorial one of the great branches of knowledge of the Gaelic world. Ireland is a small enough country, but it has been lived in for a very long time, as is attested by archaeological remains such as the Mesolithic shell middens of Sligo, or the extraordinary monumental passage tombs of the Boyne Valley from the Bronze Age, which are, indeed, older than the pyramids of Egypt. And for as long as we have lived here, we have been tramping around the countryside, telling ourselves stories about it.

The Celtic peoples who arrived in the Iron Age, bringing with them an early form of the Irish language, were amazed when they saw scattered throughout the country the works of previous civilisations, and they made of them the homes of their gods, and invented stories of them. The arrival of Christianity and literacy added another layer to an already highly encoded matrix, and once again *dinnsheanchas* flourished as Christian and Irish traditions tangoed together, interpretations of place-history mingling. Though originally and perhaps mostly a subterranean and oral tradition, *dinnsheanchas* has surfaced frequently into the literary tradition, especially in that large corpus of lore assembled in the eleventh, twelfth and thirteenth centuries and known as *Dinnsheanchas Érenn*, the *Dinnsheanchas* of Ireland. This was part of the body of knowledge that all medieval poets were expected to master, and its importance is reflected in its presence in many of the major manuscripts, such as the *Leabhar Laighneach*, Book of Leinster.

In *dinnsheanchas*, the land of Ireland is translated into story: each place has history that is being continuously told. The *dinnsheanchas* is the storehouse of this knowledge, but the mentality which it expresses is to be found throughout all phases of Irish literature. Though paramount in such early medieval texts as the *Táin Bó Cuailnge* (*The Cattle-Raid of Cooley*) and the thirteenth-century *Acallam na Senórach* (*The Colloquy of the Ancients*), it continues to imbue modern Irish literature. For poets such as Yeats, Heaney, Montague, Carson, Muldoon and many others, *dinnsheanchas* is a means of uniting psychological exploration with a larger frame-work of collective cultural understanding. And this does not function only for poets: Brian Friel's *Translations* interrogates this mentality, and his *Faith Healer* uses it to enormous effect. And I would go so far as to place the work of Joyce in the centre of the *dinnsheanchas* tradition: his first book, *Dubliners*, focuses on people who live in a specific place; *Ulysses* functions as the description of the wanderings and meanderings of two main characters around that same geographical area; and his magnum opus, *Finnegans Wake*, is another version of the same, a more deeply fragmented, encoded and metamorphosed form of *dinnsheanchas*.

Because of this profoundly woven network of interlocking stories which is the *dinnsheanchas*, life for most ordinary Irish country folk is a series of regular movements – most often on foot – over a terrain thoroughly imbued with meaning both historical and personal. The landscape itself, in other words, contains memory, and can point to the existence of a world beyond this one. 'Memories both personal and collective', the American anthropologist Lawrence Taylor wrote, 'are attached, as the Victorians liked to say, to nearly every rock and hillock, and some of these are points of power, mediating between this and other worlds.' If the site of my well suggests access to such an 'other world' as Taylor describes, there is also an access to other times: there is a sense in which *dinnsheanchas* also mediates between past and present, and allows us glimpses into other moments in historical time. And these glimpses are available to us, if only we can make the leap in realisation that is necessary, for, like the commissioning editor who cringed at the tale of the well, we see the world differently now. Charles Bowen has described these differences between our way of perceiving the world and the perceptions revealed by the medieval literary corpus of the *dinnsheanchas*: a modern road-map transmits knowledge of a kind that primitive Celts would have found inconceivably abstract. Places would have been known to them as people were: by face, name and history. The last two would have been closely linked, for as the *dinnsheanchas* illustrates again and again, the name of every place was assumed to be an expression of its history.

Thus the name of my well, and its dedication to St John the Baptist, is not accidental, and has a legend associated with it. According to this story John the Baptist had such enormous *mana* or magic power that King Herod could find nobody powerful enough to behead him. And so it happened that he sent to Valentia Island at the far side of Dingle Bay for an Irish druid called Mogh Roith (the Slave of the Wheel) to come and behead him, and Mogh Roith, with his great knowledge of magic and sorcery, succeeded where many others before him had failed. This druid was of the tribe of the Corcha Dhuibhne, who inhabited both sides of Dingle Bay, and it had been prophesied that they would be called on to pay for the crime of the beheading when certain time divisions coincided. In 1096 it was thought that the appointed time was approaching, and the people of Ireland, and especially the hapless Corcha Dhuibhne, were seized with a panic. A plague hit the area and rigorous fasting and prayer were undertaken. The holy well, which had previously been associated with some other saint, and even earlier with some other divinity ejected by that saint, was hastily rededicated in honour of St John the Baptist. The plague abated, and everyone was happy, and since that day a 'Pattern' or pilgrimage to the well has been faithfully pursued by the local people. And my small doll in the well witnessed this ritual of place that is the Pattern:

... báite sa láib
t'fhiarshúil phlaisteach oscailte de ló
is d'oíche, chíonn tú an madra rua is a hál
ag teacht go bruach na féithe raithní taobh lena bpluais
is iad ag ól a sáith: tagann an broc chomh maith ann
is níonn a lapaí ; sánn sé a shoc san uisce is lá
an phátruín tagann na daoine is casann siad seacht n-uaire
ar deiseal; le gach casadh caitheann siad cloch san uisce ...

... stuck in the mud
your plastic eyes squinny open from morning
to night: you see the vixen and her brood
stealing up to lap the ferny swamphole
near their den, the badger loping to wash
his paws, snuff water with his snout. On
Pattern days people parade seven clockwise
rounds; at every turn, throwing in a stone ...

Trans. John Montague

What my doll bore witness to was nothing less than the history of a place, the history of a landscape. And in my poem I am attempting to offer, through the guise of the doll, a sense of the absolute and even eerie enchantedness that results from placelore, as the landscape, and everything in it, takes on a life of its own and itself becomes enchanted. And as Lawrence Taylor has put it:

> The stories preserve the enchanted landscape; the well and other places like it literally hold the stories. Those raised with the stories need only hear the name of a given place or else see it to rehear the story that is tied to the place – or at least know that there is a story that someone else 'has'. Perhaps it is less a question of whether or not one 'believes' the story than of a landscape that has stories in it – stories it can tell you – versus a landscape that talks about other things or is mute.

And though the historical stories are indeed interesting and the archaeological record itself tells great stories, ultimately for me the greatest fascination is in the mythological stories, where we have poured out the powerful personages of our psyche, our collective *paysage intérieure*, so that they are writ large, and three-dimensionally, before our eyes. Such is the case, most pre-eminently, with that familiar feature of the Irish landscape, the circular, man-made structure called by a variety of names in Irish – *lios, cathair, ráth* – and which in English goes under the usual name of 'fort' or 'ring-fort' or – and more relevant to my exploration – 'fairy fort'.

Now, we know quite well from the archaeological record that these are the dwellings of anyone from a king down to what is known as a 'strong' farmer, and may date from any time from the Iron Age to the late medieval period. Yet the very fact that over 18,000 of these structures still exist scattered throughout the Irish landscape is due not to any great deference on our part for historic artefacts – and indeed, compared to, say, Scandinavians we have precious little of such deference – but rather to something else: there is a sense that these are fey and eerie places, where, quite frankly, if we are absolutely honest about it, the fairies live. I have known many a hard-headed countryman eager enough for more land who would be quite loath to interfere with such a fort, or to knock it down with his JCB. After all, we all know of so-and-so down the road who was tempted by greed to destroy a fort, and wasn't he found dead in his bed in the morning! And good enough for him! (Increasingly we are hearing of so-and-so down the road who destroyed a fort and was not found dead in his bed in the morning, which is much more worrying, as it means that nothing is holy any more and that the gods are finally powerless!)

The individual stories told about fairy forts are too numerous to detail, but taken together they produce a clear picture of the deepest hopes and fears of Irish people over generations. It is a picture of abductions of women after childbirth, and the exchange of wizened old changelings for perfectly healthy children. It is a picture that speaks of hidden gold discovered with the help of the fairies or gifts of music or poetry or healing which were taken from fairies through human acts of bravery, trickery or stealth, or in payment for a favour. It tells of milk that refuses to churn, doors which refuse to close, ghosts which refuse to lie down and animals which refuse to work. It tells of lights in the fort at night, of magic clouds which, landing on tufts of wild thyme and subsequently eaten by a favourite cow, produce pro-digious amounts of sweet-tasting milk.

One does not have to have any belief at all in the supernatural to see a wonderful and multi-layered collective psychodrama con-tinuously being remade and renewed. It is a rich linguistic vein for any writer to mine, and, as the most extensive and varied fairy accounts are in the Irish language, a veritable goldmine for the writer in Irish. I still remember the day it suddenly dawned on me that this rich heritage of stories which I had grown up with, but about which I felt a bit ashamed or uneasy, was perfectly credible intellectually. I still remember the poem I was writing when I made that discovery:

Fuadach (in *Féar Suaithinseach; Selected Poems / Rogha Danta*)

Do shiúl bean an leasa
isteach im' dhán.
Níor dhún sí doras ann.
Níor iarr sí cead.
Ní ligfeadh fios mo bhéasa dhom
í a chur amach arís
is d'imríos cleas bhean an doichill uirthi,

dúirt:
'Fan má tá deithneas ort,
is ar ndóigh , tá.
Suigh suas chun na tine,
ith is ól do shá
ach dá mbeinnse id' thí-se
mar taoi-se im' thí-se
d'imeoinn abhaile
ach mar sin féin fan go lá' ...

Abduction (in *Selected Poems / Rogha Danta*)

The fairy woman walked
into my poem.
She closed no door.
She asked no by-your-leave.
Knowing my place
I did not tell her go,
I played the woman-of-no-welcomes trick
and said:
'What's your hurry, here's your hat.
Pull up to the fire,
eat and drink what you get —
but if I were in your house
as you are in my house
I'd go home straight away
but anyway, stay' ...

Trans. Michael Hartnett

If that day I saw a distant sea glistening on the horizon and
looked far out into its infinities, it was because I was standing on
the shoulders of giants, the collective energies of millennia of
oral tradition.

Don't get me wrong: I can be as empirical as the next person.
I grew up in a medical family; my favourite subjects in school
were science and geography; I can still spend hours pouring over
conventional maps. Indeed I was quite uppity as a teenager, all

puffed up with all my newfangled knowledge and scientific certainties, and remember once, to my now undying shame, laughing to scorn an old countryman who ventured to opine the existence of mermaids. Life, and an increasing knowledge of the complexities of the human soul, has knocked some of the stuffing out of me, and made me a lot more humble in the face of the great imponderables.

At around the same time that I dismissed the idea of mermaids, during a yearly spiritual retreat for school, I had a major public run-in with a Franciscan priest on the subject of angels. He believed in them, I didn't, and the day after some altercation had occurred between us he read out from the altar in Latin that according to some Church council or other back in the year dot, anyone who didn't believe in angels *anathema sit*. I had enough Latin to know I wasn't wanted, and walked out, which caused a veritable storm in a teacup in the more-than-slightly-hysterical emotionally over-heated hothouse which was our all-girls' boarding school. The irony is that now, thirty years further down the road, the only things I believe in and am really interested in are angels and spirits and demons and merpeople and the narratives we have invented for them, a great collective narrative which confounds and transcends the limitations of the ego-envelope. We wrap it round us like a comforter as our souls shiver amidst the frosty vistas of scientific veritudes. It may all be vanity of vanities, another manifestation of the Hindu *maya*, I admit, but it is a solace nonetheless.

All cosmologies are ultimately confessional; what is sacred to one person may well be anathema to another. Like homing pigeons, we gravitate towards the narratives and landscapes that best fulfill our feelings for home, and that most fulfill our deepest psychic needs. Thus the particular repertoire of every folk-singer or *seanchaí* (storyteller) is not just an accidental accumulation, but answers to some inner valencies in both the performer and his/her audience. I can see now that by honing in on a particular well in my poem, I actually gave away much more about my own deepest realities than if I had been more overtly confessional. This is also an Irish tradition, if you like, so that there is more going on with my little broken doll than I knew myself when I wrote it:

... Tiocfaidh an spideog bhroinndearg
de mhuintir Shúilleabheáin is lena heireabaillín
déanfaidh sí leacht meala de uiscí uachtair an tobair
is leacht fola den íochtar, fós ní bheidh corraí asat.
Taoi teanntaithe go síoraí ins an láib , do mhuineál tachtaithe
le sreanganna lobelia. Chím do mhílí ag stánadh orm
gan tlás as gach poll snámha, as gach lochán, Ophelia.

... The red-breasted robin
of the Sullivans will come to transform
the surface to honey with her quick tail,
churn the depths to blood, but you don't move.
Bemired, your neck strangled with lobelias,
I see your pallor staring starkly back at me
from every swimming hole, from every pool, Ophelia.

Trans. John Montague

Thus I would be the first to admit that there is a strong element of my own personal pathology behind the stories that the landscape tells to me, or rather the stories that I have been prepared to hear from it. Nevertheless, if I constantly aver to a barely submerged female presence palpably shimmering throughout the landscape of Corcha Dhuibhne, the Dingle Peninsula, I like to think that it is not just a question of personal pathology alone, but of something bigger and more collective that I am picking up on my antennae, some cultural phenomenon beyond myself.

And the stories are there to prove it. The landscape of Corcha Dhuibhne (literally 'the land of the seed of the Goddess Dovinia') is *cailleach* country: the great personage of the *cailleach* or 'hag' haunts Corcha Dhuibhne as truly as the ghost of the murdered Banquo does Macbeth, or as the phantom of his father pursues the hapless Hamlet. Many are the stories of an old *cailleach* – whether called Mór, Mish or the Hag of Dingle – and her various manoeuvres and devices, her manifestations and avatars. Mountains are called after her, and high cliffs and headlands; other places reflect links with other of her manifestations. This shadowy presence is a distant mother of the gods who functions in the Celtic pantheon a bit like Durga does in Hindu cosmology. She is present in the three great queens of the Tuatha De Danann, who when vanquished in a battle at the foot of Slieve Mish consented to marry the leaders of the Celtic Milesians then invading Ireland, on condition that the country be called after them, Banba, Fodhla and Éire. These are still the names that the whole country goes by in Irish and the last one is to be found unchanged to this day even on our stamps, so old as to be a cognate with the Greek 'Hera', which is first found written in the Linear-B script of the ancient Minoans. Not for us the relative neologism of the Latin name for the neighbouring island, 'Britannia', thank you very much. We're talking 'UR-ur-ur' stuff here.

This female goddess figure is still venerated to this day in barely Christianised forms as the patron saints of the different parishes, like St Catherine in Ventry, or St Gobnait in neighbouring Dunquin. She also takes the form of the eponymous mother goddess of sovereignty, Mór of Munster, who is associated with many local placenames. The boat-launching site for the Blasket Islands, Faill Mhóire, is called after her, as is Dunmore Head (Dún Mhóire), the most westerly headland in Europe. She is reputedly buried at Tigh Mhóire, or Mór's House, in Dunquin, and indeed the whole parish here is often referred to jocularly as *bundún Mhóire* ('Mór's backside'), which is considered a term of pride and honour by the local people, notwithstanding the jibes that it entails. Many stories are told locally about Mór, and when I began writing poetry seriously in my late teens, it is hardly surprising that she walked unannounced and unasked for into my life and into my work without so much as a by-your-leave.

And this female presence is frequently associated with drownings. Thus the stunning Sybil Head is purportedly named after a certain Sybil Lynch, one of the famous tribe of that name in Galway city. She is said to have fallen in love with the young hero Pierce Ferriter, and the young couple eloped aboard his boat to his castle in Doon Point. They were pursued by her father and his soldiers who besieged the castle. During the siege Pierce hid

Sybil in a cave beneath the cliff for safety, but when the fight was finally over, and the two sides reconciled, they found to their horror that a particularly high tide had swept through the cave, drowning the girl.

Also most of the lakes in the area have accrued stories of drowned women; in Abhnascáil Lake she is the eponymous Scál, who threw herself in when she heard her champion Cúchulainn give out a roar of pain in his battle with the giant of Knock-mulanane. Cúchulainn finally won the battle, but Scál was already drowned at this stage. On the Flanks of Mount Brandon there is Loch na Mná, named for an anonymous woman, while beneath Loch Geal lies the legendary female monster The Carbuncle, who once in every seven years rises up at night and lights up the whole surrounding countryside as it shakes its scales down. The Carbuncle makes one of her rare appearances in a poem of mine, inspired by a visit to her lake and the image of her effect:

From Ag Tiomáint Siar (in *Feis; Pharaoh's Daughter*)

Inniu tá solas ar Loch Geal
á lasadh suas mar a dheineann an Cearabuncal
uair gach seachtú bliain nuair a éiríonn seal
aníos go huachtar na loiche is croitheann
brat gainní dhi. Bailíonn
muintir na háite na sliogáin abhann seo mar bhia.

From Driving West (in *Pharaoh's Daughter*)

Loch Geal bedazzles me today, as when,
each seventh year, the great Carbuncle
heaves up from the deep and shoulders
into air to slough her scales – freshwater
shellfish that the people gather.

Trans. Michael Coady

Whatever about her rising to the surface, there remains a question as to why she inhabits the depths. A story which gives us some clue to why this female presence became submerged is that of St Cúan and the monster that lived in Loch Cráillí. The Saint inveigled this female serpent to give him respite to make a sick-call near the lake and to stay under a huge cauldron 'go Lá an Luain'. This the serpent took, at its face value, to mean 'until Monday', but St Cúan, his mission of mercy accomplished, maintained that he had meant the phrase to hold its figurative meaning, 'until Doomsday', and so the mythical beast was bound by her own word until the end of time. A rather mean and underhand trick, no doubt, and a telling folk-comment on the sometimes rather dubious behavior of saints.

My favourite submerged monster tale of all, though, belongs to Loch a'Dúin, a lake near the Connor Pass, which takes its name from the Iron Age fort that runs across a little island in its centre. Seemingly the youthful hero Fionn Mac Cumhail was running from some enemies with his old and enfeebled foster-mother on his shoulders. Carried away by the exuberance of youth he ran so fast that the action of the wind wore away his poor fosterer, and when he looked up all that was left of her were the two shinbones he was still holding. Panic-stricken, he threw the shinbones into this lake, but there was a small worm in a cavity in one of the bones, and it grew and grew to enormous proportions, arising out of the lake one day to become his nemesis. This story surely cries out for interpretation, and would grant any Jungian analyst a veritable field day.

There is another story about a magical cow, the Glas Gaibh-neach, who could produce an inexhaustible supply of milk and was reputed to be able to fill any vessel that was put under her, and did so, until a mischievous woman placed a sieve under her and milked her into it. All day long she gave and gave, but at last she looked around, and seeing her own milk flowing away in rivulets, the great cow raised her head, and gave three great lows. At this all the other cattle in the area which were her prodigious progeny followed her into the sea, never to be seen again.

I had a gaggle of giggling five-year-olds in the back of the car recently – my youngest daughter and various cousins and friends. When they were beginning to get a bit fractious I told them this very story. Handily enough, the props were all around me in the countryside we were driving through: 'And do you see those two big standing stones over there? Well, that is where the Glas Gaibhneach used to go in the evening to check whether or not she had enough grass eaten. If her tummy touched both of the stones when she walked through them, then she felt she had eaten enough.'

Of course, there is always a sceptical member in every audience: 'And what happened if she hadn't eaten enough?'

'Oh well, then she headed off to that valley you see over there on your right – it is still called after her, Macha na Bó, the Summer Pasture of the Great Cow – and she ate her fill there until morning.'

The little sceptical voice was still not finished with me: 'But why did that stupid woman put a sieve under her in the first place?'

I was just about to deliver a lecture on sustainable growth, on the eternal cupidity of human nature, on the degradation of the environment around us because of over-grazing by sheep numbers boosted by ill-considered EEC headage-grants. I had just taken a deep breath and was about to launch into an immortal peroration when another little five-year-old voice piped up:

'The reason, you silly you, she put the sieve under the cow was because she was spoiled rotten, that's why!'

Out of the mouths of the babes. I couldn't have put it better myself. One more tiny environmentalist in the making, and hopefully, too, a future adept at *dinnsheanchas*. The great wave that swept over the Glas Gaibhneach as she disappeared into the sea is waiting for us everywhere. It is the wave of forgetfulness and unconsciousness, of denial and repression. Corcha Dhuibhne is important to me in no small part because here at least it is named and commented on, objectified in myth and folk-story. If not quite 'the return of the repressed' of Freudian orthodoxy, it is at least a marker of buried treasure, and a reminder of psychic depths, of the holy wells within us.

The Field Day Anthology of Irish Women's Writing, Introduction: Contemporary Poetry[1]

It has become a commonplace to state that one of the most salient features of Irish poetry in the last few years has been the emergence of women's voices, not as exceptional, once-off or dog-standing-on-its-hindlegs-cases, but as a collective movement. Of course many women in Ireland have written poetry in the past, but more often than not they used verse as a vehicle for ideological or political stances, whether as rabid Nationalists or as avid Unionists, which has left them rather adrift from the central currents of poetry in the twentieth century. Thus names like Speranza (Lady Wilde), Moira O'Neill, Blanaid Salkeld and Alice Milligan have faded from the main arena of Irish poetry in our time, leaving it aggressively male. In view of what Eavan Boland has called 'a different magnetic field' created by the presence of women's voices in poetry, the question you most often hear is 'Yes, women are writing a lot of poetry now, but is it any good?' This question should be seen for the red herring and not-so-subtle put-down that it undoubtably is, but first of all we must understand where it is coming from.

There is a sense in which contemporary women poets in Ireland are judged on the basis of a revived misogynistic bardic 'club'. The earliest poets in Ireland were in many ways akin to the druids, or the priestly class of the pagan Celts, or rather have subsumed many of the druids' roles once the Celts had converted to Christianity. Although there are tantalising glimpses of female poets or 'ban-fhili' in the Old Irish period, we can say very little about their status, nor with the present state of scholarship do we dare to hazard a guess.

By the twelfth century, with the emergence of Middle and later Classical Irish, the men seem to have had it all sewn up, and the bardic schools were the equivalent of the universities of the time. The bards were the king-makers and breakers, the movers and shakers, the ideologues and political journalists, the medieval versions of today's 'spin-doctors'. Bríona Nic Dhiarmada, in an excellent article on women's discourse in Irish, cites Donncha Ó Corráin's trenchant exposé of the 'extremely political motives underpinning the whole corpus of Bardic poetry'. Needless to say, part of these 'political motives' seems to have been the exclusion of women from the bardic schools.

Whatever about their pretensions to political power, which has been usurped by both PR companies and mainline journalism, some of the other roles of the bards have been successfully resurrected by the male poets of our time, especially their claim to be makers and re-shapers of the past. Since anthologies of poetry are one of the most powerful means of shaping a literary tradition, the fact that so many recent anthologies edited by male poets have marginalised or excluded women is proof of a tone-deafness to, if not a vested interest against, the voices of women. As late as 1986, the editor of *New Oxford Book of Irish Verse*, Thomas Kinsella, didn't see fit to publish as much as one contemporary woman poet, although several established female members of the profession such as Máire Mhac an tSaoi, Eiléan Ní Chuilleanáin, Eavan Boland and Medbh McGuckian had each already published a corpus of work by that time which would have well warranted their inclusion. The only real woman poet in the whole book is Eibhlín Dubh Ní Chonaill, whom some would say represented no great threat anyway, because she was already safely two hundred years dead.

The very existence of the fourth volume of *The Field Day Anthology* registers an awareness of this imbalance, an awareness which is the result of some trenchant feminist criticism both in Ireland and abroad. While the absence of women's writing from the previous three volumes of the *Anthology* created major controversy, the absence of women at the editorial level was equally startlingly and disturbing; except in those areas of contemporary literature which now have many female practitioners, one of the most important being poetry, the original *Field Day* project lacked female editorial input. The present volume seeks to restore a balance. Thus while only three women were admitted to the 'Contemporary Irish Poetry' section of *Volume III*, and two women were allowed in 'Irish Writing, Prose Fiction and Poetry 1900–1988', giving a total of five women in all, there are over forty women selected in this section, and there could have been twice as many, were it not for lack of space.

Geraldine Meaney has successfully shown how the dominant myth for the Irish prose writer was either as the 'true son' of 'Mother Ireland', a view which has of late gone out of fashion, or more recently as the literary-subversive-in-exile best epitomised by Joyce. Meaney demonstrates that the present dominant (Joycean) form is every bit as sexist and masculinist as that which went before, as '[Joyce] too is a "son" escaping from the "nets" of "Mother" church, "Mother" Ireland and perhaps "Mother" tongue.' How much more pronounced is this in the case of poetry, the creation of which in our culture has conventionally been characterized as arising from the sublimation of pre-oedipal and archaic impulses that derive from the ubiquitous Muse? If that Muse, as Julia Kristeva persuasively argues, is indeed none other than the 'never to be again accessed body of the Mother', then we might question (with Kristeva) why only the male offspring has been granted a privileged relationship to that maternal body and, because of this alliance, granted as well a privileged relationship to poetic language. To grant the masculine poet a privileged (indeed an exclusive) relationship to the Feminine is to construct the poet as a matriarchal druid/priest, a construction that in Ireland in this century has been successfully resurrected and peddled with a certain aplomb, even in its less aggressive forms as 'Green Man', or acolyte of the Muse (such as the ubiquitous Sweeney figure of the 1980s). Ontologically, this oedipal model is not only masculinist and sexist, but it also fails to take into account its predication not on the so-called 'worship' of the Feminine but rather upon the suppression of the female in the very construction of 'masculine' (which is to say 'non-feminine') poetic identity.

A lot of poets and critics have bought into the poetic status quo at such a deep level of their being that they find any seismic rumblings or shifting of the ground rules unbearably threatening. The perceived shifting of intellectual goalposts which results from the trespassing of a large number of women's voices on the hallowed male sanctum of poetry is seen as a threat to being on the basic level of self-image. And when this primary narcissism is attacked, then WHAM, all hell breaks loose. All this lies behind the hysterical outbursts masquerading as literary criticism which have heralded the emergence of women's voices in poetry and to this very day lies behind the seemingly innocent question 'Yes, women are writing a lot of poetry nowadays, but is it any good?' I do not wish to suggest that because of their gender women necessarily have any privileged access to a so-called 'real' (semiotic) underside of symbolic discourse, nor do I think that the passage from woman to 'the Feminine' is in any way a straightforward one. What I am suggesting is that there is as yet a great existential void in Western discourse which might well be filled by women, to the enhancement of all.

I think it is safe to say that something is at work in women's poetry at the moment, a genuinely new phenomenon, nothing less than an attempt to create an alternative Logos which is inclusive of the Feminine at a fundamental level. This stands in opposition to the dominant Western discourse, which, right back since the days of Plato and the all-male Symposia, was exclusive of it, if not predicated on the downright absence of the Feminine. Just as a whole world-view changed in the Romantic period or even earlier in the Renaissance to accommodate previously unknown and unthinkable realities, so now, by the sheer volume and quality of the engagement of women with poetry, is the standard being changed again. That some should consider this the remit of philosophy and not of poetry is only a symptom of how deeply the malaise of dualism lies at the very roots of our being. A less exclusive *Weltanschauung* would allow a considerable area of overlap between these two disciplines and might admit that new concepts which are genuinely bubbling up from the seething mass of the creative unconscious are often imaged in art and poetry, and indeed in popular culture, before making it into rational consciousness.

It is my firm belief that such a major phenomenological shift is upon us, and that this is clearly evidenced by what is going on right now in women's poetry. It is unprecedented and radical and being pursued by women of enormous intellectual perspicacity who are regularly trivialised as 'begonia poets' or 'wallpaper writers' or, heaven help us, 'Earth Goddesses'. Eiléan Ní Chuilleanáin has already imaged this phenomenon most powerfully as Pygmalion's statue coming to life. The image of the Feminine, which in Western discourse was until now artificially constructed and man-made, takes on a life of her own which is powerful and comprehensive and, with Medusa-like locks, arises out of the natural matrix where 'a green leaf of language comes twisting out of her mouth'. It is a powerful image of an energy on the move which is daunting and exciting to partake in and to witness.

And I think we are still only at the beginning. One of the decisions that has most broken my heart was the halving of my original selection for this volume. Another one was the need to limit the poems to material that has already been printed in book form, rather than hunted down in literary magazines or from manuscripts. This brought me slap up against what Ann Owens Weekes in her *Attic Guide to Irish Women Writers* has called half-laughingly 'the pooka in the publishing house', some unrecognised force which devours manuscripts instead of publishing them. Many writers of either gender will recognise the phenomenon, but the fact that most Irish publishers of poetry – with the exception of Attic Press, Salmon Press and the (now defunct) Arlene House – are run by men may have something to do with the fact that I found myself reading a lot of extra-ordinary manuscripts by women which really should have been published years ago. Among those whose work has been unaccountably held up I would mention Máiréad Byrne, Ruth Hooley, Eilís Ní Dhuibhne and Joan Trodden Keefe, who now lives in California but for all that is an Irish woman poet of great power and artistic excellence. The fact that some of these manuscripts are finally going to see the light of day and that publishing dates are at last materialising is of no help to me now as I finalise my selection, but rather underlines how much Irish women's poetry is in a state of flux and that we are at the start, rather than in the middle or the end, of a specific phenomenon.

But just in case some readers might think I am exaggerating the problems that women poets have had to contend with in the general publishing 'ambience' in Ireland, let me quote a little from a *comhrá* between Medbh McGuckian, Laura O'Connor and myself published in *The Southern Review*, where Medbh describes the kind of stratagems she had to resort to in her first effort to get into print.

> MMcG: Others are being published now, but I was the only one who managed to by-pass the early pamphlet stage. The by-passing was amazing. When I married I knew it was now or never and that what I had to do was win a competition. I hate competitions and judging things and even this kind of thing. I did it so clinically. I sent away for the previous year's winners and saw that they liked narrative poems of about forty lines – it had to be substantial and to flitter about the place. I wrote three poems in this style and submitted them under a pseudonym and I won.
>
> NNíD: Why a pseudonym? Was it male or female?
>
> MMcG: It was female – Jean Fisher. But they assumed that I was a male pretending to be a woman. They couldn't believe I was six months pregnant when they came over with their cameras. The big thing about it was that a well-known literary figure came second to me, and they rearranged the prize money so that I got less and he got more. I didn't care. I was pregnant and I had won this. But the *TLS* cared. They created a huge fuss for weeks, wanting to know whether my prize money was cut from £1,000 to £500 because I was Irish, or Catholic, or a woman, or unknown. And then British publishers began writing to me – Faber wrote and Charles Monteith was on the phone – and I really lapped it up. I ended getting published with Oxford.
>
> NNíD: Do you think it had to be short-circuited like that?
>
> MMcG: There was no other way. I would still not have a book out. I would still be sitting with my Emily Dickinson tome.

This may give people an idea of what women poets have been up against in Ireland, and the effects of what Geraldine Meaney describes:

> even where Irish literary and political culture opposes the dominant ideology of church and state it often merely re-presents the emblems and the structures of that ideology in more 'enchanting'

forms. One consequence of this is the cultural hegemony which the women's movement has found particularly difficult to shatter.

As have women poets. Maybe the 'pooka in the publishing house' is more than a joke after all!

I think there are other factors involved, however, rather than just the dogged recalcitrance of publishers, that explain why many women poets are often 'new' poets rather than 'young' poets. Societal expectations of women must play a part here, since women are often not allowed the space and time for themselves which is a *sine qua non* of the artistic process. The Victorian 'Angel in the House' whose demise was essential to women's creativity is still awarded pride of place in the Irish Constitution. Thus you will find women like Deirdre Brennan or Aine Miller, who have begun to write when their children were entirely, or nearly, grown up, or Máire Mhac an tSaoi, whose poetic output decreased considerably for a period following her relatively late marriage. A poignant instance of the kind of intense familial and societal expectation that weighs upon women in Ireland is provided by the woman at a writing workshop somewhere in the Irish Midlands who told Eavan Boland that she wouldn't like her neighbours to know she was a poet 'because then they would think I didn't clean my windows'. The fact that in the intense interiority which is part of the poetic process you may have to spend months and even years just looking out the windows, rather than cleaning them, would not be seen in Ireland for the hard and exacting inner work that it is, but rather as an excuse for evasion of domestic duties. It often takes a while for a young personality to emerge from under the avalanche of such expectations, and to stake out the kind of interior freedom which is necessary for poetry to happen, a decided *non serviam* which accepts a certain level of domestic chaos as a small price to pay for the joys of creativity.

And there may be something else also at work, subtle processes which have very little to do with domesticity as such, but have more to do with a genuine difference in the way that women relate to the Symbolic, and the Logos, to which I alluded earlier. I cite the American poet Amy Clampitt as an example of someone who, unencumbered by the time-consuming drudgery of children and housework, still did not start writing until well into her forties, published in her fifties and gained well-deserved renown in her sixties. Some would say that this could be explained in terms of the lack of value afforded to women writers, the lack of encouragement given to young girls, but I have a hunch that something even more fundamental is at work. Whatever the reason, however, it is already clear that the artistic trajectory of the woman poet is often quite different from that of her male counterpart, who often peaks at quite a young age, sometimes in his twenties. Thus you often have a proliferation of young male poets-about-town, a proliferation unechoed among women, the young 'star' being the exception that proves the rule, rather than the general pattern.

As it is early days yet, I would deem it hubristic in the extreme to presume to delineate in any great detail the thematics of a general psychic movement that is still in its infancy. All description tends, by a yet unnamed law of natural momentum, to veer towards prescription and therefore eventually towards proscription, and I have a personal horror of the kind of critical theory that imposes itself on the literature it purports to deal with, and cuts and chops it to suit ideological considerations, rather than looking closely and sympathetically at the literature being written and then proceeding from there. Nevertheless, certain themes have made themselves present already in women's poetry.

I have to admit at this stage that I have personally very little patience with the 'Here-I-am-looking-at-peas-falling-off-the plate' type of poem, and find that the domestic, *per se*, holds little attraction for me. I insist that filling the dishwasher is often just that, and is not necessarily always imbued with the numinosity that would turn it into a quasi-sacramental act, or the subject of a poem. I think that it is when the mythical and eternal intersect with the domestic, transfixing something as simple as lighting a fire and transforming it into a genuine symbol of metaphysical significance, that poems ensue. This frequently occurs in the present material, where the house itself, or domestic space, works as an image of the psyche in a way that is less usual for men. I would cite Medbh McGuckian's work as perhaps the most thorough example of this, where the macrocosm of the domestic space acts as a sounding chamber for the microcosm of the poet's psyche, and where the outer and the inner worlds interpenetrate through an ego-boundary so permeable and thin that it hardly seems to be there at all. The image of the house also has particular significance in the work of Caitlín Maude, where its destruction in 'Treall' transforms into an image of self-destructive tendencies and where in 'Caoineadh na Mná Tí' it is the vulnerable container for the *'loinnir fhiain'* or 'wild glare' of inspiration which, unfortunately, due to her untimely death, was not to be transformed into a *'solas sámh'* or 'tranquil light'. Eiléan Ní Chuilleanáin also has a fidelity to the uniqueness and mystery of our most ordinary perceptions, as has Moya Cannon, though in her case the 'objective correlative' of the inner world is more often or not the natural world beyond the enclosure of the domestic, especially the wild and desolate landscapes of the west of Ireland.

Another not so surprising subject which surfaces again and again is that of blood and guts. Maybe women are the supreme realists, and do not shy away from the nitty-gritties which underlie our very existence; I think it would be hard to better the description of butchering animals described by Catherine Byron in 'This was Halal' or by Rita Kelly in 'The Patriarch', while the tiniest details of the result of such activity resound with untold fascination and dread in Eiléan Ní Chuilleanáin's 'Street':

> Her shoes paired on the bottom step,
> Each tread marked with the red crescent
> her bare heels left, fading to faintest at the top.

Poetry is often the inscribing of the forbidden or taboo; such inscribing is done most powerfully by both Mary Dorcey and Anne Le Marquand Hartigan. The shibbolethic emblems of Irish nationalism are taken on with gusto by Eavan Boland in a poem such as 'Mise Éire', which is a direct answer to Padraig Pearse's evocation of the Hag/*Spéirbhean* as the personification of Ireland. His rather smug excoriation of the ordinary people as *'a clann féin a dhíol a máthair'* – the children who sold their own mother – is more than counterbalanced by Boland's precise evocation of what it was like to be the bought and sold woman of a captive nation. In other poems such as 'The Achill Woman' and 'That the Science of Cartography is Limited', the Great Famine – a momentous event in Irish history which we have dealt with, on the whole, with a singular failure of the imagination – becomes the focus of a quiet and unhurried deliberation on pain and tragedy, horror and denial.

The realities of daily life in present-day Ireland are sharply and acutely focused by Rita Ann Higgins, while myth, fable and fairytale combine to give the work of Roz Cowman an eerie and disconcerting resonance. An early life in an inner-city Dublin tenement is central to the work of Paula Meehan, but she also trawls through world mythology and the oblique techniques of the Eastern European poets to create a reality which is fierce and uncompromising and very often genuinely frightening. A faultless command of the demotic and vernacular registers of English is another feature of her work.

This successful transposition of the spoken voice into writing without loss of any of its inherent strengths or spon- taneity – something which has often been characterised as being as difficult to achieve as trying to pin a live butterfly to a page – is a feature of many of the poems I have chosen, from Catherine Byron's powerful 'Shears' and heart-breaking 'The Black and Tans deliver her cousin's son' to Roz Cowman's searing 'Shame', Rita Ann Higgins' hilarious 'Misogynist', and Eiléan Ní Chuilleanáin's mysterious 'The Informant'. The prime ven- triloquist of us all is perhaps Julie O'Callaghan, whose breathless monologues evince a black humour and wicked satirical bent not entirely artlessly concealed by the *faux-naïf* manner of their delivery, and which is perhaps best exemplified by the ending of a poem called 'Auschwitz':

I took a few snapshots and said
You're gonna be murdered if you don't get out
of that rotten old gas oven.

Mary O'Donnell writes movingly both of childlessness and of children, and brings a mythic dimension to the subject of motherhood, though this is not by any manner of means her only subject, while Clairr O'Connor brings a high level of literary self-consciousness to her understanding of women writers. Mary O'Malley's concerns are historical and tribal and engage with the general problem of language shift that is endemic to this island, but a particular problem for women:

> ... I thought this graceful foreign tongue
> was only meant for men –
> all right for the likes of Coleridge
> but it gave me unpleasant dreams.

This again may be as a result of personal preference, but it seems to me that the varied yet decidedly strong voices are already the principle achievement of Irish women poets.

When I agreed to make this selection, it was in full knowledge that it would become a poisoned cup incapable of pleasing anybody, but because I am bilingual (though not a bilingual poet) I felt I was qualified to deal equally competently with both Irish and English. This seemed important in view of the double marginalisation of women poets writing in Irish, on the grounds of both gender and minority language, and in view of the disgraceful under-representation of the Irish language in the previous volumes of *The Field Day Anthology*. Máirín Nic Eoin has pointed out that Seamus Deane's broad definition of literature in the general introduction – 'We avoid the narrow sense of the word literature, extending it to cover various other kinds of writing, especially political speeches, pamphlets and analyses' – applies only to English-language material. Therefore it seemed important to me that Irish should be put on an equal footing with English, rather than included as token 'exotica' to be trundled out on ceremonial occasions like a piece of cultural furnishing, for all the world like something from the tomb of Tutankhamun. Most of the translations from Irish the poets undertook themselves, though I took it upon myself to translate the work of Caitlín Maude (deceased). Some of the poets are bilingual writers and equally at home in either language, while others aren't, and it is important to emphasise that the translations are just that, translations, and any quality of strangeness results from the fact that the prosody of Irish differs from English in fundamental ways. One of the major differences is that the Irish language has an abomination of end-rhymes; another is its strong assonantal quality and the prevalence of internal rhyming, which gives an aural texture to the verse in many ways more akin to that of Russian rather than that of today's English. Therefore Máire Mhac an tSaoi's 'A fhir dár fhulaingíos …', though written in a bardic metre whose heyday was in the Middle Ages and whose usage fell off after the sixteenth century, still manages to be a deeply felt and moving poem, the very formality of which is an intrinsic part of its message of ritual renunciation. Likewise Máire Aine Nic Ghearailt's 'Os Tú a Mheall' is written in a traditional form of 'Meadracht an Amhráin' or the Song Metre, which, though it translates into English in a rather archaic fashion, is perfectly suitable in Irish to the smooth, majestic sweep of the moon that is the theme of the poem. Biddy Jenkinson, for reasons which I accept as entirely valid, refuses to have her poems translated into English, though I have taken the liberty of glossing them for the sake of those who have a moderate or working knowledge of the language but might not be entirely *au fait* with her wide-ranging and erudite references. Eithne Stronge is a bilingual poet and self-translator, but the literary worlds of Irish and English were so severely divorced from one another that nobody noticed at the time of publication that her first book in Irish, *Cirt Oibre*, was a translation of poems already published previously in English in *Sarah, in Passing*, and she never made allusion to that fact, either. While it is commonplace and laudable for bilingual poets to translate their own work, it still does seem to me that the genesis of a poem is undoubtably and perforcedly in one language or the other, and that one version is the original of the poem and the other necessarily the translation. Therefore, of these earlier poems of Eithne Strong's, I have chosen the English versions as more probably the originals. This problem does not arise in her later work, where the English translations, of which I have readily availed, are announced as such in various books.

The main thrust of this selection was made with an initial cut-off deadline of autumn 1993, with delays allowing for particularly good poems from 1994 to be 'snuck' in. Subsequent more serious delays in publication have allowed me to include a selection from the most important volumes published until autumn 1997. The two outstanding talents to emerge in this period have been Vona Groarke and Kerry Hardie, the latter especially bursting upon the Irish poetic world Athena-like, already full grown and fully armed. Her first volume *A Furious Place* is as good and better than many with a much more tortuous publishing history and bodes well not just for her own future, but for the state of women's poetry in general.

Finally, although so called 'verse-libre' may be seen in retrospect as the greatest gift of the twentieth century to poetry in general and as an essential stage of its development in many languages, it is not the be all and end all and definitely not an end in itself. A broad sweep of technical expertise is to be welcomed in any body of literary work. It is therefore delightful to be able to finish my selection with two poems by Enda Wyley which show a formal daring which is the result of hard work and technical application, as well as genuine inspiration, and which bode well both for her own development and for that of women's poetry.

I look forward immensely to the imminent publication of many manuscripts and of work still only available in magazine outlets and that I have therefore been unable to include in this selection. On the evidence of what is being written, it seems that many people produce their best work once they have got their first book behind them. It is as if after producing a book a radical reconceptualisation of one's work takes place, along with a (re)consideration of what it might mean to spend a lifetime working at poetry. This often leads to a more thorough commitment to the art, which in turn opens up the possibilities of enormous technical and thematic growth. As this necessary developmental process occurs in woman after woman it becomes obvious that women's poetry in Ireland is just about to break into full flower. It is a late flowering, but nonetheless a spectacular one.

1 Ní Dhomhnaill's essay proper is preceded by the following paragraph in *The Field Day Anthology of Irish Women's Writing*: 'When I first took it upon myself to make this selection, back in the early 1990s, I did so out of a sense of moral outrage at the way women poets were being treated in Ireland. It seemed obvious to me that the rules of the game for men and women poets were different. There was not an even playing field. Even at that stage the number of women who had written books of poetry was quite large and getting larger by the day. Because of the limitations of space in an anthology, and especially when only one further volume of *The Field Day Anthology* was envisaged, I was able to include only half the poets I would have liked. But when I had finished the introduction in 1994 I felt I had done my best to introduce as many poets as I could, given the space constraints. This introduction I include here, because I still stand by everything I said in it at the time, though now the situation has changed so much that in reality it could best considered a historical document. In 1997 I updated the selection, to keep in line with the changing situation. To keep the section as inclusive as possible I mainly added new poets, rather than increasing the selection of poems by authors I had already chosen. The current expanded section again makes way for new voices and is actually the documentation of a completely new poetry scene. In the last two years alone an average of one book of poetry a week has been rolling off the presses. The situation described in my introduction has been changed, changed utterly, yet I include it, since it sets out in great detail some of the reasons for the relative neglect of Irish women's poetry that existed until quite recently.'

Seal Sa Domhnan Thoir: Sojourn in the Eastern World

When I was a very small child in the West Kerry Gaeltacht, one of my great joys was listening to wondertales in which the hero had to make a perilous journey to *an Domhnan Thoir*, 'the Eastern World', usually to bring back some pearl or other without price. Whether a princess or 'the silver apples of the moon, the golden apples of the sun', a feather from a golden bird or the water of eternal life from the 'well that is at the world's end', these marvels all came from *an Domhnan Thoir*. It was as if coming from Ireland — the Western World or the Hesperides — our own apples were considered ordinary or garden or commonplace. On the principle that too much West is East, the source and site of all marvels and wonders was its opposite, the Eastern World. It has always seemed obvious to me that J.M. Synge's *Playboy of the Western World* was called such to emphasise an ironic interplay with the Eastern World of the Gaeltacht storytellers. Little did I know at the time that this very same Eastern World would play host to me for a very important and influential five years of my young adult life. It is a world in which I have kept a foothold ever since.

Years ago an applied linguist informed me that it would be hard to come across two languages that were more phonetically alike and morphologically more different than Turkish and Irish. This underlined my own deepest suspicions, though I never would have been able to put it so precisely. I had a real struggle to learn Turkish, my first non-Indo-European language, and even today my fluency depends greatly on how recently we have spent some time in the country. But there was a time when linguistically

I used to pass for an *Alamanli*, a Turk who had grown up in Germany. I remember once in Ankara, in the bazaar area of Cikrikcilar Yokusu, I demurred from such an appellation, saying that I was actually an out-and-out *gavur*, or heathen, only to find that the material I was buying suddenly doubled in price. That was the last time I looked a gift horse in the mouth, so to speak.

I distinctly remember the very first sentence I made in Turkish. I went to Turkey with my husband Dogan in October 1974 when I was six months pregnant with my first child. We travelled on the Orient Express. This was not the pampered, refurbished train of luxury tourism, but a higgledy-piggledy, mish-mash collection of run-down wagons which started off at various European cities like Paris and Munich and joined up in Belgrade before chugging their way slowly through the Balkans to the final destination of Sirkeci Station in Istanbul. As a train it was very rudimentary. It had no restaurant car, no opportunity for getting food of any sort and if it hadn't been for the *yolluk*, or travel provisions, including two cooked chickens and *bosnak boreghi*, a Bosnian-style pastry, given to us by my sister-in-law in Zurich, we would have been in a bad way.

At Belgrade I was left looking after the luggage while my husband went off to organise a couchette or wagon-lit for the rest of the journey. The carriage in which I was stranded was shunted back and forth umpteen times, sometimes an alarming distance away. Some Turkish workers spoke to me, asking what was up. I could recognise it was Turkish, but otherwise did not understand a word. But necessity being the mother, etc., I came out with 'Kocam yakinda gelecegim diyerek, gitti gelmedi,' or 'Saying he would come back soon, my husband went away and hasn't come back yet.' The Turkish sentence has an economy of words and an elegance which are due to the language being agglutinative, using participles, gerundives and gerunds where an Indo-European language would use subjunctives and relative clauses. *Kocam yakinda gelecgim diyerek, gitti gelmedi.* This sentence drew forth a torrent of Turkish. Little did they realise how much I was at a loss. It would take at least five years of living in Turkey before I could make a sentence like that again with a similar insouciance.

During those five years, the person who had the greatest influence on me and who was my chief motivator in learning Turkish was my father-in-law, Suleyman Leflef. He was a great character, a genuine 'original'. He had been the only male left at home when the new surname law was promulgated in the 1920s, and when he went to register a name for the family under the law, he just took the ending -*oghullari*, 'sons of', off the long-standing family nickname, and so their surname became *Leflef*. When his older brothers came back from military service, they were very annoyed with him, saying 'Why didn't you take the chance to give us a heroic name like *Safkan* [pure blood] or *Özturk* [real Turk] or *Demirel* [iron hand] or something like that,' just as everyone else had done. He demurred, saying that the name they had had for hundreds of years was good enough for him and should be good enough for them.

A former military officer, my father-in-law had never really enjoyed his years in the army. It was by default that he had ended up studying at Harbiye, the military academy still situated in his time in the famous Selimiye barracks on the Asian banks of the Bosporus, where Florence Nightingale had worked during the Crimean War. He had wanted to study at the Academy of Fine Arts, but did not have the necessary mathematics to be accepted, so instead he ended up at the military academy. I once saw his graduation diploma, where he got top marks only in marksmanship and horsemanship. My father-in-law was only a *yuzbashi*, or centurion, when he was cashiered for having two wives.

Being Muslims, Turks are allowed up to four wives by their religion. Since the reforms in Turkey brought about by Kemal Ataturk in the 1920s, however, the secular, Westernised state had outlawed polygamy. My father-in-law was given the choice of giving up the second illegal – but religiously accepted – wife or being court-martialled. As a good Muslim he felt conscience-bound to keep the second wife, as she had done him no wrong; so, because of his religious scruples, he resigned his commission. An Ottoman to the end of his days, he actually had eight wives, though never more than two at a time. And this doesn't take into account the temporary marriages when he was an officer in the

Southeast, where a woman's brideprice would be raised in her next marriage for having been a wife, even on a temporary basis, to a high-status official, say an engineer or a military officer.

As I said, an Ottoman to his dying day, my father-in-law refused to call Ataturk by that name. He was perfectly prepared to give Ataturk the honorific appellation of *Gazi Pasha*, because he was just that: a great war hero (*gazi*) who survives (as opposed to a *sheyit* who dies a martyr's death), Ataturk was also a great *pasha*, or general. But my husband's father refused to call him Ataturk, 'father of the Turks'. This he considered presumptuous in the extreme: 'How could anyone call himself "father of the Turks" indeed! He is not my father.'

Not that my father-in-law had two good words to say for his own father, who had been a religious teacher, or *ulema*, in the local religious school, or *medrese*. He had also been a howling dervish, who with his fellow mystics would chant the holy phrase '*yahu*' for days on end until the whole building in which they sat began to shake. As a child, my father-in-law had once looked through a keyhole and seen his own father in a trance state. He had such a shock that – though he remained an orthodox Sunni Muslim and even was a *haci* because he had made the pilgrimage to Mecca – he had no time for any of the dervish or mystic orders (the *tarikatlar*). He looked askance at anything that would be considered radical or extremist or fundamentalist in any form. He also held it against his father that he had died young, leaving his widowed mother to bring up a family of six sons on her own. His father had been blond-haired and blue-eyed, with the particular cerulean blue eyes which are not as rare as might be expected in Middle Anatolia. My father-in-law was usually scathing about light-coloured people, saying that they had no stamina, but melted like candles in the summer heat.

In spite of this he took to me enormously. Quite a demon in his youth, he had mellowed considerably by the time we met. He was in his own words '*kurt kocayinca*', 'an old wolf', which refers to the proverb 'kurt kocayinca kopeklerin maskarasi olurmus', 'when the wolf gets old and thin, he becomes the laughing-stock of the dogs'. In some ways I was a kind of honorary man for him. He would call me out of the kitchen, saying 'Benim gelin mutfakta avratlarin icinde ne yapiyor?' ('What is my daughter-in-law doing in the kitchen amongst the womenfolk?'), using in ironic fashion the old-fashioned word *avrat* for women, which might be better translated as 'female slave'. Likewise he didn't like to see me reading books, thinking it was a waste of time: time which would be much better spent in pleasant conversation with himself.

So we would spend hours at a time talking to each other. When it was time for him to say his prayers, he went into the next room with his prayer rug, said his prayers and then came in again, and we continued the conversation where we had just left off. In the afternoons I would make for him his *gelin kahvesi*, the special coffee made by the lily-white hands of the new bride, and he would drink it with great pleasure, and we would continue speaking about everything under the sun.

Comparisons of stories and beliefs held by Christians and Muslims used to keep us going for a long time. I remember in particular the comparison of the two versions of the story of Abraham and Isaac, which are actually very similar. He never suggested that I should convert, thought once he set out to teach me the Arabic alphabet so that I could read the holy book, '*Koran-i-Kerim*'. After three days of wrestling with '*ayin*', '*kayin*' and I don't know what else, I proved to be a total eejit, and he decided that conversion was a grace not vouchsafed to me by Allah: I was fine as I was, one of the 'people of the book', *kitaplilardan*. As the *Incil*, or 'New Testament', and the *Tevreh*, or 'Torah', are considered holy books in Islam, the idea of conversion never arose again. After a few years I think I became in his eyes an honorary Muslim as well as an honorary man, and we got on together like a house on fire.

I remember one day one of his cronies named Berber Huseyn called in. I made *gelin kahvesi* in the usual small cups, and, as they sat there sipping it, I was an 'ear-guest' at their conversation, as the lovely Turkish expression for eavesdropping has it.

'She is very nice, for a heathen,' says Berber Huseyn.

'Ah yes, but you know those heathens aren't bad people at all,' says Suleyman Dede.

'Oh, don't I know? I have two sons in Germany amongst the

heathens, and according to them you couldn't find a straighter or more honest people on this earth.'

'If it weren't for the drink.'

'Yes, the alcoholic drink makes animals out of them. Animals entirely.'

'Yes, it is a real pity about the drink.'

This would have been amusing in itself even if it hadn't reminded me of similar conversations about Turkey I had had in Irish with Thomas Murphy, my aunt's husband, and his cronies in the Gaeltacht.

'And do you mean to tell me they don't take drink at all?'

'No. They think that drinking is a mortal sin. It is against their religion.'

'God, that's hard. They must be very straight people.'

'Oh yes they are.'

'And tell me this if ye tell me no more: is it true what they say that Muslims have more than one wife?'

'Yes, sometimes they have more than one wife. Their religion allows them to have four.'

'Four wives. That's awful, they must make right animals of themselves to even think of having four wives.'

Same difference. *Plus ça change.* The sort of thing that has always made me aware of the fact that so many things, whether ideas of dirt and pollution or ideas of inward and outward, edible and inedible, sacred and secular, are just lines that are drawn in a way that is highly culture-bound and pretty arbitrary, if not gratuitous altogether. All cultures draw these lines; it's just that they draw them at slightly different places. Living *à la turca* for five years at an early age made me something akin to an anthropologist. It was sharpened by feeling myself at home in a language so entirely different to Irish and, paradoxically, helped me focus more than ever on Irish. Being outside an English-speaking world for so long also made me aware of my other mother-language. This all came to me from learning Turkish.

The language that Suleyman Dede taught me was Turkish that was colloquial, slightly old-fashioned and basically Middle Anatolian, rather than the more precious language spoken in

Istanbul. Just as in Gaeltacht Irish, this is a language which has a large stock of proverbs and formulaic phrases. Suleyman Dede's Turkish is located somewhere between the written language and the spoken, perhaps with more emphasis on the spoken. This is best illustrated by its marked reliance on context. Who says what and to whom is very important, because of the very construction of the language, where a single word may have an autonomous function to an extent unknown to us. For instance, *Irlandalilastira-madiklarimizdanmisiniz*, which means 'are you one of those whom we could not turn into an Irish person?' Unlike the amazingly long words in German, which are really chains of words, this is one single word with the function and meaning of a whole sentence.

Nevertheless, in spite of the huge differences in syntax, I recognised something in the language that made me feel very much at home. Like the Gaeltacht Irish I had learned as a small child, the appropriate use of a key word from a well-known story or from a proverb can either clinch an argument or cause general hilarity. All one has to mention are the words *ahu gözler* or *sirma sacli*, 'almond eyes' or 'golden hair', and everyone knows you are referring to the apotropeaic over-praising of the dead, from the proverb 'Kör ölür ahu gozlu olur; kel ölür, simra sacli olur' ('When the blind man dies, they say that he had almond-like eyes; when the bald man dies, they say that he had golden hair'). This is a good example of a Turkish proverb in that it contains the highly characteristic parallelism and balanced structure of two complementary clauses. Also the two verbs *olur*, 'to be', and *ölür*, 'to die', have an alliterative and euphonic charm almost too strong to resist.

There are many proverbs contrasting 'one' and 'a thousand'. Rather than being attributable to Oriental exaggeration, these proverbs come about because of the closeness in sound between *bir*, the word for 'one', and *bin*, the word for 'a thousand'. Thus, 'one trouble is worth more than a thousand warnings' or 'a thousand worries do not pay a single debt'. I even found proverbs that were identical to each other in languages so different as Irish and Turkish – for example 'Dagh dagh kavusmaz; insana kavusir' ('Mountains do not come nearer to mountains, but men to men'), which in Irish is 'Casann na daoine ar a chéile, ach ní chasann na cnoic ar na sléibhte.'

Then there is the whole range of colloquial language which stems from the stories associated with Nasraddin Hodja. They say there really was a person by this name, and, according to the most reliable sources, he was born in 1208 in the Anatolian village of Hortu. He has become the delightful and inimitable personification of Turkish humour. He has also become an international celebrity, with his stories having been translated into many languages, including Russian and Chinese. His fame at home is assured, and many towns in Anatolia vie for the exclusive honour of being his birthplace. The Hodja stories have passed down to us chiefly by word of mouth, and wide knowledge of Nasraddin Hodja stories can be taken for granted among all Turks. He is the archetypal Turkish Everyman, and his down-to-earth humour and the sagacity of his repartee are redolent of the best of Turkish culture. His stories are so renowned that usually you only have to mention a key phrase from a story in an appropriate place in conversation to raise a laugh. By a process of metonymy, the audience supplies the rest of the story. And if somebody doesn't get it, well this is as good an opportunity as any to tell the story all over again from the start: 'Bir varmis, bir yokmus, bir gun Nasraddin Hodja ...' ('Once upon a time Nasraddin Hodja was walking along the road and ...)

Many stories about Nasraddin Hodja require some basic knowledge of Turkish life. One such story might very well be understood by an older generation of Irish people for whom 'DV' or 'Deo Volente', 'by God's will', would be a phrase that was written in every letter and that tripped readily off the tongue. In this story Nasraddin Hodja looks up at the sky one evening and says to his wife, 'Tomorrow morning, if the weather is fine, I will go out and work in my vineyard. If it is not fine, I will stay in and work at home.' 'Oh, Nasraddin Hodja,' says his wife, 'you mustn't forget to say "inshallah", "by the will of God".' 'Woman,' he says to her, 'it has nothing to do with the will of God. Either the day will be fine or it won't be fine.' Next morning when he woke up, the day was fine, so he hopped up on his donkey and set off for the vineyard. But on the way he was set upon by robbers who robbed him and beat him and then loaded up big loads on his back and

on that of his donkey and made them carry the loads all day. Late
that night his wife heard a very feeble knock at the door. '*Kim o?*'
she asked, 'who is there?' '*Benim,*' said a very weak voice, which she
recognised as her husband's, '*benim, inshallah*' ('It is I, by the will of
God'). He had learned his lesson the hard way.

During my five years in Turkey, I came under many literary
influences. According to Chinese sources, Turkish literature began
in the second century BC, but the first extant records are those of
the Orhon cuneiforms, generally dated to the eighth century AD
As the Turks moved westward, different branches of the language
came into existence. The most important is Caghatay, which
evolved its own literature quite separately from Ottoman. There
is also Oghuz, the forerunner of Modern Turkish: the most
notable work produced was *Dede Korkut Kitabi* (*The Book of Dede
Korkut*), which like the early Irish sagas has a prose narrative
punctuated with superb poetry insets. Ottoman literature began
in the early thirteenth century, with poets like Yunus Emre and
Esrefoglu soon founding a mystic tradition of considerable value
in Islamic culture. A riveting sample of this mystic tradition
voiced seven centuries ago comes in the following stanza from
Yunus Emre's poem titled 'Askin aldi bendin beni' ('Your love has
wrested me away from me'):

Askin aldi bendin beni
Bana seni gerek seni
Ben yanarim dün ü günü
Bana seni gerek seni.

Your love has wrested me away from me
You're the one I need, you're the one I crave
Day and night I burn, gripped by agony,
You're the one I need, you're the one I crave.

Trans. Halman

This tradition of syllabic folk poetry, much of it marked by a
mystic quality, was always sung to the poet's own accompaniment
on the stringed instrument called the *baglama* or *saz*. It has

continued to our own time, and competitions for extempore composition of folk poetry are still held.

Persian forms gradually began to exercise an influence on Ottoman poets, who gradually adopted and used them to create a new Turkish language now known as Osmanli. Poetry inspired by Persian forms began in the mid-sixteenth century, reaching its peak perhaps in the work of Nedim, the most prominent and the most Turkish poet of the *Lale Devri*, the 'Age of Tulips'. Westernisation started in the late nineteenth century, and the work of Ahmed Hasim and his contemporaries combines Persian metre with themes prompted by the French symbolists. The emergence of modern Turkey produced poetry far more aware of its local, popular roots. Poets turned to take up the syllabic metres of folk poetry, and the old Osmanli literary style gave way to the more direct language characteristic of most Western poetry.

In both Persian and Arabic, the literary language is poles apart from the colloquial language, but in Turkish, because of the extremely robust and widespread tradition of folk poetry, the language as it exists since the reforms of the 1920s is not so polarised. Most famous of the folk poets called *ashiks* (literally, 'lovers') of recent times is Ashik Veysel from Sivas province; following is a selection from 'Kara Toprek' ('The Black Earth'), perhaps his most famous composition:

Dost dost diye nice nicesine sarildim
benim sadik yârim kara topraktir
beyhude dolandim yâr, boşa yoroldum
benim sadik yârim kara topraktir.

I embraced so many, thinking them a friend
My true love is the black earth
In vain I wandered, exhausted myself for naught
My true love is the black earth.

The kind of poetry composed by Ashik Veysel became possible not only because of the depths of the folk tradition in Turkey, but also because of the work of several major Turkish poets of the twentieth century. Nazim Hikmet is one of four poets who brought Turkish poetry howling and screaming into the twentieth century. The other three – Melich Cevdet Anday, Oktay Refat and Orhan Veli – followed Nazim Hikmet, who was half a generation older than the others. He was a committed Communist, which meant that in the New Turkish Republic of Kemal Ataturk he spent many years in jail, finally absconding to Russia, where he died in the 1960s, with much of his poetry unavailable in his homeland until its full publication in 1965. What poetry was available prior to this was tremendously influential: Nazim Hikmet used a mixture of Vladomir Mayakovsky's loose lines and the patterns of Turkish folk poetry, developing a clear, fluid style where personal and political themes combine easily. When Melich Cevdet Anday, Oktay Refat and Orhan Veli began to write in the 1930s, they found in his poetry the existence of a new Turkish which would have enormous consequences for their own work.

Nazim Hikmet's influence is seen in Orhan Veli's colloquialism, which is radical in transcending the middle class from which he came and attacking conventional language. Orhan Veli's poetry features people who are low-level civil servants (many poor but few utterly dispossessed) coping with daily life. Surprisingly, however, there are few slang expressions in his work, that is to say, very little that belongs only to a subculture: his colloquialism is instead central to the language, a *classic* element of it, you might even say. In its pared-down naturalness and its selection of the most immediate cadences, it is also quite abstract. Despite the relative narrowness of his subject matter, his poetry remains fresh, continuously contemporary. In this respect he shares the virtues of major folk poets such as Yunus Emre, Pir Sultan Abdal and Karacaoglan; his relationship to the long tradition of folk poetry has been, surprisingly, often overlooked. Folk poetry is marked by repetitions, by rhymes and the repetition of lines at the ends of stanzas. Orhan Veli's work is also full of repetition and parallelisms, and while he doesn't use rhyme or refrain as does Nazim Hikmet, he often relies on lists or disguised lists. Such repetitions give his work its lyrical, contemplative tone, as seen in 'Istanbul'u Dinliyorum' ('I am Listening to Istanbul'):

Istanbul'u dinliyorum, gozlerim kapali
Önce hafiften bir ruzgar esiyor;
Yavas yavas sallaniyor
Yapraklar, agaçlarda,
Uzaklarda, cok uzaklarda,
Suçnlarin hic durmayan cingiraklari
Istanbul'u dinliyorum gozlerim kapali.

Istanbul'u dinliyorum, gozlerim kapali;
Kuçlar geçiyor, derken:
Yukseklerden, suru suru, ciglik, ciglik.
Aglar çekliyor dalyanlarda;
Bir kadinin suya degiyor ayaklari;
Istanbul'u dinliyorum, gozlerim kapali.

I am listening to Istanbul with my eyes closed.
First a breeze is blowing
And leaves swaying
Slowly on the trees;
Far, far away the bells of the
Water carriers ringing
I am listening to Istanbul with my eyes closed.

I am listening to Istanbul with my eyes closed.
A bird is passing by,
Birds are passing by, screaming, screaming,
Fish nets being withdrawn in fishing weirs,
A woman's toe dabbling in water,
I am listening to Istanbul with my eyes closed.

Trans. Nemet-Nejat

In November 1950 Orhan Veli Kanik died of a brain hae-
morrhage in Istanbul at the age of thirty-six; his last unfinished
poem, 'The Parade of Love', was found wrapped around his
toothbrush after his death. The type of modern poetry that he
pioneered has continued to develop and grow. Its most recent
excellent exponent is the young Kurdish woman Bejan Matur,
who, though Kurdish is her mother tongue, writes in Turkish. She

is doing for her generation what Orhan Veli did for his own and for all time: creating a whole new language of poetry.

Two other main strains of Turkish poetry affected me during my half-decade in Turkey: the mystic tradition of Mevlana Djellal a-Din Rumi, and the Osmanli tradition, written in Persian form, mostly as *gazesl* or *rubai's*, as the Turkish pronunciations of those forms go. Of particular interest to me at the time were the poems of Mevlana Djellal a-Din Rumi, so much so that I went by bus to Konya every December to watch the dancing dervishes of his religious order perform the *Sema*, the 'dance' of the whirling dervishes. In one poem he writes:

> Come, come, whoever you are
> Wonderer, worshipper, lover or leaving.
> It doesn't matter.
> Ours is not a caravan of despair.
> Come, even if you have broken your vow
> a thousand times
> Come, yet again, come, come.

Trans. Annemarie Schimmel

I took tremendous pleasure in my exposure to Turkish literature. Imagine my amazement and delight when a few years ago 'Toircheas I', a three-stanza poem of mine, was translated into one short and three long Turkish sentences, each sentence taking up almost a whole stanza. Similarly 'Ceist an Teangan' was translated into two complicated sentences. These two poems and fifteen or so others were translated during a week-long seminar on one of the Princes' Islands, Heybeli Adi, by a group led by the noted poet and translator Cevat Capan. After listening to all the different possible suggestions, Cevat Bey would keep his pen poised in mid-air until he was satisfied. Then, as I watched in amazement, he would come out with one perfectly enunciated, complicated, long agglutinative sentence which left me spellbound. I could appreciate enormously the verbal virtuosity involved but could never hope to match it myself.

Living in an almost hermetically sealed Turkish lifestyle for five years was the greatest inducement I could possibly have had for writing in Irish. Outside an English-language *mentalité*, I felt freed to deal with Irish on its own terms, free of the conflict between my two mother-languages that I often feel when in an English-speaking environment. The five years I spent in Turkey contributed greatly to my ending up as a poet writing in Irish. Strangely enough, losing myself in the delights of my new environment – in the carpets and kilims, in the handcrafts of all kinds, in Turkish classical music and calligraphy – I came to appreciate my own language more acutely.

In the beginning I had a hard dose of culture shock and let all things that reminded me of home fall into desuetude. I had a whole shelf of books in Irish – the 'classics', including Tomás Ó Criomhthain's *An tOileánach* (*The Islandman*) and Muiris Ó Súilleabháin's *Fiche Bliain ag Fás* (*Twenty Years A-Growing*) – but there were times early on when I looked at them like creatures from another dimension. I used to dust them occasionally and occasionally listen in the dark of night to Seán Ó Ríordáin and Máirtín Ó Direáin speaking their poems from the two Claddagh records I had brought with me. Their voices mixed with Arabic *illahis*, prayers like the once common 'ejaculations' of Catholicism, beaming from Riyadh on the radio in the depths of night. It was in such circumstances that I received a deep emotional shock and responded to it in the only way I knew how, by writing poetry in Irish, to help me deal with the acute separation anxiety I felt. Here is a verse from one of those poems, 'Bliain tar éis Imeachta', 'A Year after Your Leaving' (in *An Dealg Droighin*):

Tá na duilleoga ag titim
duilleoga móra crainn plána
ag titim ar rian do choise
mar ar shiúlais chugham tráthnóna.

The leaves are falling down,
broad leaves of the plane trees,
falling on the imprints of your footsteps
where you walked to see me of an afternoon.

Trans. Nuala Ní Dhomhnaill

The vast distance from my own culture helped me see things in a more objective way. I could see clearly the dysfunctional family – Irish style – in a way that I'm sure I could not have done closer up. The result was two poems, 'Athair' and 'Máthair' ('Father' and 'Mother'), which described the two sides of the same shilling, the Irish family where the father was mostly absent – an absentee father – and the mother was correspondingly too caught up in her children, living vicariously through them, for she could not go out to work because of the marriage ban.

Gradually I began to write more and more, and before long writing in Irish had become the core of my daily life in Turkey. I found that I didn't miss Ireland as such, and in fact in many ways I execrated it. But I began to feel that I was losing any fluency I might have had in the Irish language. The final result of that loss would have been devastating to me. There was only one thing for it: to get back home to the Gaeltacht and see if I could manage to live there.

I applied for an Arts Council bursary and got it. I was very driven: I broke up my Turkish household and decamped to West Kerry. Back in Ireland I managed to eke it out so that we could live in the West Kerry Gaeltacht for three years. When I finally had to move to Dublin, I was directed by Seosamh Ó Dálaigh, the famous folklore collector, to the collections of the Department of Folklore, University College Dublin. I discovered that I had fallen into a goldmine: this was the selfsame Irish that I had learned in the Gaeltacht in the 1950s, the selfsame language that had cured the extreme pain of separation from my family when I was a very small child. This was the language that was a balm to my soul. I wanted never to be without it again.

Gradually I began to see the artistic advantages that accrue from this ineffable material. Like modern Turkish poets who also turned to their folk traditions, I just go on and use this material, and sing praises that the modern folk material in Ireland is so rich and rare, with the early Irish material even richer still. I don't write folktales as such, but use the motifs in them to talk about the ghoulish spectres that haunt our modern times. I feel I have enough to write about in the Department of Folklore archives for as long as I live, and then some.

But all this was given to me because of my time in Turkey. If I brought nothing else home with me from that five years — and in truth, I brought much — I brought a keen appreciation of what it was like to live outside English, to live in a cultural space that was genuinely decolonised. The constant tug-of-war inside me between my two earliest languages had lessened somewhat. This gave me a great surge of energy and inspiration that was to last unabated for years. It was as if I had touched an inner tripswitch and released a level of language that I had known as a child and long since forgotten. The delight was in the language itself and not the agendas with which it had become burdened.

The sheer life-saving act of escaping from those 'nets' was what had brought me to Turkey in the first place. Like much of the disaffected youth of my generation, I went straight for 'silence, exile, and cunning'. Unfortunately, in my case loss of contact with the Irish-speaking community meant a gradual diminution of fluency: I had cut off my nose to spite my face. As is probably obvious, I am long converted to the idea of identity being an ongoing and constantly reconstructed thing. In fording a welter of changing meaning, only the choice of language for writing poetry is a fixed horizon. I still can only write poetry in Irish, and I do not translate my own poems, as I am not a poet in English. This leaves me rather at the mercy of my translators, but what is surprising is how many fine poets have done me the enormous favor of translation. Many of my fellow poets in Irish refuse to allow translations of their poems into English, and I understand their position implicitly. I am painfully aware of the lack of tolerance of cultural diversity often found in Ireland. I understand the context of a threatened minority language attempting to resist the colonial pressure to assimilate. We all make our peace with the language in a different fashion, and it would seem that I have a 'vocation to the missions'. I allow translations, indeed encourage them, so long as the books that result have a dual-language format. There are still problems: most of the translated poems, for example, are taken out of context, and the architectonics of the original publications therefore mislaid.

Yet the whole act of translation seems to me vitally important. What we gain is still so much greater than what we lose. It is another precarious purchase on reality in the often uncomfortable, even at times downright pathological, life of continuous dualism. Many are wont to praise the stereophonic and stereoscopic world-view gained by knowing a major world language and a less-spoken local one which has a long and august literary reality. I am more inclined to be aware of the vertiginous swoon and sense of headlong rush into incomprehensibility which often accompanies this dual view. I know full well what it is like to feel like a trapeze artist who has forgone Joyce's famous nets. In 'Na Múrucha a Thriomaigh' (in *Cead Aighnis*), translated by Paul Muldoon as 'The Assimilated Merfolk', I have tried to image the condition as being a fish out of water, part of a whole tribe of conflicting merfolk in an intertidal reality:

Fágann na rabhartaí a rianta fós
an chlathacha cosanta a n-aigne; gach tonnchosc díobh
ina ghlib ag bruth farraige is ag brúscar raice –
focail a scuabtar isteach mar a bhéadh caragháin charraige
ar líne bharra taoide nuair a bhuaileann an ré rothleacáin
aimsir ré an tSathairn, focail a thugann scáil
na seanré fós leo, focail ar nós
'más reamhar, com seang, meanmain ualliagh'.

The high spring tides leave their mark
on the sea-walls of their minds, the edge of every breaking wave
ragged with flotsam and jetsam and other wreckage,
words carried ashore like the shells of sea-urchin
and left at the high-water mark where they get the head-staggers
at the time of the Saturday moon, words that are still imbued
with the old order of things, phrases like
'wide thighs, narrow-waist, hare-brain'.

Trans. Paul Muldoon, unpublished

And if I have succeeded at all in imaging the linguistic world that is Irish, it is due in no small part to the happy chance that transformed those childhood tales of the Eastern World into a reality. My sojourn to the Eastern World brought me many pearls, but among the most precious are the Turkish language, and a renewed commitment to the Irish language, that marvel of marvels.

Unalive Beings and
Things That Don't Exist

I would like to focus here on a theme of which I never tire, one
of the things that has given me great enjoyment and pleasure as a
person as well as the best literary matter as a poet – this country's
folklore and, in particular, the folklore of Corca Dhuibhne. I
have always been interested in folklore, although at first I couldn't
have given it such a high-falutin name. It was simply little stories
interwoven as warp and woof throughout the speech when I was
that little five-year-old exile over in my Aunt Máire's house in
Cathair an Treanntaigh in Ventry parish in the mid-fifties. 'Folklore' back then was something else: small things that happened
from day to day that would be associated with an old story or
some unusual reference. One day when I was a young girl, for
example, I happened to be walking up the Cathair road in a silk
dress made of two strips of material that I had sewn together and
sewn a hem around the bottom of – the only attempt, and the
last one, at sewing I had ever made.

'O,' said John Sé, a cousin of my Grandad, whom I met on the
road, 'I like your dress.'

'Yes,' I said with sheer pride, 'it's silk.'

'Isn't it well I know it,' said John Sé. 'There was so much silk
came into that cliff over there called Faill a' tSíoda [The Cliff of
Silk] that the people of the parish tied up the animals with it.'
'Bhí leaincaisí síoda faoi chaoire na Cathrach [The Cathair sheep
were spancelled with silk],' as the poet said – a sentence that
would stay in my head forever and would leap out at me when I'd

be writing a poem years later. 'Folklore' was, back then, the everyday learning, the way that people looked at the world.

I've often spoken or written about my aunt's husband Tomás Ó Murchú or Thomas Murphy, as he was better known, a source of infinite wisdom in our very own house. Here was a man very knowledgeable about his own parish, but also about the lore of the seven parishes west of Dingle. I heard him one night in Dónal Ó Catháin's, when Breandán Mac Gearailt had assembled Oireachtas na nGael in An Buailtín. Máirtín Ó Cadhain was among those present. A dispute arose between Thomas and Art Ó Beoláin about the site and building of a Carraig chapel.

'It's built on the Carraig [Rock],' said Art.

'Devil the bit', said Thomas, 'it's on the Bóthar Buí [the yellow road].'

'It's built on the Carraig,' said Art again.

'Who told you that?' said Thomas.

'Didn't I read it? It's written in the book.'

'O,' said Thomas, 'whoever wrote that book wrote the devil of a lie!'

'There's no limit,' said Máirtín Ó Cadhain, 'there's no limit to the real native speaker.'

Around this time I gave Thomas a copy of the book *Romantic Hidden Kerry*. A few days later I went to see him.

'Well, Thomas, how did you like the book?'

'It's not bad,' said he. 'It goes back two hundred years. That's not bad, now, but I'd go four for you.'

It wasn't an exaggeration entirely, because he knew that it was a shot from a big gun vessel out in Dingle Bay that had swept the head off the Trant castle in the townland, instead of a felling from a boat in Ventry harbour, as one would have expected. There hasn't been a stone on top of a stone of that castle left for hundreds of years: maybe it was in the time of Dún an Óir or at the latest during the Cromwellian wars that the castle was destroyed. And there hasn't been anyone of the Trant race on the Corcha Dhuibhne peninsula for a long time, although there are three townlands in Ventry parish called after them and the name is common enough in north Kerry. Unlike their fellow Normans the Ferriters, the

Rices, the Fitzgeralds and the Husseys, they didn't survive on the peninsula. And yet Thomas knew this about the gun and the castle.

Thomas could go back seven generations of his own ancestors; he had all their names and knew much about their lives. He used to say that his own grandfather was born in Cuan Uachtar, a townland that survived the potato blight during the Great Hunger. This survival was of little luck and benefit to the tenants, however, because the townland and two others on the Cuan, Cuan Íochtar and the Cúilín Bán, were cleared in the year 1867 by a land steward of Lord Ventry, a Cork man called Leahy. His grandfather was six-and-a-half when they were put out of Cuan, Thomas said. Many of the tenants went to America or west to Fán or into the Great Blasket or were scattered throughout the district. And some of them came to Cathair.

'How did they manage to get possession of this place in Cathair?' I asked him.

'Because the birds had flown,' said he, 'the place was empty.'

He knew how the chapel had been moved in Ventry from its old spot over in the east of the parish, where the school is now, to a site on Imleach Shlat bestowed by the Shea family of Imleach. His granduncle Micheál, who died tragically just after he went to America, was the last person to have public prayers said for him in the old chapel, and his aunt was the first person to be baptised in the new one. He knew of my own people, and had information you would prefer not to hear, at times. 'Sulky Léan of the scaldcrow eye,' he used to call my great-grandmother, Léan Ní Chearna, whom I was supposed to be like.

When I began taking a real interest in Irish and in folklore as a young girl and teenager, I picked up this lore mostly from him, although my memories of him and of other old-timers do go back to my youngest childhood days among them. When I was five, Johnny Long, Jacksie Shea and his sister Nell were in the house above in the townland. John Sé's house was at the top of the townland and the pump that they had in the yard was said to always be sure not to run dry in summer. Each man of them would stand on top of his own compost heap and he'd throw backchat at the other man. I don't remember any one particular sentence they said, but I well remember how poetical and intelligent their talk was. These were people full of argument and sarcasm, and it was no bother to them to take you down a peg if they so wished. 'Leá bumbóire, nó leá mún Móire ort' was often their prayer, or curse I should say, and 'How would you know, it's not that you know the Reason for Everything' was also a saying of theirs. Was it any wonder, so, that when I began my first poems, it was on this level of language I set out, picking up the tales I'd been told and the rhythms of the speech:

Mór Cráite (in *An Dealg Droighin; Selected Poems / Rogha Danta*)

Tá Mór go dlúth fé ghlas
ina meabhairín bheag fhéin; 3"/4"/2"
ábhar liath is bán –

dearg (a bhíonn na créachta
a bháthann leath na gcuileanna
faid is a dheinneann an leath eile a mbiaiste
ar fheoil na n-imeall)

'Éistíg', in ainm Dé,' ar sise leis na préacháin
is cabairí an Daingin a thagann san iarnóin
ag suathadh a mbolg.

'Tá na héinne dúnta isteach
ina ifreann féinín féin.'
Scaipeann na mion-éin
nuair a chuireann sí scrabhadh scraith
lastuas dóibh.

Mór Anguished (in *Selected Poems / Rogha Danta*)

Mór, firmly under lock and key
in her own tiny mind
(2" x 4" x 3")
of grey, pinkish stuff
(here be the wounds

that drown the flies
while other flies survive
to make their maggots
on the carrion fringe).

'Listen, in God's name,' she begs
the magpies and the crows
that come at evening
to upset their guts,
'everyone's enclosed
in their own tiny hells.'

The small birds
scatter and spread
when she flings up at them
a sod of earth.

Trans. Michael Hartnett

There were other people in the townland at the time with a wonderful gift of language: as well as being native speakers they were good speakers. The best Gaelic speaker of them all, Tomás Mháiréad (Ó Sé), had been dead since 1956, just a year before I arrived in Cathair. He was the last monoglot speaker in the parish, reputed to have no English. I'm not saying that I ever believed that entirely:

'How could he have no English, living in this townland, where there were coastguards for over a hundred years?'

'Because he didn't consort with them, didn't go among them.'

Perhaps there was a strong hint of politics there as well. He was among those at the first meeting of the Land League during the Land Wars, a meeting held in curraghs in the middle of the harbour – some two hundred of them – when Lord Ventry wouldn't allow it to be held on land. (His people were called 'The Parnells' for many a day.) And like the histories and genealogies of Old Irish, the tales preserved those who attended that meeting on the waters: Fitzie and John Sé and Jacksie and his sister Nell, and Joeen, and Annie Sheehy and her brother Jackie, and Johnny Long and his son Mike Long of Cathair.

When I came back to Kerry from Turkey thanks to an Arts Council bursary many years later, I came back with my two children, and we settled into our family summer home in Cathair an Treanntaigh. (The children were called the 'White Turkeys' because they were so fair: 'Nuala and the White Turkeys' was a common saying.) I was busy with many things at the time: a novel that got the better of me, a collection of short stories that I finished and never published. But above all else, I laid into poetry. My husband hadn't returned to us yet and I was very lonely in the house on my own when the children were asleep, looking out at Ventry shore, the tide ebbed. If I revealed that loneliness at all, it was in terms of folklore that I expressed myself, drawing on the persona of the Mermaid:

From An Mhaighdean Mhara (in *An Dealg Droighin; Selected Poems/Rogha Danta*)

… Má tá eireaball éisc féin orm
nílim gan dathúlacht éigin.
Tá mo ghruaig fada is buí
is tá loinnir óm' ghainní
ná chífeá riamh ag mná mhíntíre.
Dath na gcloch an tsúil acu
ach féach go cúramach isteach
im' mhogailse
is chífir an burdán fearna
is róinte groí
ag macnas
im' Mhac imreasán.

Ní gan pian
a thángas aníos
ar thalamh.
Do bhriseas
an slabhra réamhordaithe,
do mhalairtíos snámh
ar luail cos,
ag priocadh liom
ar nós na gcuirliún.

Creid uaim gur grá, ní Dia,
a dhein é a ordú.

D'imís
is thógais leat mo chaipín draíochta.
Níl sé chomh furast orm teacht air,
is a bhí sa scéal
i measc cearachaillí an díona.
Tá's agam;
dheineas tocailt síos 'dtí an gaíon
is níl aon rian de.
Theip an taoide orainn chomh maith
is tá francach ag cogaint na gréine.

From The Mermaid (in *Selected Poems/Rogha Danta*)

... Though I've got a fish's tail
I'm not unbeautiful.
My hair is long and yellow
and there's a shine from my scales
you won't see on landlocked women.
Their eyes are like the stones
but look into these eyes of mine
and you will see the sturgeon
and you will see fine seals
gambolling in my pupils.

Not without pain
have I landed:
I broke
the natural law.
I swapped swimming
for walking on earth,
picking my steps
like a curlew.
Believe you me
it was love, not God,
who gave the order.

You left
and took my magic cap.
It's not as easy to get back
in the roof's rafters
as it was in the fable.
I dug to the subsoil
and saw no sign of it.
The tide also fails us
and a rat
gnaws at the very sun.

Trans. Michael Hartnett

It was about the same time that Seán Ó Tuama introduced me to Joe Daly and the Bab Feirtéar, who provided me with not only blazing fires and cups of tea but also reams of folklore. I recorded a few tapes of the Bab telling me stories, and would even play them to myself in bed until I'd fall asleep; it's no exaggeration to say that they influenced me greatly. Not only did they give me titles and frame stories for my first two books of poetry, but they taught me also how to transform the raw material of feeling, taught me to make it a thing more universal than small personal or too personal events of my own life. The stories helped me to tell the truth in a way like that described by Emily Dickinson: 'tell the truth, but tell it slant' – to say things that I couldn't say outright. An example of this approach is the poem 'Féar Suaithinseach' ('Marvellous Grass'), the title-poem of my second collection. The first time I recorded the story that lurks behind the poem, the Bab gave me a version on which I based the poem. The tape wasn't long recorded, how-ever, when my sister destroyed it by taping pop music over it, as though it were a blank tape because there was nothing on it but talk! I went back to the Bab and got another and another version, but they were all different from the version on which the poem was based. As it happens she never again told it as I first remember it: saying that the priest grasped the sacred host '*go haiclí*' ('dexterously'). I wanted that particular expression above any other. The version I used eventually as an intro-duction to the book was a version I got from Professor Bo

Almquist, a version recorded and then transcribed by Dr Ríonach Uí Ógáin.

By this point there were great changes in my life. We had just spent three years in Corca Dhuibhne. One of those years my husband was working in Dublin, returning only every second weekend. We appreciated that the journey was too onerous for him and that we'd have to move to Dublin. It was a horrible struggle for me to leave the western coast and for long I was very homesick for the Gaeltacht. Indeed, initially I was forever playing Radio na Gaeltachta, and for a number of years after that I'd do a bit of a programme with Mike Shea on local history, drawn especially from what I was reading in the Department of Folklore.

It was Joe Daly who had directed my feet towards the Department of Folklore the first day. He told me that it would do me good; 'See all that you'll see,' he said to me.

First I went searching for my own people, and I began, of course, with Thomas Murphy. And he was there! Three of his stories had been collected: a story about the greatest wonder, a story about the boy and the holy pictures and the beginning of a certain story 'An Luch is an Dreoilín' ('The Mouse and the Wren'). Joe had told me about this last story, which appears in the *Seanchaí Muimhneach* (*Munster Seanchaí*) collected by Pádraig Ó Siochfhradha, better known as 'An Seabhac' ('The Hawk'), at the beginning of the last century. By the time Joe was collecting in the thirties and forties, the story no longer remained in the memory or mouth of the people: he had found parts of the story here and there, but no one knew the beginning. Then he came south to Cathair an Treanntaigh, as he had heard that maybe it was there – with Thomas. According to the account at the beginning of the story, Thomas heard it from his mother some twenty years earlier. He is said to be a farmer's son, twenty-eight years of age. That was true because he hadn't yet received the land from his father.

And that same father, Peats Ó Murchú, was the greatest gem I discovered in the Department of Folklore. I had already heard much of Peats, as he had been a very well-spoken man and phrases of his were still being recited by people during my own time. One such utterance that stayed in people's memories was elicited by his anger with some man who argued with him at Dingle fair. 'The cheek of you,' said he, 'for a man with nothing to his name but two auld broken-down knacks to be talking against a man with the grass of eight cows, and that in a city,' very proud of himself. But it wasn't until I saw all the material Joe Daly collected from him that I understood how excellent a *seanchaí* Peats was. He had the long Fenian cycle stories: a story about Balor of the Blows, a story of Fionn and the King of Athadonáis. Not only that, but he had the formulaic 'runs' of the battles: the battle array of the hero, the battle array of the ship, the battle array of the sea.

For a while, these 'runs' went to my head:

'Which would you prefer,' said the giant, 'hard fierce wrestling or to strike above and below each other's ribs with sharp shining swords?' 'I'd prefer hard fierce wrestling for that's what I practised on the playing fields with the other noble children.'
They set about each other, they struck a blow above and a blow below and a blow in the height of the wrestling on each other and the person who would come from the bottom to the top of the world to watch two wrestlers it's these two he should come to see. They'd make soft land of hard land, hollows of heights and heights of hollows. They'd bring springs of fresh water through the heart of the grey stones and up through the hard stony soil and the clods that shot from their feet, they'd take three teeth from the hag sitting in London city reddening her pipe, and those three teeth wouldn't stop through bogs and mountains until they'd knock down three castles in the Eastern World.

I learned all this by heart as a kind of madness gripped me. I went from *seanchaí* to *seanchaí* examining different versions of the battle array, and, unsurprisingly, the poems I wrote at the time were full of battle arrays of different kinds. It was the battle arrays, their language, rhythm and forms, that came to my mind as I fed the baby, as I tried to describe the kind of world where the newly born child lived – a world full of views and sounds that she couldn't yet distinguish from each other, that world of pre-symbolic sound, or the 'chora', as the French feminist theorist Julia Kristeva calls it:

From Ag Cothú Linbh (in *Féar Suaithinseach; Selected Poems/ Rogha Danta*)

... An eol duit an lá ón oíche,
go bhfuil mochthráigh mhór
ag fógairt rabharta,
go bhfuil na báid
go doimhin sa bhfarraige
mar a bhfuil éisc is rónta
is míolta móra
ag teacht ar bhios is ar bhais
is ar sheacht maidí rámha orthu,

go bhfuil do bháidín ag snámh
óró sa chuan
leis na lupadáin lapadáin
muranáin maranáin,
i go slim sleamhain
ó thóin go ceann
ag cur grean na farraige
in uachtar
is cúr na farraige
in íochtar?

From Feeding a Child (in *Selected Poems/Rogha Danta*)

... Do you know day from night
that the great early ebb
announces spring tide?
That the boats
are on deep ocean,
where live the seals and fishes
and the great whales
and are coming hand over hand
each by seven oars manned?

That your small boat swims
óró in the bay

with the flippered peoples
and the small sea creatures
she slippery-sleek
from stern to bow
stirring sea-sand up
sinking sea-foam down.

Trans. Michael Hartnett

Other poems were also full of the battle arrays, poems like
'The Race'. I wanted to describe the zest and excitement of a mad
session of driving up the country, and I adopted the hero's battle
array to express this:

From An Rás (in *Féar Suaithinseach; Selected Poems / Rogha Danta*)

Faoi mar a bhéadh leon cuthaigh, nó tarbh fásaigh,
nó ceann de mhuca allta na Fiannaíochta,
nó an gaiscíoch ag léimt faoi dhéin an fhathaigh
faoina chírín singilíneach síoda,
tiomáinim an chairt ar dalladh
trí bhailte beaga lár na hÉireann.
Beirim ar an ghaoth romham
is ní bheireann an ghaoth atá i mo dhiaidh orm.

Mar a bhéadh saighad as bogha, piléar as gunna
nó seabhac rua trí scata mionéan lá Márta
scaipim na mílte slí taobh thiar dom.
Tá uimhreacha ar na fógraí bóthair
is ní thuigam an mílte iad nó kiloméadair.
Aonach, Ros Cré, Móinteach Mílic,
n'fheadar ar ghaibheas nó nár ghaibheas triothu.
Níl iontu faoin am seo ach teorainní luais
is moill ar an mbóthar go dtí tú.

Trí ghleannta sléibhe móinte bogaithe
scinnim ar séirse ón iarthar,
d'aon seáp amháin reatha i do threo
de fháscadh ruthaig i do chuibhreann.

Deinim árdáin des na hísleáin, isleáin de na hárdáin
talamh bog de thalamh cruaidh is talamh cruiadh de thalamh
    bog, –
imíonn gnéithe uile seo na léarscáile as mo chuimhne,
ní fhanann ann ach gioscán coscán is drithle soilse ...

From The Race (in *Selected Poems / Rogha Danta*)

Like a mad lion, like a wild bull
a wild boar from a Fenian tale,
a hero bounding towards a giant
with a single silken crest,
I blindly drive the car
through the small towns of the west:
I drive the wind before me
and leave the wind behind.

Arrow from bow, bullet from gun.
Sparrow hawk through flock of small March birds
I scatter miles of road behind.
Figures flash on signposts –
but in kilometres or miles?
Nenagh, Roscrea, Mountmellick
(but have I travelled through these towns?)
mere things that limit speed
mere things that slow me down.

Through geographic barricades
I rush and dart from the west
I gallop towards you where you wait
I speed to where you stand.
Heights are hollows, hollows heights
dry land is marsh, marsh is dry,
all contours from the map are gone:
nothing but shriek of brakes and sparks of light ...

Trans. Michael Hartnett

While so immersed in my study of Irish folklore, I came on a book: *Italian Folktales Selected and Retold by Italo Calvino*, an English translation of a collection of tales Calvino had originally translated from local Italian languages. Calvino's foreword described what happened to him when he got caught up in this world of fairy tales:

> To me it was a sheep's leap in the ocean. An ocean into which many people before me had jumped already, over some 150 years, not seeking novelty or the usual thing in itself, but with a deep belief that there was some dark secret element lying on the sea bed, an element that had to be rescued for the sake of the language.

From what he wrote I realised that my own disease didn't just belong to me. By this time I had deserted the battle arrays and the Fianna stories for fairy stories and other storytellers: Tomás (Mhárthain) Mac Gearailt; Tadhg Ó Guithín; Seán 'ac Gearailt from Márthan who was married in Gorta Dubh and whose nickname was 'Danger'; Peig Sayers and her son Mike ('the Poet') Ó Guithín; Domhnall Ó Mainín from Cill Uraidh (Domhnaillín of the Smoke) who gave Joe Daly the longest story he ever wrote, a story that took twelve nights to take down. Then there was Seán Ó Grífín from Cathair Boilg, a man not renowned as a storyteller in the community since he wouldn't tell in public because of a touch of stammering. But he had spent his life in the house of Peats 'ac Loinsigh, listening to him carefully and learning every story: The Black Thief, Balor of the Blows, Cuid, Céad and Céatach, Farmer Shepherd of the Weather and many more. By the time Joe Daly was collecting stories Peats was dead, but he discovered Seán Ó Grífín and recorded all the stories from him.

Those stories are wonderful: all of them. Calvino's description of his feelings while working on his Italian folktales captures the magical essence that I also experienced:

> As I pursued the work, always picking up all the material at hand, sorting and cataloging it, a kind of madness took hold of me, an excessive eagerness with no let up, to discover every kind of version and alternative version, of certain motifs. It was as if a fever had taken over me. I felt a passion in me as in an entomologist, so that

I'd have been more than happy to give up all that Proust had written for one more version of the story 'Shit Gold, Little Donkey'.

(The most widely known Irish version of this story is called 'Cac airgead, a chapaillín bháin'.)

It gave me great mental satisfaction to know that another writer had gone through the same madness as myself – and not only that but had come out on the other side. Because it was this period that he spent afloat in the unconquerable ocean of folklore that changed greatly the form of Calvino's writing. He left realism behind him and set his face on what is now called 'metafiction', as in his remarkable novel *If on a Winter's Night a Traveler*. His experience was so close to my own that it seemed to me he had taken the words out of my mouth:

> For two years I lived in woods and castles bewitched, torn between the urge to reflect and the urge to act ... During these two years the world around me adopted features of the fairy world and everything that happened was caused by magic or by some sleep charm or by metamorphoses of one kind or another. Nests of snakes opened under the soles of my feet and just as suddenly they became streams of milk and honey. Kings whom you thought faultless until then became ruthless parents. Kingdoms that were bewitched became alive again. It seemed to me that the forgotten rules of folklore life came falling head over heels out of the little magic box I had opened.

And when Calvino finished working on his book of folktales, something was affirmed for him: 'that is, that there's truth in fairytales'. I too had happened on this truth, and my poems had changed from bottom to top.

As I continued researching, my interests changed. After indulging in the battle arrays and the international motifs, I began taking a particular interest in the women storytellers, people like Peig Sayers, Cáit Ruiséal and especially Máire Ruiséal. I suppose I fell in love with Máire Ruiséal, whose approach wasn't at all like Peig Sayers'. There was something almost baroque about Peig, little twists of rhetoric about her. She liked hard words or 'rocks', and a given word often reminded her of a story. For instance, when potatoes called 'minions' are mentioned, she says, 'It was the year of the minions when my father was in the house. A woman of the roads came into the house to him ...' and away she went.

Although she, like everyone else, has battle arrays in her stories, Máire Ruiséal has a very straight storytelling style. There is one place in the middle of a story that I love, when she says in an aside to Joe Daly:

'The king's children were out on the ... Joe, can I use the English word here?'

'Say away', says Joe.

'The king's children were out on the piazza ...'

I'm very pleased to note that Eilís Ní Dhuibhne chose a story of Máire Ruiséal's for the chapter on 'Oral Tradition' in the *Field Day Anthology of Irish Women's Writing*: she tells a story called 'The Story of the Little White Goat', a fine example of a 'feminine fairytale' that is a version of 'Psyche and Amor'. Commenting on what Vladomir Propp says about this story in his essay 'Historical Roots of Russian Fairy Tales', Calvino says:

> Although the customs of millennia are disregarded, the plot of the story still reflects the spirit of those laws and describes every love thwarted and forbidden by law, convention or social disparity. That is why it has been possible, from prehistory to the present, to preserve, not as a fixed formula but as a flowing element, the sensuality so often underlying this love, evident in the ecstasy and frenzy of mysterious nocturnal embraces.

This sensual love may be felt in Máire Ruiséal's version of the story and, as in Peig Sayers' storytelling, there is openness of mind about human nature that you wouldn't expect, perhaps, in a woman storyteller from a country where women are meant to serve as national monuments:

> They went into a fine court. He spoke to her then:
> 'Muise, well now,' said he, 'which would you prefer now,' said he, 'that I be a goat by night and a man by day or a man by night and a goat by day?'
> 'O indeed,' said she, 'I prefer the night company – you to be a man by night and a goat by day.'
> That's how it was.

Recently it's little bits of *seanchas* that interest me most, the little trivial tales of what happened to people: Sheehy of Baile Eaglasta telling how many houses were knocked down in every townland during the Famine; Peats Dhónail (Ó Cíobháin) of Muiríoch talking about fishing or about Tomás na bPúcaí, a relation of my own. Peats had one story about Tomás that I'd have to refute. There were three young women who were pregnant at the same time in Leataoibh Meánach. Tomás na bPúcaí had the second sight, and he said there'd be a great tragedy in the townland but he wouldn't say which of the young women would be carried off. As it happened the woman who was taken was the woman most closely related to him, the wife of his sister's son. She died of puerperal fever after bringing a baby daughter into the world. 'And,' said Peats Dhónail, 'the young woman died shortly after that, and the daughter died as well.' Well, the daughter didn't die. How do I know that? If she hadn't survived, I wouldn't be here now, because she was my grandmother.

I mentioned at the beginning my fascination with the 'The Cathair sheep ... spancelled with silk'. I was in the Folklore Department the other day and happened by chance upon more information about it. I had always understood that this was a mythological incident: it was a significant example, I thought, of people's poetic prowess and of the wonderful imaginative power always to be felt strongly in the language of Corca Dhuibhne. I had never dreamed that there was any historical basis for it, but indeed there is. A big sailing boat called *The Lady Nelson* was wrecked on the Sceilg full of wine along with the silk. After this ship was wrecked the lighthouse at Sceilg was built:

> It was a foggy night and the captain was saying they were three leagues from any shore. Some of the crew disagreed and they were right, because it wasn't long before she hit the Sceilg. All in her were wrecked, drowned and crushed but three who climbed unto a plank of wood. Two or three days of mist and rain from the west and south followed and the pipes of wine were moved east. Boats were searching for them. Ventry Bay was full of boats and Cathair a' Treanntaigh. There was a man called Scainlin with a boat and crew back in the bay searching for the wine when they saw the wreckage well away from them and the men on top of it. There were two of

them when they got to them. The other man had fallen into the
water asleep a little while before. They lifted the two and saved them.
That's all that survived. The survivors sent Scainlin and his crew a
mast and two sails in thanks after that.

I give thanks too, for the survival of such tales, and so arrive safely
at the end of my own journey on the oceans of material that we
have as a resource in this country. These stories remind me of the
concision of a language I heard people tossing across the fields at
each other when I was a child. But they also enter into my
imagination: when the story motifs and even the snippets of
seanchas scattered here and there in manuscripts bring me such
marvellous imagery that I can play with them, sporting and
cavorting, throwing them in the air and catching them again. And
of course, that sporting is one of the necessities in creative work.

I want to return, finally, to one thing concerning the title of
the talk: 'unalive beings and things that don't exist'. Until recently
I'd have sworn that there was such a title on one of the sections
in the general catalogue of the Irish Folklore Commission, a
catalogue compiled by one of the Department's founders, the
collector Seán Ó Súilleabháin. But unfortunately, when I went
looking for it for this lecture, it was gone. I searched and searched
but could find no trace of it, which suggests that maybe it never
was there and that I was hallucinating from start to finish. Such a
thing could happen.

Gearóid Ó Crualaoich, in his book *Leabhar na Caillí – The Book
of the Cailleach: Stories of the Wise-Woman Healer*, writes of the material
he examines that it

> bear[s] witness, hopefully, to the way that traditional material,
> frequently seen as outmoded, naïve, parochially-bound, can
> constitute a rich imaginative resource for our own times and our
> own circumstances in a world where the local and the global are
> intermeshing at an increased rate for greater numbers and in ways
> not previously imagined.

We have precisely this 'rich imaginative resource' in the oral
traditions of Ireland, whether from the Department manuscripts,
or from the plain speech of good storytellers. I have no interest
in introducing ranges of language or models of literature into

Irish, although I'll go search for a dictionary of science, physics or chemistry if I have to, for example, when I want to describe the natural phenomenon of the Northern Lights that I saw when visiting Fairbanks, Alaska. But what I do want to do above all else is to supply something, through the natural resources of the Irish language, that hadn't been there before in poetry. It's for that purpose that I continue rummaging in the Department of Folklore, and with the help of the gods and demons, the unalive beings and things that don't exist, I'll do that for whatever number of days I manage to live.

Bibliography

'Why I Choose to Write in Irish, the Corpse that Sits Up and Talks Back' appeared first in *The New York Times Book Review*, 8 January 1995.

An earlier version of '*Dinnsheanchas:* The Naming of High or Holy Places' appeared in P. Yaeger, ed., *The Geography of Identity* (Ann Arbor: University of Michigan Press, 1996).

A version of '*An Bhanfhile sa Traidisiun:* The Woman Poet in the Irish Tradition' first appeared as 'What Foremothers?' in *Poetry Ireland Review* 36, 1992.

An earlier version of 'Patterns' appeared in *The Los Angeles Times Magazine*, 5 March 1995.

An earlier version of 'A Ghostly Alhambra' appeared in T. Hayden, ed., *Irish Hunger: Personal Reflections on the Legacy of the Famine* (Dublin: Wolfhound Press, 1997).

An earlier version of 'Mis and Dubh Ruis: A Parable of Psychic Transformation' appeared in R. Welch, ed., *Irish Writers and Religion* (Gerrards Cross: Colin Smythe, 1992).

An earlier version of '*Cé Leis Tu?*' appeared in *Éire-Ireland*, Spring/Summer 2000.

An earlier version of '*Dinnsheanchas:* Holy Wells and Psychic Depths' was presented as a lecture in Sweden in 1996.

A slightly different version of 'Contemporary Poetry' appeared in *The Field Day Anthology of Irish Women's Writing* (Cork: Cork University Press, 2002).

An earlier version of '*Seal Sa Domhnan Thoir*: Sojourn in the Eastern World' appeared in *Éire-Ireland*, Spring/Summer 2003.

An earlier version of 'Unalive Beings and Things That Don't Exist' was presented as the Ó Cadhain Lecture 2003 and was subsequently translated from the Irish for *Irish Pages* by Cathal Ó Searcaigh.